Between Two Towers

Between Two Towers: The Drawings of the School of Miami

Vincent Scully

with Jorge Hernandez, Catherine Lynn, Teofilo Victoria

photographs by Teresa Harb Diehl

THE MONACELLI PRESS

First published in the United States of America in 1996 by
The Monacelli Press, Inc.,
10 East 92nd Street, New York, New York 10128.

Library of Congress Catalog Card Number: 95-75839
ISBN: 1-885254-07-5

Printed and bound in Italy

Designed by Michael Rock.Susan Sellers Partners

Front cover: Roberto M. Behar, *Temple for Seaside* (plate 117)
Back cover: Rosario Marquardt, *South Florida* (plate 28)
Frontispiece: Eric Vogt, *Roman door* (plate 42, detail)

Contents

FOR JACK

¡Oh blanco muro de España!

¡Oh negro toro de pena!

– Garcia Lorca, "La Sangre Derramada"

Preface

This book is neither a history of the School of Architecture of the University of Miami nor a detailed analysis of its pedagogical method. Those topics are touched upon only enough, it is hoped, to put the drawings of the school in context. Those drawings are, in my opinion, much the most beautiful being produced by any school of architecture at the present time. They can be enjoyed as works of art in their own right. They have also played a central part in re-creating a kind of architecture long lost and much needed today, and they are, finally, the only contemporary architectural drawings that have, however unconsciously, been done in large measure in the spirit of John Ruskin – in the spirit, at least, of the Ruskin of *The Two Paths* and the drawings from nature. That spirit, as Catherine Lynn points out, has played much less a part than it ought to have done in the formation of Modern architecture and has, moreover, come down to us in a seriously distorted and diminished form. These drawings do, I think, put a lot of things right concerning contemporary architecture as it might have been and perhaps ought to be.

I am grateful to Jorge Hernandez, Catherine Lynn, and Teofilo Victoria for their help in putting this book together. It could not have been done without them. Joanna Lombard deserves special thanks for help with the bibliography. Alina Hernandez and Maria Nardi also gave unselfish assistance.

I am grateful to all the students and faculty of the school who permitted their drawings to be reproduced and were willing to talk to me about them. It goes without saying that there are many other faculty members whose work is important to the school who are not represented by drawings here.

I think that under the professional and moral leadership of Andres Duany and Elizabeth Plater-Zyberk the young faculty and students at Miami have created something unique: a school young in years, as they are, but already special in the world of architectural education, within whose fairly murky purlieus we can hope that its way of work will survive to change things for the better. Here one tends to look for support to Miami's Latin culture, and to its multinational character as a whole. They are potent factors for continued growth and have already played a central role in the burgeoning of the school. Moreover, the appointment of Elizabeth Plater-Zyberk as dean in May 1995 indicates that the school is now decisively headed in the direction that is appropriate to it. Along that line of advance, during the next decade, we may expect great things.

On a more personal note, I cannot forget the incomparable professional community, some of it retired, of artists, businessmen, and lawyers, whose frequent presence in class makes teaching in Miami so much fun. One thinks especially of Mrs. Harry Hood Bassett, Roger and Shirley Feldman, Joseph and Betty Fleming, Benjamin and Rita Holloway, Peter and Lily Knize, Robert and Lyn Parks, and many others. Finally, I am grateful to Edward T. Foote, president of the university, and his wife, Roberta Fulbright Foote, for their continuing support of the school.

As always, I owe a debt for typing and much other help to Helen Chillman of Yale and Fay Bernardo of the University of Miami.

Vincent Scully
Coral Gables and New Haven, 1995

Vincent Scully

Between Two Towers

The first tower was Phineas Paist's, for the Administration Building of the University of Miami; the second was Aldo Rossi's, for the architecture school (plates 1, 2). The first was never constructed; the other, too, may never be built. They exist only as drawings, the former of 1925, the latter of 1989. Between them, however, they illustrate, and indeed have partly shaped, the special history of the School of Architecture of the University of Miami. That history involves before all else the development of a special kind of drawing, one which, by the late years of the twentieth century, has begun to affect the course of contemporary architecture profoundly, has in fact begun to restore architecture in the United States and around the world to its former glory as the shaper of the human community, as the fundamental intermediary between humanity and nature's invincible laws.

Strange and wonderful, perhaps inevitable, that this should have occurred in Miami, where nature is so vivid and so often terrible, able to show a face before which no works of humankind can survive, where human life itself can barely endure. Strange, too, that the kind of drawing that came to trace that face with love, and to design human structures in relation to it, was one that had been recognized, revived, and acclaimed by John Ruskin in the cold and misty North more than a hundred years before. To draw directly from nature, not to "conventionalize" it, was Ruskin's answer to Owen Jones, and it is exactly this that distinguishes the drawing of the University of Miami from that of other architecture schools and from the abstraction, the conventionalization, of almost all Modern architecture from the time of Frank Lloyd Wright and the Bauhaus to the present day. Ruskin's enthusiasm had also helped create in his time a new excitement about Italian painting of the late middle ages and the early Renaissance, of the period before Raphael; and a strikingly Pre-Raphaelite impetus from the Latin south has also played an essential part in the development of drawing at Miami.

In 1916, William Jennings Bryan, a year after resigning as secretary of state, called in Miami for the foundation of a string of Pan-American universities along the southern border of the United States, the first to be constructed in Miami itself. Teachers were to be bilingual in English and Spanish. The idea languished but never died, and in 1924 it was revived by Bryan himself with the support of his good friend George Merrick, the developer of Coral Gables. It was also endorsed by Judge William E. Walsh, of Miami Beach, who called for "a great outdoor university . . . a great park"; and that is exactly what Paist's Edenic scheme of 1923 for the University of Miami turned out to be. Paist's splendid aerial perspective of the campus shows the Administration Building on axis behind its reflecting lagoon, while many little Greek theaters nestle in the trees behind it (plate 3). There are also splendid dormitories like cloisters with deeply shaded colonnades. This is what the university would have looked like if there had been no hurricane in 1926. Its quality as architecture and planning, with its monumental grouping of buildings and its pedestrian scale, was even higher than that of Coral Gables as a whole, of which it was to have been the crowning ornament.

Coral Gables had been developed by George Merrick as an automobile suburb designed to be a true town, with a strict perimeter of gridded streets within which the English garden-as-golf-course opened the space into flowing patterns of streets ideal for motoring. These spilled out southward to a grandly planned seaside town with an urbane boulevard along the shore of Biscayne Bay. As part of this noble plan Merrick had richly endowed the University of Miami with land and with his own money (and prophesied that many of the students would be Cuban), and by 1926 the Administration Building (plate 1) was well along in construction. It was being erected almost as fast as the Biltmore Hotel had been a year or two before, and its tower, like that of the Biltmore and the Miami Herald Building (later the "Freedom Tower" of Cuban immigration) based on the Giralda of Seville, would have joined those two and that of a hotel on Miami Beach as the only tall spires along the flat South Florida shore. The gaggle of skyscrapers that has proliferated in and around Miami since that time has eaten up the shoreline and so diminished the haunted grandeur those lonely relationships once possessed. But the hurricane struck before the university's tower was completed, ruining Merrick financially and leaving Coral Gables wonderful in many ways but not what it might have been, especially in its loss of the democratically conceived township along the shore, currently the setting for elaborate gated private estates. The concrete frame of the Administration Building, known as the Skeleton, existed in that form until 1949, when it was clothed in an undistinguished Late Modern skin. Most of the buildings at the University of Miami were built in this guise, possibly representing the nadir of human architecture of all time.[1]

The general planning of the campus was even worse, as was typical of the Late Modern period. There is no shape whatsoever to anything. The contrast with what Paist, Denman Fink, and Merrick's other architects had proposed was total. We are far enough away from it now to recognize that the contrast is hardly less than that between civilization and barbarism. It illustrates that curious failure of nerve, that despair of civil tradition, which seems to have overwhelmed the architectural and planning community directly after World War II. Some of this was partly repaired, or concealed, in the early eighties, when President Edward T. Foote and his wife, Roberta Fulbright Foote, landscaped the campus and planted it heavily. But an underlying structure was still absent, and later schemes for expansion were equally amorphous.

The history of the architecture school at Miami reflects that general development. When the university opened in 1926 the first courses in architecture were taught by Paist, Fink, and the other designers of Coral Gables. They were organized around drawings similar to Paist's for the university. Indeed, Eunice Peacock Merrick, George Merrick's widow, has said that all the major projects for Coral Gables were the result of group design in which everyone sat around and drew their ideas and worked

1 *The little semi-Bauhaus buildings designed by Marion Manley in 1949, of which four were discreetly remodeled by Jan Hochstim in 1982 to house the architecture school, should be excluded from this category. They are early modern architecture still, and remain quite appealing in their awkward simplicity, suggesting a curious innocence of the knowledge that more sophisticated architectures had ever existed.*

them out together. Such collaboration has become a hallmark of the practice of the school today, as has a special interest in landscape architecture and the natural environment. Such courses were indeed taught for a while around 1931 by Ernest F. Coe, best known as "Father of the Everglades National Park." But the architecture school was abolished in 1932, apparently as the result of an unattractive administrative squabble, and perhaps also because of the Depression. The study of architecture did not reappear until 1947, when it was incorporated into the School of Engineering. There it remained, with all the limitations inherent in such an affiliation, until it was set up in 1984 as a school of its own by President Foote, largely through the efforts of then-chairman John Steffian, who is enshrined as an administrative hero in the mythology of the school.

Well before that time, however, the teaching of architecture at Miami had begun to develop its own special qualities. The arrival of Andres Duany in 1977 and that of his wife, Elizabeth Plater-Zyberk, in 1978 were surely the decisive events. The continuous teaching presence of Plater-Zyberk since that time, accompanied by the more sporadic cameo appearances of Duany, along with the office work and "charrettes" all over the Americas that their firm, DPZ, made available to students, coupled with, most of all, the special renewal of traditional town planning that DPZ brought about, all changed the school decisively and endowed it with the unique character it possesses today. In this Duany (a refugee from Cuba) and Plater-Zyberk (the same from Poland) were blessed by Fidel Castro, who since 1959 had been instrumental in building up the richly endowed and energetic Cuban population of Miami, which, in less than a generation, was to transform that city from a provincial town into the capital of the Caribbean. It was also to become the most potent enclave of Latin culture in the United States, the one that was without question to exert the most critical contemporary effect upon its host culture – especially, it would now appear, in the field of architecture and urban planning.

The young Cubans, joined, as the cultural pot began to boil, by increasing numbers of other Central and South Americans, became Duany and Plater-Zyberk's students and then their collaborators; soon many of them were teaching in the school. A surprising number were originally hired to teach drawing and could hardly avoid coming under the influence of, or reacting against, Thomas Spain, who had been teaching drawing at the university since 1966.

Fig. 1
John Ruskin.
Study of Gneiss Rock at Glenfilas, 1853. Pen and watercolor. Oxford, Ashmolean Museum

For Spain, drawing is nothing less than the way that reality can be known. "Reality is shrouded in veils," he says, "and, as you draw, those veils begin to be removed." Only through drawing, he believes, "can visual experience be permanently registered on the brain." In his own drawings (plates 4, 5), the physical reality of the object drawn is in fact "realized": the South Florida öolitic limestone of the wonderful Coral Gables Police and Fire Department building by Denman Fink and Phineas Paist; the madly proliferating root buttresses of Coral Gables' magic banyan tree, the strangler fig. The obsessive linearity, the determination to depict every accident of surface and to make everything real and clear, markedly recall Ruskin's drawings from nature (fig. 1). Moreover, Spain's meticulously developed technique succeeds, like Ruskin's, in identifying itself with the object, which – rather than, as in abstraction, the artist – becomes increasingly real itself, more and more the focus of attention. Spain says it better: "A reverence develops for the thing more than for the interpretation of the thing." This is Ruskinian, indeed the very essence of Ruskin's approach to the teaching of art as distinct from that of Owen Jones: not "conventionalization," with its eventual deification of the designer, but "naturalism" in the reification of the thing seen (figs. 2, 3).

Frank Lloyd Wright, whom we should probably regard as the first great abstractionist in architecture, was to write that he "read" Ruskin but "traced" Owen Jones. And Wright linked this activity with the abstract blocks and strings of the Froebel kindergarten system, through which, he said, he felt that he was "designing" the world rather than merely "representing" it. This is the artist as divinity. And so it has generally been through the "Modern" years: Ruskin read and paid lip service to (though less and less after the nineteenth century waned) but Owen Jones and others like him used, with abstracted forms deriving from his work but, as time went on, more and more attributed mistakenly to Ruskin as well – in part, it is true, because of his own endlessly contradictory remarks on every subject over his long and tragic life. Hence Ruskin, though still occasionally evoked, had never really affected twentieth-century Modern architecture at all – at least not the canonical Modernism of the International Style, taking shape as it did while the more nearly Ruskinian forms of the English garden cities of the early twentieth century and the Dutch and Viennese housing of the nineteen-twenties were dying away. Abstraction was everything and, concomitantly, the personality of the designer.

Fig. 2
Owen Jones. **Moresque Ornament from the Alhambra.** Color lithograph. Plate 41*, *The Grammar of Ornament*, London, 1856

So, in turn, the fabric of the traditional city had to be despised, even outraged, by architects, because its demands were a brake on abstraction and anarchic individuality alike. All this rose to a crescendo in the Late Modernism of the 1950s. It was then presumably killed off in the revival of more architectural traditions by Robert Venturi and others, but was resuscitated with a shot of Russian Constructivism (which many of us tried to inject during the seventies) in the recent Deconstructivist fad of so many architectural schools. There it is *de rigueur* that drawing must transform the object drawn, or see it from an impossible angle, certainly subject it to the designer's ego but, most of all, invent forms rather than describe them. Not Spain's. His major drawings celebrate the primacy of the object drawn, and he may spend almost a year on each one. In terms of architectural education, we might ask if such concentration on one drawing is worthwhile. Duany himself was to offer an answer when he said that once students had spent weeks trying to make perfect and faithful drawings they could never bear to do shoddy (or conceited) work again.

Fig. 3
John Ruskin. **Roses from dress of central figure of Botticelli's *Spring*,** not dated (c. 1845–75). Watercolor. Isle of Wight, Bembridge School, Ruskin Galleries Trust

There can be no doubt that the drawings produced at Miami are of a quality that can hardly be matched. In this, their sources are not only Ruskinian but more generally Pre-Raphaelite and, specifically, Latin as well. I am tempted to write "Hispanic" here, particularly under the circumstances at Miami and also because of the beautiful old word itself, now out of favor. It has more bite than "Latin," evoking as it does Lorca's "white wall of Spain" and his "black bull of sorrow." But the fact is that the source in Miami is truly Latin, that is, Mediterranean: Spanish and Italian together, as Merrick's inspiration for Coral Gables had been long before. The vehicle that brought a special Latin mode to the school seems to have been the painting of Rosario Marquardt, an Argentine; Marquardt's husband, Roberto Behar (whose work will be described later), says, "The average Argentine is Italian, speaking Spanish, pretending to be English, and wishing he were French." That cultural mix has been especially evident in Argentina's lively and often obscure contributions to modern literature and criticism. But in Marquardt's work, in part reminiscent of that of Frida Kahlo, the mix is most intensely Spanish and Italian, and it is in the peculiar luminous freshness of its Magic Realism that it is farthest from Kahlo's and most Pre-Raphaelite in character.

Marquardt's parents were both architects; one of her sisters was murdered by the Generals, and her brother was imprisoned by them for five years. Rosario and Roberto had been together since they were sixteen; in 1982 he left for New York, and in 1983 she went to relatives in Miami, where they were reunited. In 1984 Behar began to teach in the school and Marquardt to do some coloring for Duany and Plater-Zyberk and to paint on her own. One of her earliest works, "Memories of Mar de Plata," shows the Pre-Raphaelite flavor (plate 6). Roberto intrudes into Rosario's little *trecento* cubicle of space (she a puppeteer) and offers her the globe of the world, the architect's sphere. She seems entranced and soon begins to paint portraits of persons equally possessed, like Dean and Jania Ziff, patrons of architecture and good friends of the school (plates 7, 8). They would soon build a house on Biscayne Bay, designed by Teofilo Victoria, a Colombian, Jania's brother, and one of Duany and Plater-Zyberk's students, now teaching in the school. The Ca' Ziff was strongly influenced by the work of Aldo Rossi, itself Italian and Spanish and Magic Realist in character, and when Rossi came to Miami on one of the visits that led to his commission to design a new architecture school, he was painted by Rosario in one of Duccio's spaces (fig. 4), arriving *a trecento* at the Miami International Airport (plate 9).

In 1989, Rossi presented his proposal for the school to the trustees of the university, but money was never forthcoming to carry out the work. By 1992, it was proposed to build only a small part of it, a version of the tower that was intended to stand between the lake and Manley's buildings. It was designed to contain three large and much-needed class and jury rooms of exquisite proportions, but its major effect was clearly intended to be symbolic. Rossi's drawing (plate 2) shows it in the foreground, revealing the beautiful geometry of its rooms, while the ambitious project of which it was originally a part now recedes, lost in the distance of dreams. But the tower alone would have been an object of mysterious power, like all of Rossi's work, probably even more effective in white stucco (and much cheaper to construct) than in the stone cladding Rossi originally intended for it. At any rate, Dean Ziff offered to assume a very large percentage of its cost. Despite this, it continued to be the subject of various delays and has not yet been constructed. It may be lost to the school. An older member of the faculty called it "fascist" in the local press.

Fig. 4
Duccio. **Maesta: The Way to Emmaus** (detail: rear, center), 1309–11. Tempera. Siena, Opera del Duomo

Whatever the case, Rossi's architecture, shaped as it is by the types and images of the Mediterranean tradition, is closely related to Marquardt's painting, which by 1987, in the portrait "Roberto" (plate 10), was showing the architect as the creator of fantastic, towered Tuscan towns like those to be found in so many Sienese landscapes of the fourteenth century (fig. 5). Behind them, the presence of Ambrogio Lorenzetti's monumental fresco in Siena of the ideal republican town in its landscape may be surmised. Thereafter, Marquardt's work began to focus ever more closely on the human individual, whose presence was progressively to dominate the surrounding space. Her series of the early nineties on the Conquest gives us an Aguirre filling the frame like a *quattrocento* portrait, but here he is unforgiving, bemused, and sad, with only darkness around him (plate 11). The mask of the Jaguar Knight screams in the forest, but the man within hates in silence (plate 12). The richness of the palm jungle, the tropical American environment, which was to become a central image in the joint work of Marquardt and Behar, is purposely contrasted with the emptiness around the conquistador, where all environments are eaten up by the European will.

The dignity of Rosario Marquardt's work, the clarity of its forms and their magic intensity, perhaps most of all the proud, tragic stance of its people – all had a profound effect on the students and faculty of the school. They touched a Latin chord, perhaps a peculiarly Latin-American one where pride and nobility are poised on the edge of violence and torn by conflicting cultural forces. So with Rosario's coming the students at the school began to paint self-portraits, set in environments meaningful to them. As student work the level of achievement was remarkable. Juan Camillo Caycedo from Medellín, Colombia, paints himself alert, a little suspicious, in front of a columned atrium space, with a strong red dadoed wall that stretches deep behind him (plate 13). One column stands far back on that axis, suggesting a peristylar garden, but instead, dark distant mountains show beyond it. In that disquieting setting, Caycedo sees himself as a kind of *campesino*. He holds what is apparently a painting of the tiled roofs of his town, his country remembered. It is an uneasy picture, suggesting some disjunction, some wariness in the classical space.

Roberto Orosa, on the other hand, puts on a clean-cut classical face as does the Augustus of Prima Porta (plate 14). Orosa holds Augustus like a doll in his hands. He is the soul of dignity and decorum, as Augustus was. But he floods the background blood red, like the shower of bull's blood that played a central part in the rituals of Mithras, of which the later soldier emperors were so fond. Jose Valencia paints himself in the uniform of a Union officer of the American Civil War (plate 15) but more directly suggests one of those cadets perennially butchered in South American political upheavals. He faces the firing squad bravely, holding as a target the only work he has yet had time to accomplish. Deborah Verley, from Jamaica, in a drawing whose colors are roughly applied, blazes darkly before a Tuscan sky (plate 16). She too holds a little building in her hand but is herself a much vaster architecture, her majestic shoulders standing out in front of the gentle clouds. We are struck again by how splendid it must have been for the students at that time to have been led to look at themselves and choose their several roles – all dramatic

Fig. 5
Ambrogio Lorenzetti.
View of a town, c. 1340.
Tempera. Siena, Pinacotheca

ones. Indeed, the series seems to have released them to identify themselves as interesting individuals, here specifically Latin or Caribbean, confronting new cultural experiences.

Growing out of similar formal impulses but directed outward, toward the surrounding world, is Ana Alas' "Massacre of the Innocents" (plate 17). Its Latin legend tells us that it records human encroachment on the Everglades in 1938. It was drawn for a studio called "The Recovery of Nature," and perhaps owes more to Uccello than to the *trecento* masters. Soldiery of a sinister grace floods in from the left onto a fairly deep stage of space defined at the rear by a columned facade like a *scaena frons*. Delicate white birds, who lend their tone to the composition, flee to the right, are caught by their wings, bend their long necks to the knives. They are helpless, ineffective intellectuals in the face of a military coup. But they are also the birds of the Everglades, the cranes shot, the egrets butchered for women's hats, their young left to die in the hatcheries. They are treated as people. One identifies with their agony, and beyond them thinks of the Everglades as a whole, always threatened by human greed, and of the heroic individuals, like Marjorie Stoneman Douglas, who defended them almost alone for so long. It is the beginning of the school's preoccupation with the fauna and flora of its region and with larger environmental concerns.

So in the drawings the area of interest begins to widen far beyond that normally considered relevant in architecture schools. The alligator, architect of the Everglades, who hollows out the caverns in the öolite rock, is drawn meticulously, line by line, scale by scale (plate 44). He is as reverently seen as in a drawing by Ruskin but has in fact been subjected to an architectural discipline. That is to say, one is made to sense his weight, his muscular flesh, and he is wholly natural; but his back is drawn in pure plan, like a roof plan. On the other hand, the mosquito, that ultimate tensile structure, has to be drawn as a volume, defined by the thinnest of lines (plate 20) – indefatigable mosquito, who once kept most of humankind out of South Florida and drove shipwrecked sailors mad; immortal mosquito, guardian of the shore, drawn lighter than air on the page. There, in elevation, is the turkey of the Yucatan (plate 19), many-colored, tipped with bronze. He is big; he looms like a Greek akroterion. Red-legged, deep-chested, he pouters along across a yellow sky. The drawing was a revelation to the locals, who had never looked at their common domestic bird with such wonder before. All of these are student drawings, as are those of flora that accompany them in the same years, such as "Yuca" and "Red Mangrove" (plates 18, 21). The pervasive clarity of the technique allows a great variety of focus: the yucca is treated as a botanical specimen; the mangrove builds the shore line. The school soon came to think of drawings of this kind as "Documentary." They were intended to recover the nature of particular environments and to lay the ecological groundwork for the architectural projects to follow, which were to be marked by an equal respect for the architectural vernacular of the place.

By this time, too, the drawings of the school, of whatever subject, had taken on the universally architectural quality of decisive linearity. They were normally in ink and/or colored pencil (for which *lapiz* is the lovely Spanish term). Both are essentially linear media, though the colored pencils were often used on their sides, rubbed into the paper to produce broad planes of color, but watercolor and oil do not appear. Hence the drawings remain Wölfflin's "linear" rather than his "painterly," and their fundamentally tectonic quality is affirmed.

The drawings of Rocco Ceo were to play a central role in this formulation. Ceo came to Miami from the Rhode Island School of Design and Harvard and began to teach at the school in 1988. He had wanted to be a painter but was by then wholly committed to architecture and so found a way to put painting skills to the service of an architectural discipline. He paints (draws) a baobab seed in three dimensions across a mechanical drawing of a folding drafting table used to make such drawings in the field (plate 22). The colored pencils become a doubly pictorial architectural medium in his hands, used point and sides, as they then are by the rest of the school. With them he draws the magic tree of the Caribbean, the "Traveler's Palm" (plate 23), so called because it is always oriented north-south. The "Balsa" (plate 24), a tree that always grows at the edge of the water, is probably Ceo's most beautiful of that series, flaring out into space as it does, its leaves glossy and enormous, apparently blown up far out of scale but in fact entirely accurate in their dimensions.

The student drawing "Conch" (plate 25), by Graciela Torres, shows the influence of such faculty example, its glossy surface not at all the kind of thing one associates with colored pencils (which are in fact chewed up very fast in this process) but suggesting in its great scale the booming of the sea that can always be heard within it.

Fig. 6
John White.
Indian village of Secoton,
1585. Pen and watercolor. London, British Museum

And so we come to maps and charts, which by the late eighties the school had begun to focus upon as the essential environmental beginning for architectural projects. And – how appropriate here – they can be seen first as charts of the waters north of Cuba (plate 26), from Cuba to the Keys. They are the charts of the *balseros*, the rafters on light balsa logs who entrust themselves to the sea, driven out of Cuba by political repression, economic deprivation, and it must be said, a cruel blockade. The raft is the basic image of migration for the Cubans of Miami, and if the *balseros* are fortunate, it floats them to the Keys themselves (plate 27), here drawn in beautiful clear ink, a string of pearls on the sea. Then South Florida at last, here colored by Marquardt (plate 28), with Miami blazing like a nest of rubies against the richly articulated green of the Everglades, while angels float in with the legend as for the Spaniards long ago. It is the city of refuge and opportunity, glowing in a river of grass, almost exactly at the level of the sea, one flowing into the other across the sea's ancient limestone floor. So the gardens of Florida, like those of seventeenth-century France, are as perfectly flat and thin as parchment on the water, which seems to slide in just below the plane of the ground.

Perhaps largely for this reason, Ceo and Joanna Lombard, an architect specializing in landscape design who joined the faculty of the school in 1980 and became a formidable administrator as well as a brilliant teacher, directed their students to make Documentary drawings of Florida in a series called "Historical Landscapes," which were kept as flat as the terrain and were indeed true maps with dimensions that could be measured (plates 29–31). On these mapped landscapes students drew the trees in elevation, each one as meticulously rendered as the bricks Mies van der Rohe once had his students draw, while the buildings were made to lie back in a kind of axonometric projection showing one facade and the whole roof plan. "Chinese perspective" Ceo sometimes calls it, and it does recall some of the devices employed in Chinese landscape scrolls. John White's sixteenth-century drawing of the Indian village Secoton on the North Carolina shore is also recalled (fig. 6), as is, though in a more typically perspective rather than cartographic guise, Peter Gordon's great view of Oglethorpe's Savannah in 1734 (fig. 7). It is appropriate that two of the earliest masterpieces of topographical drawing in the Americas should be recalled at Miami, where there was a renewed intention to depict cities that were beginning to take shape, rising upon the flat land. The method can show a lot, more than normal perspective can, and in a vision always strictly measurable, as in an architectural plan. Here it differs from its early sources, and from the cartographic perspectives of the late middle ages. McKee's Jungle Gardens are turned into a jewel-like filigree through this device, though every plant is carefully shown (plate 29). Thomas Edison's house, laboratory, and experimental gardens at Fort Myers, of about 1886, stretch up like a vertical scroll (plate 30). This, like the drawing of the Jungle Gardens and many others, is a group effort, drawn in this instance by many students working together in a seminar called "The Construction of Eden." Each keeps the level of technique up to standard, planting each tree, as it were, building a landscape together. The great panorama of the Koreshan Unity Settlement, drawn by Adib Cure, is probably the masterpiece of this particular group of ink drawings (plate 31). A whole agricultural landscape of streams, forests, and farms is as fully realized as the balsa tree or the alligator (plates 24, 44). The members of the Koreshan sect believe that humankind inhabits the interior face of a great hollow sphere and looks inward toward the universe it contains. That wonderful image is drawn here, perhaps for the first time.

Fig. 7
Peter Gordon.
View of Savannah.
Engraved by
Pierre Fourdrinier,
London, 1734

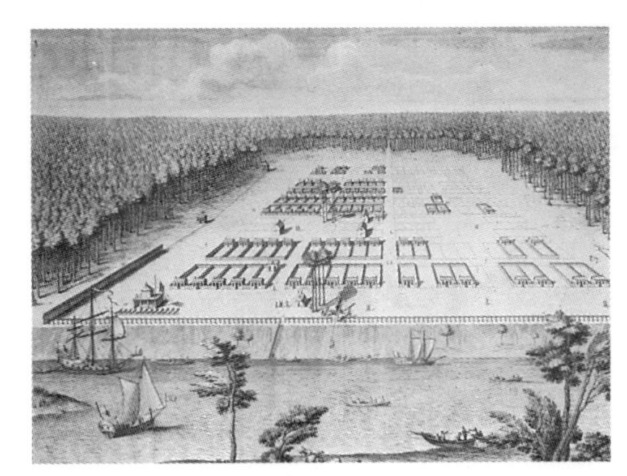

Hence the Documentary drawings may be said to have started from individual representations of flora and fauna and, at the other scale, from maps, and to have found ways to depict whole places, with architecture playing its proper, often subordinate, part. Ceo and Maria Nardi's map of Coral Gables is another demonstration of this (plate 32). The north-south axis is horizontal, as is rarely seen on maps, to emphasize the city's relationship to the shore, especially to that fine long extension that Merrick intended to project southward along the bay. The old shoreline, the edge of the öolitic ridge, can be seen tremulously sweeping along behind its modern, partly manmade position. Tall thin pines, once the only local trees (before Merrick's citrus and all the marvelously gaudy imports that followed), frame the grid of the city, enhanced by scenes from it; we feel Coral Gables in relation to its place and its time. In comparison, the great scroll by Joanna Lombard and Thomas Spain which shows Coral Gables with north at the top comes as a real shock, involving a physical reorientation (fig. 8). It was perhaps in this drawing that the axonometric device of "Chinese perspective" was used for the first time. The view of the city tumbling southward with its richly sculptural Mediterranean buildings shown in three dimensions was so vivid that the city administration had it colored and issued as a municipal document, and it still offers the best graphic representation of Coral Gables and its major buildings as physical realities. The university lies just north of the savage diagonal created by U.S. 1.

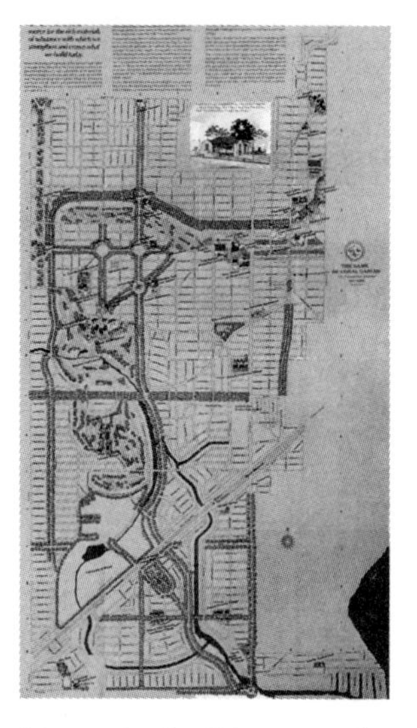

Fig. 8
Joanna Lombard and Thomas Spain.
The Landmark Map of Our City Beautiful: Coral Gables,
1982. Published four-color map based on mixed-media original

As an institution packed with Latin Americans, who have always retained a more tenacious cultural link with Europe than has normally been the case in North America, the Miami school has also emphasized its European connections, especially those with the Mediterranean. This is nevertheless also traditional in Coral Gables; after all, Merrick himself was awarded the Order of *Isabella la Católica* by the king of Spain for his sympathetic revival of Spanish architecture. It is probably unfortunate in this regard that the school's appointment of the distinguished Basque architect and scholar Xavier Cenicacelaya as its dean in 1991 did not work out in terms of the exacting temporal demands of American collegiate bureaucracy, unknown in Europe, but it is probably true that the very heart of the school is so special and idiosyncratic that it can only be directed without injury by a simple, regular succession of chairmen drawn from its own teaching ranks.

However that may be, the school has for some years supported a lively program in Rome (and for a time, an exchange program, run by Gary Greenan, with the Architectural Association in London – which, however, had to be abandoned as the A.A.'s pedagogical objectives became increasingly dotty). One of the first monuments of the enduring Roman connection was the fantastic drawing "Veneziano Anonimo," made by Teofilo Victoria and Roberto Behar for the Venice Biennale of 1985 (plate

33). Here the Documentary type is joined by another, the "Composite," in which, for example, Santa Maria della Salute may exist in a scene with Palladio's Basilica in Vicenza, with one of his projected bridges, never built, and with Victoria's own intervention, a new tower rising from the water – a structure much influenced by Rossi and somewhat recalling Rossi's own project for Miami. A student drawing of Michelangelo's Campidoglio (plate 34) from a Roman seminar directed by Thomas Spain and José Gelabert-Navia shows the general level of student work, in the encouragement of which Spain's drawings continue to play an important part (plate 35). Two of the most striking drawings to come out of Rome are by Eric Vogt, a student from Connecticut, by no means Latin. One is of Trajan's column with all its reliefs magically clear (plate 36); the other, directed in this case by Ceo, is a gigantic Roman door, drawn at full scale on a roll of heavy paper laid out on the ground (plate 42). Both are enormous drawings, that of the door especially, so close to being the door itself, with the accidents of its long, hard, noble Roman life displayed before us. It is hard to believe it took only about three weeks to complete. Again we ask, is it worth it? The same answer seems relevant: once a student has realized something so faithfully, no work of lesser quality, lesser presence, can be tolerated again.

That fact became increasingly true as the school's unique system of charrettes took shape. These grew directly out of the planning of new communities and the healing of old ones that DPZ initiated. But it took the school a while to realize what the charrettes had become. In 1987 Michael Crosbie's perceptive analysis of the school, published in *Architecture*, incorporated many statements of intention by students and faculty, and stressed the Latin aspect, but barely mentioned the urban side. Nevertheless, the relevant seminar in the school on town planning and community development, generally taught by Plater-Zyberk, fed directly into the charrettes. Architects from the DPZ office and students from the school were sent to the communities concerned for periods of up to six or eight weeks and would produce solidly drawn Documentaries and Composites of the place and, finally, new "Projects" for it. The students were normally accompanied by faculty on an almost one-to-one basis, as in the seminars. Funding was partly local, partly institutional, always erratic, and if less so than that for the seminars, ad hoc. Enthusiasm was enormous. Ways were always found, sometimes antithetical to usual business practices. Andres Duany led the very first such charrette to Key West in 1977, but the procedure was not wholly worked out until almost 1990, when a charrette to New London, Connecticut, took place. It was grandiloquently and rather confusingly titled the New London Institute of Art, Urbanism, and Architecture, and was directed by Teofilo Victoria and Jorge Hernandez, with Jorge and Luis Trelles also taking part. Even former chairman John Steffian played a role, reaching out from his post at the Boston Architectural Center to provide studio space and liaison with city hall and the local museums. Somehow, everything came together, and the school's unique character as an urban force became obvious to itself. The great drawing of H. H. Richardson's railway station in New London (plate 37), surely the most powerful building in town, was given an incomplete because the vertical mortar joints were never drawn. (One is again reminded of Mies' students with their bricks.) Here that reverence is directed toward an existing building, preserved from the horrors of Redevelopment almost by chance alone and now once again loved, respected, revered as it deserved to be, and taken, most of all, as a suggestion of what new buildings in the town might be like.

It is interesting that an inordinate proportion of the finest drawings of this charrette were done by Anglos. For whatever reason, New England was seen by them, touched as they had been by the Latin spirit, with an astonished wonder and clarity, and in Composite drawings of magical intent. "Stonington Green" opens like a flag with twin cannon rampant (plate 38). "Obelisk Churchyard" suggests the influence of Shaker drawings, quilts, and American folk art of many kinds (plate 39). The obelisk is an icon of the place, rising at its center. Most familiar is the device of the map with its "Chinese perspective," now modified by the elevations of buildings facing each other across an open space, a street or a green, such as can be seen in the most famous old plan of Boston (fig. 9) and in the eighteenth-century perspective of Savannah (fig. 7). Eric Vogt's "Green" (plate 40) combines these elements in the most graphically

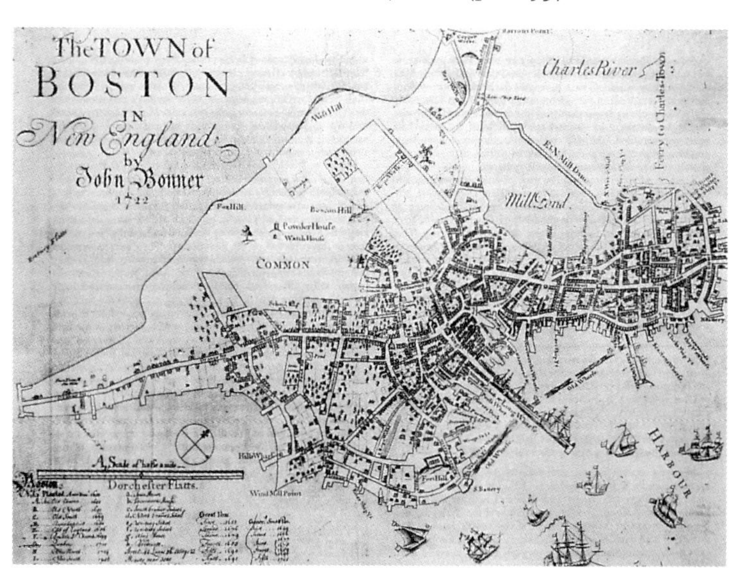

Fig. 9
John Bonner.
Plan of Boston,
1722. Engraved and printed by Fra. Dewing, Boston

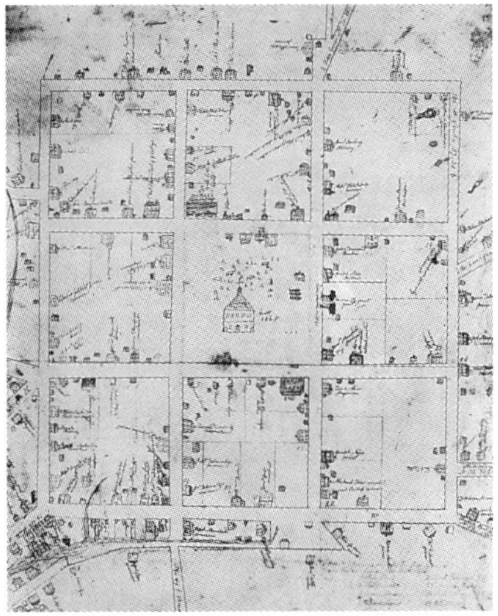

Fig. 10
William Lyon (after the Hon. Gen. Wadsworth of Durham). **A Plan of the town of New Haven, with all the buildings in 1748.** Redrawing published by T. Kensett in 1806 showing the plan laid out in 1638 by the surveyor John Brockett. As published by D. Lyman in *Atlas of Old New Haven,* New Haven, 1929

arresting way. It is the New England of dream: clean, cool, bright, laid out like a quilt before us. The houses, cows, monuments, graves, trees, stone walls, fences, crops, barns: all assume their positions. The church faces us with its spire and states the time. The building types are clear and are surprisingly like those of Rossi's Italian tradition, though Rossi himself loves the specifically American types as well. A place is made, shaped by its physical structures and by their associations. This is surely one of the most moving student drawings ever; it should be compared with the Roman door (plate 42) to show Vogt's range. It can hardly fail to stir a New Englander, since the nine squares of New Haven with their Green (fig. 10) are, as it were, joined in it to the Spanish grid of the Laws of the Indies, with its plaza, to shape the urban typology of the school.

In "Old Glory" Chris Whittaker takes the vernacular houses of New London straight on and identifies them with the flag (plate 41). The buildings face each other to define straight streets, of the type along which the wives of sailors once stretched their ropes of hemp, otherwise keeping them piled in the intervals between the houses. In other drawings we see the Obelisk monument in Groton across Connecticut's Thames and the harbor from downtown (plates 45, 46). Finally, spanning that river, I-95 leaps horrifically across the night sky, while a range of new brick houses, reminding us of Richardsonian as well as Colonial precedent, climbs the slope below it (plate 43). This drawing, also Eric Vogt's, is of a Project, since the houses are an invention, but the magical effect owes a good deal to those of the Composite type, like Behar and Victoria's for Venice (plate 33).

The lighted arc of the bridge also suggests drawings done in seminars in Miami, like the splendid "Firestone," showing a sign near Calle Ocho that marks a place much favored for congregation by the Cuban community in its early days (plate 47). It becomes a flag, an icon of Miami, as heraldic as the massed tailfins of airplanes at Miami International Airport (plate 48). The M.I.A. is peculiarly sympathetic as an urban symbol because it is almost in the center of town, rather than out destroying the Everglades where special interests had intended to put it until Marjorie Stoneman Douglas and her supporters foiled their schemes. The heraldic verve of those tailfins, massed like Kurosawa's snapping banners, is complemented as an image of Miami by the patterns of a Seminole sampler (plate 49), where the city is shown symbolically as absolutely flat and demarcated in bands primarily of green for the land and blue for the water. Then two of its domes appear, riding above the green canopy, a Composite drawing of a watertower and a famous church, here improved by the substitution of Brunelleschi's cupola for its own (plate 50).

A competition for the redesign of Brickell Bridge, which spans the Miami River and is the major traditional entrance to downtown from the south, produced drawings by Jorge and Luis Trelles (plate 51), adorned by the great MIAMI from the Orange Bowl, and by Jorge Hernandez, Raphael Portuondo, and Miguel Sardinas (plate 52), whose combined effort was premiated and is now under construction, though with a few modifications, probably unfortunate. Statues of heroes of Miami's short history will stand at the four corners, Douglas among them. Other members of the school, like Teofilo Victoria and Roberto Behar, also submitted designs to the competition (plate 53), which was directed for the city by Dennis Hector, who teaches structures at the school.

Other seminars focused on Miami gave rise to a design for a boat for the Everglades, drawn in plan, section, and elevation (plates 54–56), shallow in draft (indeed, intended to float in mud), and worthy of Cleopatra, along with a plaza for alligators (plate 57) and a subtly foliated beach towel (plate 58), to which should be added a splendid hibiscus rendered as a kind of wallpaper pattern, even though it was drawn for a seminar in another place (plate 59). These drawings also suggest Ruskin, and after him William Morris, in their "naturalistic" development of figured design as decoration, in contrast to the abstracted patterns of Owen Jones. Robert Pilla's "Atrium," which recalls Ruskin's admiration for Correggio and Mantegna in this regard, is surely one of the most spectacular drawings from the several Miami series (plate 60). It was intended as a ceiling mural for the rather fine new Physics Building at the University of Miami; we look up through it to the clouds, while birds balance precariously on cords strung in space between the ceiling and ourselves. Less obviously architectural, perhaps, but wholly characteristic of Cuban Miami and, in the end, grand and tragic in its space, is the "Gallo Fino" ("fine cock," or "fighting cock") by Marcelino Marrero (plate 61). In a room off a little alley in West Miami the victor stands at the bottom of the cockfighting pit which confines him and is the setting for his glory and, one day, his death. His spurs are red with his adversary's blood; coins thrown by his admirers lie on the ground around him. He crows in triumph, saluting his destiny. It is his *Moriturus*. Marrero is now working on a similar study of the fighting bull in his ring, the black bull in the red ring under the white walls. Marrero is clearly moved by the ritual of courage and death that put the hot blood, the ultimate reality of terror, into Spanish and Latin American Magic Realism, much as they did, one supposes, in America itself in pre-Conquest days.

It is therefore natural that a significant part of the energy of the school in seminar and research should be directed southward toward the Colonial and Pre-Columbian civilizations of Central and South America. The influence of those cultures has of course always been significant in North American architecture during the twentieth century, in Florida and California generally, and in the buildings of Frank Lloyd Wright and the great skyscrapers of the nineteen-twenties and thirties. So, turning southward, a town for migrant workers near Florida City is largely Maya in feeling: a village of Maya huts wholly electrified (plate 62). Farther south, in the Yucatan, not really so far from Florida, the cultures sleep together under the night sky: church and little houses, lighted from within (plate 63). But "A Maya Christmas Card" sets a somber tone. It may be Christmas, with angels upholding a girdle of lights – the Dominican cord embracing the heavens – but the hard red church, clearly one of the high fortified churches of Colonial Yucatan, broods over the roofs of the subject Maya huddled below it, glares over them, just as one of its direct ancestors, the cathedral of Albi in southern France, looms darkly over the conquered Albigensian city at its feet.

In another panel, painted in tempera on wood (because of a shortage of paper), red churches and temples alternate in the thick green scrub jungle (plate 64). A Maya temple base opens like a cubical flower (plate 65), and an ink drawing of the Castillo at Chichen Itzá (plate 66) fills a vast sheet, every stone exactly traced, the mass looming like Richardson's railroad station (plate 37) or the black alligator of the Everglades (plate 44). Finally the city of the dead assembles, each little house in the cemetery lighted by its own candle (plate 67). One of them stretches up to a stepped tower-spire, suggestive not only of the skyscrapers of New York and their Maya precursors but also of Coral Gables' Biltmore and of Rossi's work. All these images, deeply sympathetic as they are to the students of the school, seem to be condensed in this drawing. It is another of Eric Vogt's, its nighttime illumination glowing in colored pencil as, in ink, his Roman door broods (plate 42) and his "Green" shines (plate 40). So the school has found itself in Italy and New England and among the Maya of Pre-Columbian and Colonial Yucatan.

By 1994, charrettes had penetrated as far south as Peru, under the leadership of Teofilo Victoria, Jaime Correa, a dedicated young architect and planner who had begun teaching at the school in 1990, and Jean-François Lejeune, a Belgian urbanist and historian who joined it in 1987. In Lima, the students clearly reveled in the splendors of Spanish urbanism. The urban grid, regularized by the Laws of the Indies, is laid out on the landscape between the mountains and the sea and is brought up into three dimensions by means of the axonometric "Chinese perspective" (plate 68). It is the Spanish *quadrata*, the pure right-angled imprint of human architecture on the land that was to move Le Corbusier to some ferocious abstractions in South America. Here the urban fabric is dense; solid and void suggest one hollowed-out mass of stone. It is a *manzana urbana*, an urban block of blocks. The color is harsh, brilliant, and powerful, as of rough jewels, and the whole sheet is laid out, along with its title, according to the format of the illustrations in the *Nueva corónica y buen gobierna,* written between 1580 and 1620 by the half-Inca Guaman Poma de Ayala (fig. 11). The drawings "Lima, Plazoleta" and "Lima, Plaza Mayor" (plates 69, 70) are organized in the same way. In the latter, giant masonry arches frame everything: the surrounding mountains and the volume of the plaza nearby. Its considerable expanse is dominated by cubical masses of buildings, picked out in bright colors and looming over the cathedral, which, itself not large under the cliffs of the *palazzi*, seems to be advancing up into the light of the square. Human figures everywhere are of uncertain scale; the space is strange, the architecture gigantic, glaring. It is a magical theater for the dramatic deployment of human beings in the special topography of the city, and it suggests some of those created in Rossi's drawings, derived from similar Mediterranean urban sources. "Plazoleta" (plate 69) especially recalls Rossi, with its broad barrel-vaulted masses and high, domed tower surmounted with crosses, all echoed in the miter of the giant prelate, himself resembling one of Rossi's colossal saints. Ink drawings of Cuzco trace the plan of an elegantly irregular palace (plate 71) and sketch a

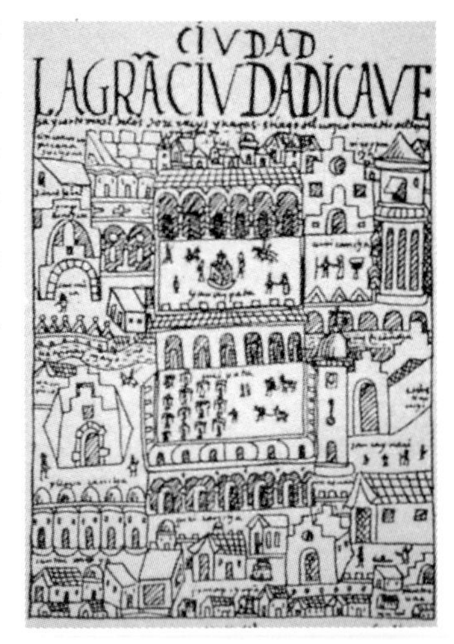

Fig. 11
Felipe Guaman Poma de Ayala. **Cuzco.** Published in *Nueva corónica y buen gobierna*, c. 1580–1620

street staircase framed in flowers (plate 72), a border typical of the great Colonial school of painting that flourished there. Another drawing shows a splendid dome rising before the mountains, whose faces are brutally scarred by nationalism's brash slogans and insignia (plate 75) – which, however, also recall the vast Nazca tracings on the earth of Pre-Columbian times.

The drawings from Peru show that the school has gained confidence in its system of traveling seminars. They study architecture in its place and at its proper scale as the city in landscape. But probably nothing farther away has been more important to the school than its seminars in Key West, where Andres Duany held the first one in 1977. It is especially in the ability to grasp the character of a place in drawing, and to make use of the suggestions for new work embodied in its vernacular architecture, that the recent seminars differ markedly from those of only seventeen years before. They clearly demonstrate what the school has accomplished in the intervening years. Charrette leaders and students alike have now learned to have confidence in the vernacular; they are in no way driven to abstract it or to subject it to "inventive" distortions. They trust the type. They affirm that the revival of the vernacular and classical traditions of architecture and the concomitant revival of traditional urbanism, which have been developing for close to a generation, have been almost wholly realized. The problems of architecture and urbanism now seem to be explored at once more accurately and with more solidly human sense and emotion than had been the case before.

The drawings from Key West demonstrate all that. "Camaroneros" shows a gentle, cosmic unity: the lights of the shrimpers merging with the stars, all floating on the velvet blue of sky and water (plate 74). In "Water Plaza," too, the vernacular houses of Key West sail in on barges around Key West's famous buoy through a wonderful, linear, dancing sea, rather Japanese in feeling (plate 73), while in "Overseas Highway," the engine marked "Progress" pulls wooden houses along a railroad track (Flagler's track of the eighteen-nineties) just above the water (plate 76). We can feel the Cracker frame structures quiver as they speed along; we then stand in the porch of one of them, within a totally realized volume of architectural space (plate 77). Every board is set in place by the drawing, every nail driven; the porch is as tautly framed and sheathed as a ship, and a little boat hangs from its rafters. It is the surfboat that the builder of this house once used to reach wrecked ships; his porch at that time had a wide sea view, restored in the drawing. Models of these structures are also made in the seminars, large in scale and structurally accurate, each framing member and sheathing plank faithfully reproduced. They therefore complement the drawings with their physical realization of architecture as specific buildings in specific places; they are not abstract study models but structural, commemorative ones.

In this, the method of the school may be said to extend Ruskin's where his is most limited, that is, in its preoccupation with architecture as an affair of surfaces and edges. Ruskin projected his reverence for nature onto architecture in terms of ornament, preferably naturalistic. As in his drawings from nature, most of his thousands of architectural studies thus affirm the solid materiality of the building and the dignity of its intersections, richly enhanced, but they seldom embrace its wholeness, and only rarely its structure, plan, space, massing, or context. One of Ruskin's most volumetric drawings, the famous perspective of the loggia of St. Mark's, is still dominated by detail, here by the stupendous, bulging, blooming capitals (fig. 12). The Miami drawings of Key West display no such monumental wonders, indeed have none to deal with, but they try to show buildings as structural wholes or, as in the wrecker's porch, to shape their major spatial units.

Fig. 12
John Ruskin.
Loggia of Ducal Palace, Venice, c. 1849.
Pencil and wash.
Philadelphia Museum

In *The Stones of Venice*, Ruskin himself does just this just once: in a perspective of the Doge's Palace (fig. 13), which is so "steep," as he terms it, that it resembles the "Chinese perspectives" of Miami. It is a unique drawing for Ruskin, and he introduces it only toward the end of his second volume. Elsewhere he draws only details or hazy picturesque perspectives at which he is much less adept; it is not his style. Nor is it that of Miami, where the drawings are always crisp and hard-edged. A corner-house type in the old town of Key West is presented in this way (plate 78). Again we are made to see how it is built, to feel how the boards are sawn at the mill and nailed onto the frame and how the structure adjusts to the corner. This, like that of the porch, is a Documentary drawing, a straight description, unlike the Composites on the water, which are environmental speculations and fantasies. All these qualities are then combined in Projects, like that for "Casa del Balsero," intended as a kind of house-shrine to shelter refugees from Cuba for a few days. It is placed like a little temple on an existing street (plate 79), and then its haunted interior is shaped (plate 80). Again, it is the *balsero* as rafter, one who floats over on the light balsa of Rocco Ceo's tree (plate 24). He sleeps in a strange, empty space like a Shaker bedroom in a tiny iron bed under an American flag; in the crawl space below the floor a Cuban flag is folded away and other objects from the old way of life can be seen. A hand pushes up the cover of a hatchway to the bedroom above. No body accompanies it, but pungent memories flood into the room. We are struck again by the poignancy of the recollections so many of the students at Miami have. It is a rich heritage in every way, involving as it does exile, loss, the courageous outfacing of an alien Anglo world, the projection nevertheless of a golden age long past, and the inevitable cultivation of those rich meadows of regret that are such a fine field for art. It is all in the *balsero*'s room, and in Key West it joins the wonderful older Cubano-American culture of the tobacco rollers, whose little houses float on the brown billows of a richly aromatic tobacco sea (plate 81). These are the people who through several long generations pooled their earnings to hire lectors to read the Spanish classics to them, and sometimes the newspapers, as they rolled their dark death-dealing tubes.

Fig. 13
John Ruskin.
The Doge's Palace Bird's Eye View. Etched and engraved illustration from *The Stones of Venice*, volume 2, London, 1853

One of the most recent of the seminars held in Key West was aptly entitled "Ferry to Havana" and involved the rehabilitation of the old ferry slip which once served that busy route. One of the liveliest drawings the seminar produced was "The Sinking of the Maine," in which the famous ironclad is seen bow on, heavy in the water, shooting off what appear to be firecrackers in all directions (plate 82). The Project drawing from the seminar required a panorama of Key West's waterfront, with the proposed new ferry terminal set in place on it (plate 83). One proposal was for a fine tall thin building, like a Lombard church, that enclosed a single high volume of space through whose windows the panorama of the town could be seen, with the same view painted in a thin horizontal band high up on the walls (plate 84).

Most of the drawings described so far have been by students, and as we noted earlier, the faculty regards the encouragement of students to learn through drawing as its most important function. To do so they have had to be devoted to drawing themselves. Moreover, they have all continued to practice architecture and planning on their own. University administrators have not always recognized how important such practice is for the health of an architecture school. Faculties stay alive by pursuing their own work, some of it scholarly research as in the humanities, but most of it professionally architectural, involving building and design. Such practice at Miami culminates in the work of DPZ, wherein all the best energies of students and faculty have tended to come together in the creation of new towns. There the system of seminars finds its environmental fulfillment. But a good deal of work by other members of the faculty has also been of considerable importance and has involved the continued development of the school's ways of drawing.

The Ca' Ziff, designed for Dean and Jania Ziff by Teofilo Victoria, with his wife Maria Della Guardia and his colleague Tomas Lopez-Gottardi, is perhaps the best known of such work so far. The ink perspective of it as seen from Biscayne Bay (plate 86) has all the breadth and power of Behar and Victoria's drawing "Veneziano Anonimo" (plate 33), which it strongly recalls. Here the bay side of the house, strictly cubical in form, is closely paired with the rich mass of La Vizcaya, the splendid Mediterranean villa by F. Burrall Hoffman Jr. for James Deering, which was completed in 1917. La Vizcaya does lie in that direction, but it is too far away to be seen with Ca' Ziff. The same is true of the tower of the Biltmore (also in the perspective), which rises well inland and can only be seen from much farther out in the bay. As in Behar and Victoria's Venetian drawing, the group is pulled together to demonstrate the underlying urban relationships and to suggest how delightful such a direct association might have been. The land side of Ca' Ziff (plate 85) shows the stark white face of the building, with balcony details suggesting those to be found in Columbus' house in Santo Domingo. The plans seem calculated to infuriate a functionalist (plates 89, 90). Their neo-Palladian proportional relationships are obsessively concentrated into a dense geometric figure, apparently purely self-referential. There is no north arrow. Questions about where one sleeps and dines, not to mention where the johns are, are all ignored. One of Wittkower's diagrams is suggested. In fact, the scheme makes considerable sense: the older Ziffs were to be housed on one side of the symmetrical puzzle, the young Ziffs, Dean and Jania with their children, on the other. Each side has a stair. An open atrium in the center at once divides and unites them and acts as an integral cooling system, pulling warm air up and out of the house and cooler air through it (plates 87, 88). A drawing of the floor with its pool shows a Pompeiian delicacy of pattern. One spectacular feature of the house, especially attractive to those with strong nerves, is its location directly below one of the M.I.A.'s major flyways. Jets constantly thunder overhead and, if one waits long enough, will sooner or later pass directly, and with deceptive slowness, across the great square opening in the ceiling, always suggesting, perhaps because of the palatial setting, dragons, or at least the larger flying saurians of an earlier time. These baroque wonders are set off by the austere Roman elegance with which the walls of the house are painted and detailed (plates 91, 92).

The work of Victoria's good friend Jorge Hernandez also deserves recognition. Hernandez, whose father had been a liberal in politics and sympathetic at first to the revolution in Cuba – until he was forced to flee before Fidel's insistent totalitarian drift – was trained at Miami and the University of Virginia and has been more directly concerned with North American Colonial and Classical architecture than some of the other members of the school. His drawing of the green in front of the Governor's Palace in Williamsburg (plate 93) underscores that fact. Again, it is a map, with the buildings facing each other in elevation. Hernandez then takes his Palladian forms and plunges them into the jungle (plate 94). His "Tres Villas" shows three of his own houses engulfed in all the luxuriance of the subtropical hammock that can be so easily achieved in any garden in South Florida, even in Coral Gables. The smallest of lots there may be planted with four or five gumbo-limbos, a live oak, a satin leaf, several bottle-brush, a monumental ficus hedge, bougainvillea, *thunbergia grandiflora* (that invincible vine), and every kind of palm. But few lots will be lucky enough to play host to a roseate spoonbill of the kind Hernandez draws here, though a great green-and-gold intruder from Parrot Jungle may fly in at any time. The presence in Coral Gables of Lyman Philips' Fairchild Tropical Gardens – though that institution is in fact deeply involved with ecological questions – innocently encourages these horticultural excesses, which are without question among the major delights of building in South Florida. Their combination with the Palladian villa is one of the more sympathetic achievements of Miami's school, wherein its Mediterranean architectural tradition is passionately merged with the more violent Caribbean landscape. Something of the sort had already taken place in the great classic gardens of La Vizcaya. So Hernandez' drawing of his own house produces a sheet right out of Palladio (plate 95), deceptively cool on the page. One way such classicism is adjusted to the subtropical setting is seen in the Side-Yard House, a type which – in part through the earlier experiments by Scott Merrill with Charleston side-yard houses in Seaside – has become something of a standard in DPZ's new town of Windsor, north of Vero Beach. Hernandez' design for one such house, with Joanna Lombard and Dennis Hector, combines the plan and the laid-back axonometric with which we have become familiar (plate 96). The Martinez House by Spain and Rolando Llanes is in a similar vein (plate 97), though, involved as it is in Coral Gables' setback and on-lot parking, it lacks the solid street frontage of the Windsor designs.

Scott Merrill is one of the most promising of the young architects associated with DPZ. He was town architect of Seaside for some years and is now that of Windsor. Since he has not taught in the school, none of his drawings is shown here, but Thomas Spain has done a spectacular perspective of his project for the Village Center at Windsor (plate 98). It shows his strong condensation of Mediterranean traditions with a strict Modernist discipline suggestive of that of Mies. Here, though, the bold wooden pedimental structure recalls the primitive Classicism of Inigo Jones' St. Paul's, Covent Garden, which has in general had a special effect on the school.

Charles Barrett is another of the school's most talented designers. Like Merrill, he trained at Yale but began to teach at Miami in 1989. He is more strictly classical than most of his colleagues and, in a traditional classical sense, may be the most distinguished draftsman of them all. One of his two drawings of the Belvedere House in Windsor (plates 99, 100) shows an atrium especially elegant in detail, sharply black and white with the frieze picked out in orange gold. Here, as elsewhere, Barrett's work suggests the cool English Neoclassicism of the early nineteenth century. There is nothing Latin about it somehow, as there is not in Merrill's work either, despite its rich and disciplined development of a Caribbean vernacular. These architects, along with Vogt, Kevin Storm, and others, represent the Anglo component in the school's generous ethnic mix, and their interaction with the Latin majority is good for everybody. Barrett's drawing for a proposed bathhouse at Seaside is especially striking in this regard (plate 101). It seems pure Pompeii of the second or even the third style, with attenuated columns – which Barrett calls Ionic – as flat as ribbons or sawn boards, where the thin planes slide behind each other against a black background. This elegantly skeletal pavilion should be contrasted with Barrett's project for a brick building in DPZ's town of Mashpee, on Cape Cod (plate 102). If built, it would go far toward bringing that developing project – the conversion of a shopping center to a town center – up to urban scale. Its expression of brick wall and spatial volume is especially intense, with the decidedly vertical voids of its windows pulled well in from the corners and tightly grouped. Barrett is also the finest master of traditional European perspective working with DPZ, and he has done some of the most effective landscape views of their projected townscapes.

Barrett's perspectives of his own work are, however, especially eloquent and accomplished. Two drawings of his proposed library quadrangle for Mashpee bring us into a space fully realized with all of Western architecture's traditional richness of columns, walls, building masses, and mullioned windows (plates 103, 104). His strange view out through a columned landing toward a sunlit grand canal for Coral Gables as it ought to be is the most evocative of them all, sibilant with the lap of water echoing in the noble volume of the place (plate 105). But Barrett's stunning perspective of a proposed town for San Francisco Bay (plate 106) is most striking in terms of what was to come later. It dates from 1979, before DPZ began to do town planning schemes, and it stretches out across the dark water loaded with a panoply of classical monuments of a grandeur as yet unrealized by them. Leon Krier's epoch-making perspective of La Villette (fig. 14), of only two or three years earlier, is strongly recalled, but Barrett's layout organizes a much more sophisticated mix of architectural types and urban situations. It is one of the great civic visions, perhaps the most memorable created in this context and clearly predating those produced at the school.

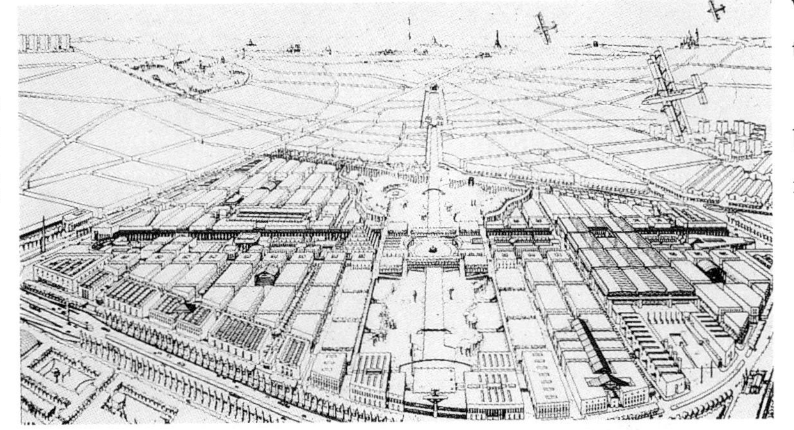

Fig. 14
Leon Krier.
La Villette Competition Drawing: Paris, Air View, 1976. Ink

Frank Martinez, who was trained at Princeton and began teaching at the school in 1992, works in a very different way. His drawings are linear and precise, directly concerned with communicating structural facts and working out architectural details at once simple and refined. His wooden house (plate 107), an uncompromising box, is drawn with a precision of wooden structure that recalls the drawings from Key West (plates 76–78). Designed for a very hot climate, it features a delicate perforation of the overhang to ventilate the rafters. Martinez' drawing of the gate to the pool complex at Tannin, a DPZ town in Alabama (plate 108), is in a more heroic and fanciful vein, its marvelously eccentric masonry evoking that of Hawksmoor and its wood detailing, as often in the school, that of Inigo Jones at Covent Garden. It is a fantasy worthy of English Mannerist and Baroque architecture, and in this Anglo vein is perhaps a bit more like the work of Barrett than that of the other Latins in the school. The ethnic differences can be overstressed, however. There is generally a broader urban discipline that connects everyone's work to the major issues of town design. So Eric Valle shows us the house types of Charleston, strung together to shape a street (plate 109).

Jorge and Luis Trelles have also played central parts in some of the school's most important seminars and charrettes. In addition they have designed a number of fine buildings themselves and have done some lively drawings for them. Putting a pervasive Latin American addiction to graphic use, they love to work in coffee, and a rich aroma of the lethal *cafe cubano* arises from the sepia surfaces of the renderings of their stables in Redland (plate 110) and their own house on Tigertail Road in Coconut Grove (plate 111). The latter is so beautiful an adjustment to the climate of Miami that air conditioning, normally essential in summer, can often be dispensed with. Gentle breezes from the bay always seem to blow through the fine shaded Caribbean courtyard and the open gallery on the second floor. The combination of warmly painted stucco and unpainted concrete block around the window voids lends a welcome toughness to design in an area, like Miami, where the surfaces are normally pristine, and the general air of rough *posada* is in a tradition Cervantes might well have recognized. The Trelles brothers have also designed some rather Arabic fantasies with Teofilo Victoria, like their Blue House for

Fig. 15
Bernhardt E. Mueller.
Perspective of the Administration Building for Opalocka, Florida,
1925. Pencil and watercolor on illustration board. Archives and Special Collections, Otto G. Richter Library, University of Miami

Fig. 16
Abdel Wahed El Wakil.
Island Mosque,
Jeddah,
Saudi Arabia, 1986

Miami Beach (plate 112), unfortunately never constructed, as well as some towers for South Beach which, if built, would shape a kind of Arabian Nights profile, not necessarily unwelcome, at the entrance to Miami harbor. Glenn Curtiss' doomed Opa-Locka is recalled (fig. 15).

A more integral connection with Islam exists in Miami in the person of one of the world's greatest architects, the Egyptian Abdel Wahed El Wakil, who is at present teaching in the school as a visiting critic. El Wakil has said that when he was a student in Cairo he especially admired Ruskin and hoped to shape his career according to Ruskin's "Lamp of Truth." He then came to emulate Frank Lloyd Wright and was about to travel to America on a grant to study his work when Nasser seized the Suez Canal and all grants were off. It was then, the West failing him, that El Wakil turned to Islam, and to Hassan Fathy, who was at that time designing beautiful buildings in the Egyptian vernacular tradition. In a sentence that itself recalls the opening of a tale from *The Thousand and One Nights,* El Wakil says of their first encounter, "I met him near the Citadel, under the old wall." Since that time El Wakil has become a master of the grandest classical and vernacular tradition of them all, that of the building of domes. His teaching is based on descriptive geometry, an architectural science now more than half lost. Expounding on it he sounds like Christopher Wren and brings Hadrian and Sinan to life before us. With it, he has shaped domes of brick, never of concrete, for the loveliest mosques of the modern age, in Saudi Arabia and elsewhere (figs. 16, 17). Since the Gulf War, that noble building program has fallen off, and El Wakil has closed his offices in London and the Near East and is in truth a wanderer – Miami's gain. Here, for one of the area's most conspicuous developers, he has designed a house like a small city with an eloquent hierarchy of spaces, now close to construction (plate 113) and, better yet, a mosque for Miami's growing Moslem population, not yet in building. His continued presence in Miami cannot help but raise its level of architectural discourse, while

Fig. 17
Abdel Wahed El Wakil.
Construction detail, Island Mosque,
Jeddah, Saudi Arabia, 1986

nourishing at the same time that bright vein of fantasy so close to its heart.

Fantasy has always played an important part in the architecture of South Florida. Much of the buildable land – including most of the islands in Biscayne Bay, for example – is manmade, pulled up by dredge from the bottom of the sea. Even Merrick on his limestone ridge in Coral Gables aimed for a Mediterranean atmosphere, certainly more urban in character than the meager Cracker vernacular that preceded it. Cracker building, of which all too few examples remain, was normally of wood frame construction, with deep porches and overhangs and good ventilation through the house, including through the crawl space underneath and by vent under the roof, as in Martinez' house (plate 107). It grew out of the board and batten, Stick Style vernacular of the American pattern books of the mid-nineteenth century, and it was entirely appropriate to the area, as it is in slightly different form in Key West. The eloquent little shelter for the homeless that was built by the students of the school in 1992, in a seminar directed by Gary Greenan, was of that kind of construction (fig. 18). Hurricane Andrew blew right through it at the peak of its force and disturbed it not at all. Too bad that the jerry-builders of South Dade were not (and are not) held to its standard.

Fig. 18
Students of the School of Architecture, University of Miami.
Shelter for the Homeless, 1992

Appropriate as the Cracker vernacular was, however, Merrick and the others turned away from it precisely because it seemed too rural to work well in urban groupings or, further, to suggest the kind of Mediterranean urbanity that the climate of South Florida also seemed to encourage. Duany has said that South Florida has had three major styles: the Cracker, the Mediterranean Revival, and the Frivolous Modern of Miami Beach, from which Arquitectonica took some suggestions in its early days in the nineteen-seventies when Duany was with the firm. It is indeed toward fantastic imagery that contemporary South Florida most seems to tend. And into that atmosphere has moved the brilliant Magic Realism of the South American temperament, best typified, as we have seen, by the paintings of Rosario Marquardt (plates 6–12). The architectural projects of Roberto Behar, done alone or in collaboration with Marquardt, are also in this vein. In one of his early schemes, conceived for a Mexican neighborhood in San Diego (plate 114), the sacred image is drawn on a background of script, part Spanish (Bernal Díaz), part English (the Declaration of Independence). The same device is used in Behar's "Motel Room," where a little wheeled caravan trundles across the text (plate 115). This seems quite Argentine, suggesting at once the pampas and that country's well-known obsession with European semiotic theory, but in Behar's and Marquardt's work the simple and overwhelming magic of the physical image always dominates. So Behar's "Table Clock" (plate 116), featuring a base that turns to indicate the hour, creates a disquieting mouse-eye scale. The tiny doll figures (which sometimes appear in Marquardt's paintings) seem especially sinister here. Best of all, though, is Behar's "Temple for Seaside" (plate 117). He shows us where the monstrous structure should be placed, more or less on the central axis of the town with flat forest lands behind it, but the drawing shows it silhouetted against a vast and tragic American sky, the canopy of an open desert, like those that flare in Cormac McCarthy's *Blood Meridian*. The cylinder itself is open to the sky; its vast hat brim – John Wayne, Frank Lloyd Wright? – is a banal North American image gone terribly wrong, misread by the Latin imagination and so transformed into a sublime continental presence not suspected before.

In a way, Behar's imagination suggests Christo's. They are in fact linked by projects for Miami Bay. Christo wrapped the manmade islands; Behar proposed the creation of yet another island, to be called the Star of Miami (plates 118, 119), and to be seen best, like the others, from the airliners letting down toward the M.I.A or lifting off from it. The Star was to be mostly garden, choked with the great palms Marquardt loves, a place for contemplation about what Miami is and what the tropics may mean. Drawings of its "Coral Gate" and "Blue Bench" show the giant green palm fronds, as dark and heavy as those of the Douanier Rousseau (plates 120, 122). Implicit in them is the affronted Indian image emerging from the jungle, as it does in Marquardt's paintings of the Conquest series (plate 123). Like them, too, is Behar and Marquardt's most effective urban project to date: "Jungle Cab," wherein the cars of Miami's Metro Mover would be painted with jungle palms and flowers (plate 121). There is now considerable interest in Miami in seeing this proposal carried out, and well there should be: the Metro Mover is elevated; its cars string out across the great skies, the "cloud-mountains of Florida"; and in this guise, as if wrapped by Christo, how marvelous they would be, and what a disarming symbol of itself for a Miami perennially worried about its image in the tourist world.

Behar and Marquardt's big "M," designed as a symbol of Miami, is in fact going forward (plate 124). It is being built in the embrace of the elevated People Mover, the Metro's extension around downtown. It will surely become a decisive presence among the rather straggly towers that have come to shape Miami's skyline. As in Rossi's work, very much admired by Behar, time plays a part, and a clock will hang, perhaps rather disconcertingly, between the creature's knees.

Behar's work is generally directed by a lively concern for social justice, from which his project "Little Guatemala" derived. It was designed after Hurricane Andrew for the Guatemalan migrant workers of South Dade – people who, as Behar points out, had nothing whatever left after the storm, no mobile homes, no belongings, no insurance. He projects a town for them (plates 125, 126) which, as drawn in plan and axonometric, recalls those of the *manzana urbana* of the Spanish Colonial tradition (plates 68–70). The color is hot; it is clearly a tropical settlement of solid street facades, courtyard houses, and monumental public spaces. The plan shows us how to read the three-dimensional image of the plan-axonometric. A great plaza has its own star and a baroque staircase rising to elevated groves. The church gets special treatment (plate 128), and a grand rough color sketch shows a red clock tower, recalling downtown's M, at the entrance to the square (plate 127). As always, Behar's design is the most powerfully, even brutally, Magic Realist of any produced by the school. The black bull roams through it. Behar and Marquardt rise together to a kind of Latin sublime hard to match, a tragic art full of awe and terror, with a special Hispanic resonance of its own.

A drawing by Rolando Llanes for Armando Montero (plate 129), an alumnus of the school, for housing after the hurricane is for the same site in Perrine as that for which Little Guatemala was intended. But it is wholly different in feeling, proposing a much gentler architecture of columned porches and hipped roofs, developing a more Anglo urbanism of grass plots and trees.

All this work carries the drawings toward the program that is the logical outcome of the pedagogical system that produced them: the building of the community as a whole, the design of towns. Here, naturally enough, the central, generating work has been that of DPZ, but other members of the faculty of the school, though also working with Duany and Plater-Zyberk over the years, continue to do important studies and projects of that kind on their own. Two of them who have concentrated largely on urban design are Jean-François Lejeune and Jaime Correa, who sometimes work alone, sometimes in collaboration. The charming drawing of the *Dorfplatz* at Vockerode (plate 130) is Correa's; it is the most solid and original of a series done during a seminar in Germany. The drawings produced by that seminar explored the kind of primitive classicism or simplified medievalism (*ur*-classicism and *ur*-medievalism might be better terms) that had first appeared in Leon Krier's stunning drawings of the nineteen-seventies, which, more than any other graphic agency, had helped spark the vernacular and classical revivals of his generation. They, too, embodied a physical reality impossible to ignore, and they were combined by Krier with an equally solid sense of the city as a whole, as a grouping of simple types put together under apparently timeless architectural laws. Krier's effect on Duany and Plater-Zyberk was critical and has indeed been felt by everyone involved in the new urbanism. Correa's drawings reflect that influence and bring some of Miami's own brio to it.

It is interesting to note that the seminar for which Correa did his drawing of Vockerode was fortuitously able to make a study of the Bauhaus in Dessau, during which the students from Miami were quite taken with the more traditional housing that had later been built directly across the street from the Bauhaus itself. The German students, by contrast, were not yet able to look at that housing with open eyes because it was not "Modern" in style. The Bauhaus, as published, normally seems to exist in space all by itself, because Gropius and his colleagues were accustomed to airbrushing out the surroundings in the old photographs. It was in fact sensitively adjusted to the existing street pattern, as is the later housing across the way, which indeed complements the famous old revolutionary building in shaping a reasonable urban space. The Miami students were able to look at both because they had come to understand that type is infinitely more important than style in urban situations, and that these were equally simple blocks of buildings defining streets. Correa's drawing of the Latin American city, the *manzana urbana* of the Colonial period (plate 131), shows that type clearly enough. This drawing is computer-generated. Here the computer, with the study of its capacities very advanced at the school, is used according to what Thomas Spain regards as its strength: "to study an idea, not to formulate one."

Seminars directed by Correa and Lejeune have produced studies of classical city plans like that for a "New Caribbean Town in Florida" (plate 132). This goes to the heart of the Mediterranean tradition with its archetypal Roman plan based on the intersection of the *cardo* and the *decumanus* and laid out more or less on the fixed pattern of the legionary camp as described by Polybius. The North African city of Timgad is recalled. This plan is one of the clearest expressions of the enduring authority of Rome which the great classicist Frank E. Brown of the American Academy in Rome was so successful in communicating to Modern historians and architects, most notably Louis I. Kahn, in the early nineteen-fifties. Traditional American urban layouts are also studied in these seminars, as in the black-and-white, solid-and-void renderings of Georgetown and Nantucket (plates 133, 134). Finally, Lejeune and Correa focus on the climax of the American planning tradition, before it was engulfed by Modernism and instantly forgotten, in the work of John Nolen, dean of the American planners of the period 1910–30 (plate 135). The cul-de-sacs of Clarence Stein and Henry Wright, more modest but hardly less wrongheaded in conception and destructive in effect than the cataclysmic utopian schemes of Le Corbusier and American Redevelopment, still lay in the future in Nolen's time and now give way at last to a revival of the sounder principles developed by him and his contemporaries out of the City Beautiful and Garden City movements of the early days of the century.

That revival has been brought about largely by the work of Duany and Plater-Zyberk, and it came to light in Seaside first of all. That work has at one time or another engaged the talents of almost all the faculty and students mentioned in this book. Most of them have done drawings for one or more of DPZ's projects. Among them is the monumental plan for Seaside by Jean-François Lejeune and his students, showing the earliest buildings on the site (plate 137). The houses are drawn in plan, the larger buildings in one of the first examples of that "Chinese perspective" the school was to employ so consistently later on. Here are the grid, the radiating avenues, and the hemicycles of Nolen's tradition, employed in the first coherent town design in America since his time.

The drawings of Seaside that the school most values are those that describe its building code and the sections of its streets (plates 138–42). They are more historically significant than graphically rich, though they are conceived elegantly enough. The streets recall drawings by Nolen and his generation of a kind that had gone wholly out of style under Modernism, which felt nothing but contempt for the street and was therefore incapable of designing one. The graphic representation of the code is of a kind that Nolen might well have employed as a way to bring his plans up into three dimensions as he imagined them: to enforce, as he could rarely do, their realization in the way the town was actually built. Poor Nolen. He believed that if buildings were "controlled by standards such as those recently adopted by the Federal Government to serve war needs . . . we may safely take chances on [their] appearance." He was right so far as World War I housing was concerned, but those controls were not in force when he designed his towns of Venice and Clewiston in the twenties, and there the whole thing tends to break down in three dimensions. By contrast, Duany, Plater-Zyberk, and Robert Davis, the developer of Seaside, learned to value a strict building code in Coral Gables, where Merrick had been determined to ensure that his new town was shaped in every particular as he wanted it to be and as owner and developer was able to control the process far more strictly than Nolen as hired planner was ever able to do. It is symptomatic of the change that has come about in architectural thinking during the past forty years or so that many of us who applauded Frank Lloyd Wright's tussles with town building codes during the first half of the century (in which the town was right more often than not) now positively welcome the code as an essential device in the building of coherent communities. All human societies are built on law; their architecture is no exception to that rule and indeed has never in past history been exempted from it.

By the same token, design at DPZ is a group activity, as that of Merrick's architects was. The contributions of individuals in the office, often university faculty and students, have been important from the beginning. That group interaction grew directly out of the teaching of the school – or each drew strength from the other. In it the individual was released from divine conceits in order to focus on architecture's grand, human problems and to explore the subjects and techniques of drawing that we have traced: to shape places most of all. So the process of design in school and office does move in one way or another from flora and fauna to maps and axonometrics and buildings and gardens, while Documentaries and Composites do come together in Projects and all combine at last to shape the town as a whole, to which everyone involved in the community has something to contribute.

So Marquardt colored an early project for Orlando (plates 143–45) and did portraits of Duany and Plater-Zyberk (plates 146,

147), the former looking deceptively like a chocolate soldier, the latter not at all deceptively like a young she-wolf with pale lanterns for eyes. The portraits should be seen side by side, so that the masonry wall in both portraits unites them.

One of DPZ's most important projects, that for the large town of Wellington in Florida, fell foul of the recession of the early nineties and had to be abandoned (plates 148, 149). Almost everyone in the school was responsible for the design of one of the neighborhoods. The last complete plan of the project was done, like so many of the school's drawings, by many different hands. It is a true group effort that can produce a town precisely because, while they require codes, towns also need variety, which is best supplied by different individuals (if they all know what they are doing and obey the same laws). That is why Duany and Plater-Zyberk consistently avoid designing all the buildings in their projects themselves. Wellington is also a classic expression of the South Florida made by dredge. Here, the land areas were to have been scooped up from the bottom of the bay, so that land and water would have existed in a true one-to-one relationship. This close interaction, coupled with the utter thinness of surface which is its visual result, recalls the character of the great French classic gardens of the seventeenth century, especially those of Vaux-le-Vicomte, Chantilly, and Versailles. The Fairchild Tropical Gardens, which were so important for the education of architects and clients alike in South Florida, are equally thin in surface where ponds and streams meander through the made-land lying seaward of the öolitic limestone shelf that was once the shore. At Wellington, land and water would have interacted dynamically, each perhaps seeming to push the other and to react to pressure, thereby expanding and contracting along the major paths of movement in a very lively way. One of the neighborhoods was designed by Hernandez and Lejeune but drawn by Charles Barrett (plate 149), who also did the classic perspective of DPZ's town of Windsor (plate 150). A fine plan of Windsor at an early stage, showing some of its first projected buildings, was constructed in the same manner as the Seaside plan by Lejeune and his students (plate 151).

It is curious that Barrett's incomparable drawings were criticized by California planners, who otherwise regarded themselves as more or less in league with DPZ, as being too attractive, too apt to seduce the public with their charm. This odd point of view seems a relic of the dour German Modernism that was determined to discipline humankind into its own reductive image. It also recalls the sinister judgment of the congressional investigating committee that condemned the magnificent low-income housing built in Bridgeport, Connecticut, during the First World War (the finest group of all was called Seaside Park) for its "undue elegance in design" (fig. 19). In other words, it was too good for the poor. The World War II housing that was built directly across the street from Seaside Park, Bauhaus-barrack in character, successfully avoided that error. It is now a center of drug-dealing in Bridgeport, while Seaside Park remains an Eden, lovingly maintained, jealously guarded. It was successful vernacular housing for center city – something that contemporary critics of DPZ's similar urban vernacular say the firm cannot do. Bridgeport's old Seaside says that it can be done, and is surely an illustration of the truth of Duany's comment, "Once we did architecture right in the United States, and now we are doing it wrong."

Windsor, of course, has nothing to do with the poor – it has two polo fields. But its progress suggests how pervasive the desire for community has become among Americans. Windsor offers houses by the ocean and others around the golf course (an old Florida favorite), but every client so far has chosen to build in the gridded town that lies in the center of the development. Those who are free to choose here choose community. The poor, who need it most but have lost it to urban connectors, high-rises, and Redevelopment, had it once and can surely have it again.

Fig. 19
R. Clipston Sturgis with Andrew W. Hepburn (for the United States Housing Corporation). **Emergency wartime housing at Seaside Park,** Bridgeport, Connecticut, 1918

At any rate, Barrett's graphics are neither self-referential nor misleading. DPZ designs the towns as Barrett draws them. A characteristic example is the aerial perspective of Pathways, a retirement community in Miami (plate 152). A solidly traditional architecture with a hierarchy of building types clearly defines the streets and other open spaces. The streets are kept as narrow as is practical, which is much narrower than departments of transportation, in these days the most sinister urban force of all, normally demand, so that in most new developments they are much too wide and all sense of community is lost, and blacktop and automobile take over. DPZ shows that the automobile can be disciplined; it need not obliterate everything, as it is threatening to do. The basic question – whether the automobile and civilization as we have known it can permanently coexist – has not yet been answered. DPZ, counter to what its critics seem to think, believes that coexistence may be possible so long as we design for some time against the automobile rather than for it. Why should it alone be exempt from larger laws? So Barrett's retirement community looks and feels like a true town and is indeed generically linked to the town traditions of the pre-automobile era.

DPZ's confidence in the specialness of places and their local ways of building, long explored in the drawings of the school, informs all their work. Houses in the wooden vernacular of Turkish architecture, suggestive of the American Stick Style, shape the new town of Kemer (plate 153), designed for Esat Edin, who studied at Yale and is now in Turkish government service. DPZ is also designing community environments made up of very low-cost housing indeed. The group called Rosa Vista in Tempe, Arizona, is intended for mobile homes (plates 154–56). Adobe walls and portals create an urban frame, shaping streets and squares into which the mobile homes can be plugged. The curse is, as it were, taken off them, and they can take their places in a town built according to the most enduring traditions of its region. Even more to the point is the Nehemiah neighborhood group in Cleveland (plate 157). This is an inner city African-American community which Duany and Plater-Zyberk here bring to participate in the architectural environment of which most Americans have dreamed, that of the single-family house on its own lot, set on a street with a sidewalk and a strip of grass, planted with trees (plate 158). One hopes that it will be only the first of many such neighborhoods to be built. It is today's equivalent of Bridgeport's Seaside, but Robert A. M. Stern's Subway Suburb, of 1976, conceived for the South Bronx, should not be forgotten (fig. 20). Here, for the first time as a complete and integrated system of design, the principles of the traditional suburban town, studied by Stern and published in an important book by him, were brought to bear on the rebuilding of center city, now generally destroyed. Its inhabitants, literally betrayed by the modern age and Modernist planning into disorienting high-rise compounds in devastated cities, were considered American enough to enjoy the architectural types of house, suburb, and town that more affluent Americans had consistently preferred. The project was never realized, but its influence was considerable, since Duany, after receiving his architectural degree from Yale, worked for Stern during this period.

Fig. 20
Robert A. M. Stern.
Subway Suburb project, 1976. Ink

Finally, prevented from realization by the political clout of the builders of the area, whose own products could not compete with its low price, there is DPZ's Migrant Workers Housing for Florida City (plates 159, 160). In layout and scale the group shares some of the Central American characteristics of Behar's "Little Guatemala" (plates 125–28), despite the fact that the houses are based on mobile-home technology, employing its spatial units and methods of wall construction. But the dominant image is of low, flat-roofed rows of houses painted in bright colors, recalling those of the Caribbean and Mexico. They bring to mind J. B. Jackson's article "Chihuahua as We Might Have Been," which describes the differences in the similar topographical environments created by human culture on the two sides of the border. In South Florida, perhaps a bit as William Jennings Bryan hoped, the border has broken down, and the little houses affirm it. Each would have cost $30,000, half the going local rate for considerably less. Maybe workers in the endless baking furrows of South Dade might just have made it in this housing, and enjoyed something of the cultural stability and dignified family life they deserved. The rendering is endlessly appropriate, stretched out as it is into a narrow horizontal band on the big page, like the houses themselves on the flat fields under enormous skies.

It seems wrong, however, to end on a blithe note of architectural achievement, however frustrated by the character of the world. It is true that the drawing of the school, as it has developed over only a very few years, has come together to create and support the architecture of community that constitutes the school's special contribution to American society at the present time. But in the end the drawings are not primarily about success or simple achievement. They are, as we might hope Ruskin would have recognized, concerned most of all with reverence for the thing seen, especially for the reality of the South Florida land. There are the Everglades, with the thin Dade County pines leading out into the sky across the flat expanse (plate 161). There is the grass that Marjorie Stoneman Douglas made us understand (plate 162); the boardwalk of Everglades National Park leads us toward it. There finally is the Hammock (plate 163), South Florida's glory, packed with vegetable and animal life, and there are the graves before it, just barely above the level of the water. They will be swamped at flood time, like those of Uruk, and like them they are all that is left of the human beings who tenaciously worked and shaped the land.

Then the great drawing by Ceo and his students unfolds (plate 136). In it we witness the human hold on the earth as it takes shape in agriculture, the foundation of all community since Neolithic times, the mother of all its arts. The drawing was made after Hurricane Andrew in order to study the fundamental structure of the farming communities in Redland. It is a holistic drawing, showing everything. The straight line of the road links the grid of individual holdings; we travel along it as along a Chinese scroll. The relation of building to field is shown with every tree and all the crops, like the bricks drawn by Mies' students but so much more. It is a map and can be measured, and it becomes a three-dimensional place through the axonometrics we know. Only a drawing so unconscionably long could have revealed the structural fact of this place: the fact of the road. Something like Vogt's door (plate 42), this drawing is big enough to be almost the thing itself, in this case a place to cultivate and inhabit for a lifetime, to be known wholly only through the long hard work of many years. It shows us what architecture is, a space of nature shaped by human beings, here reality realized and community promised in the order of farms. It is the beginning of everything and the underlying structure of everything, and those who draw it here are determined to make us see that and remember it however old we grow.

1. Denman Fink. **Administration Building, University of Miami (Phineas Paist, architect),** 1925. Watercolor, 36 x 24"

2. Aldo Rossi. **Ziff Tower, University of Miami,** 1989. Mixed media, 21 x 30"

3. Phineas Paist. **Campus aerial, University of Miami,** 1925. Pencil and watercolor, 36 x 24″

4. Thomas Spain. **Coral Gables Police and Fire Department building (Denman Fink and Phineas Paist, architect),** 1992. Colored pencil, 15 x 18"

5. Thomas Spain. **El Prado entrance (banyan),** 1982. Colored pencil, 17 x 15″

6. Rosario Marquardt. **Memories of Mar de Plata (after Fra Filippo Lippi)**, 1985. Colored pencil, 15 x 21″

7. Rosario Marquardt. **Dean Ziff,** 1986. Colored pencil, 20 x 37″

8. Rosario Marquardt. **Jania Ziff,** 1986. Colored pencil, 20 x 37″

9. Rosario Marquardt. **A Arrivato: Sampano! (Aldo Rossi)**, 1986. Colored pencil, 15 x 21"

10. Rosario Marquardt. **Roberto,** 1987. Pencil and pastel, 16 x 26″

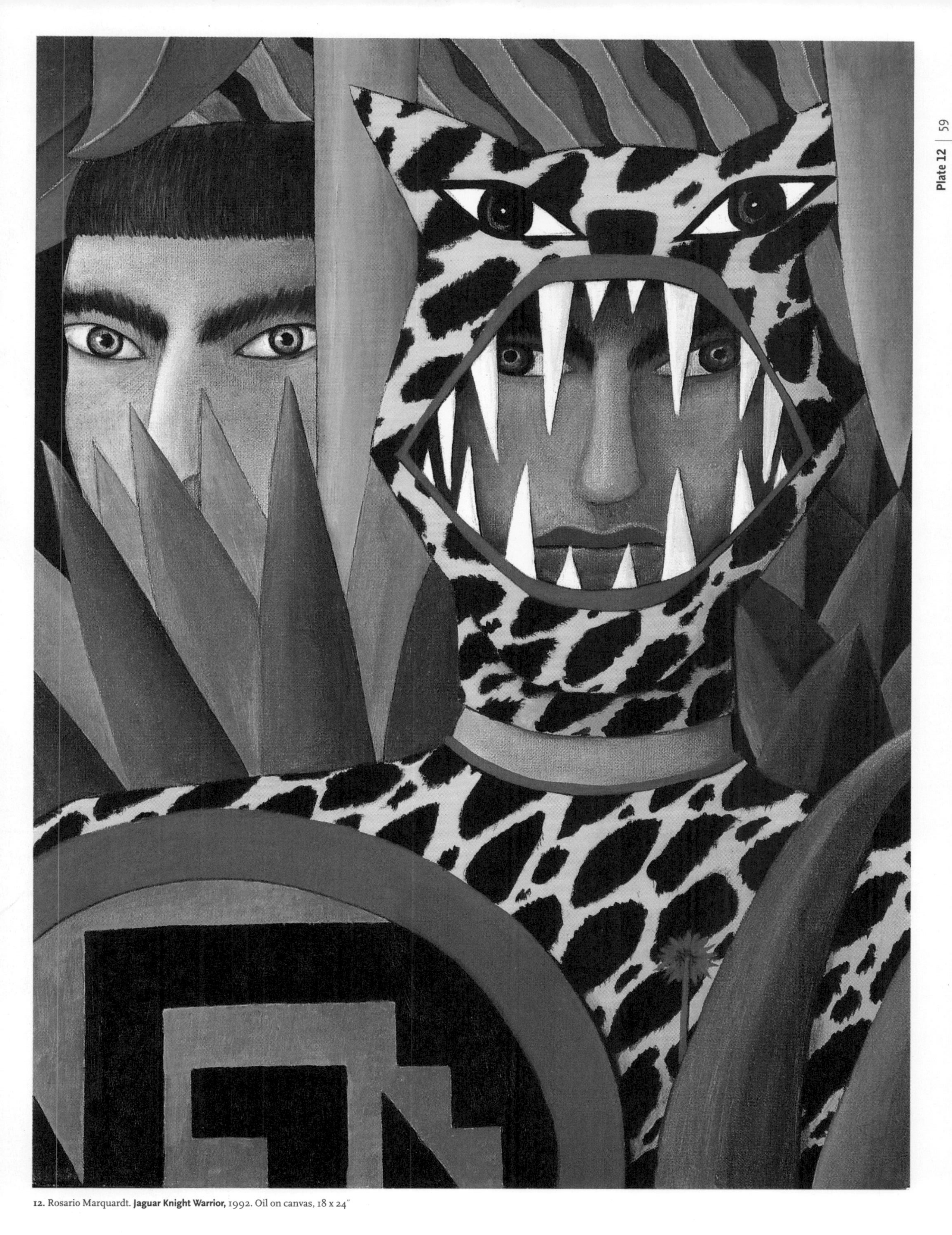

12. Rosario Marquardt. **Jaguar Knight Warrior,** 1992. Oil on canvas, 18 x 24"

11. Rosario Marquardt. **Aguirre,** 1991. Oil on canvas, 18 x 24"

13. Juan Camillo Caycedo. **Self portrait,** 1988. Colored pencil, 24 x 36"

14. Roberto Orosa. **Self portrait with Augustus,** 1988. Colored pencil, 24 x 36"

15. Jose Valencia. **Self portrait with project**, 1988. Colored pencil, 24 x 36"

16. Deborah Verley. **Yard: self portrait,** 1988. Colored pencil, 24 x 36″

17. Ana Alas. **Massacre of the Innocents,** 1988. Colored pencil, 36 x 24″

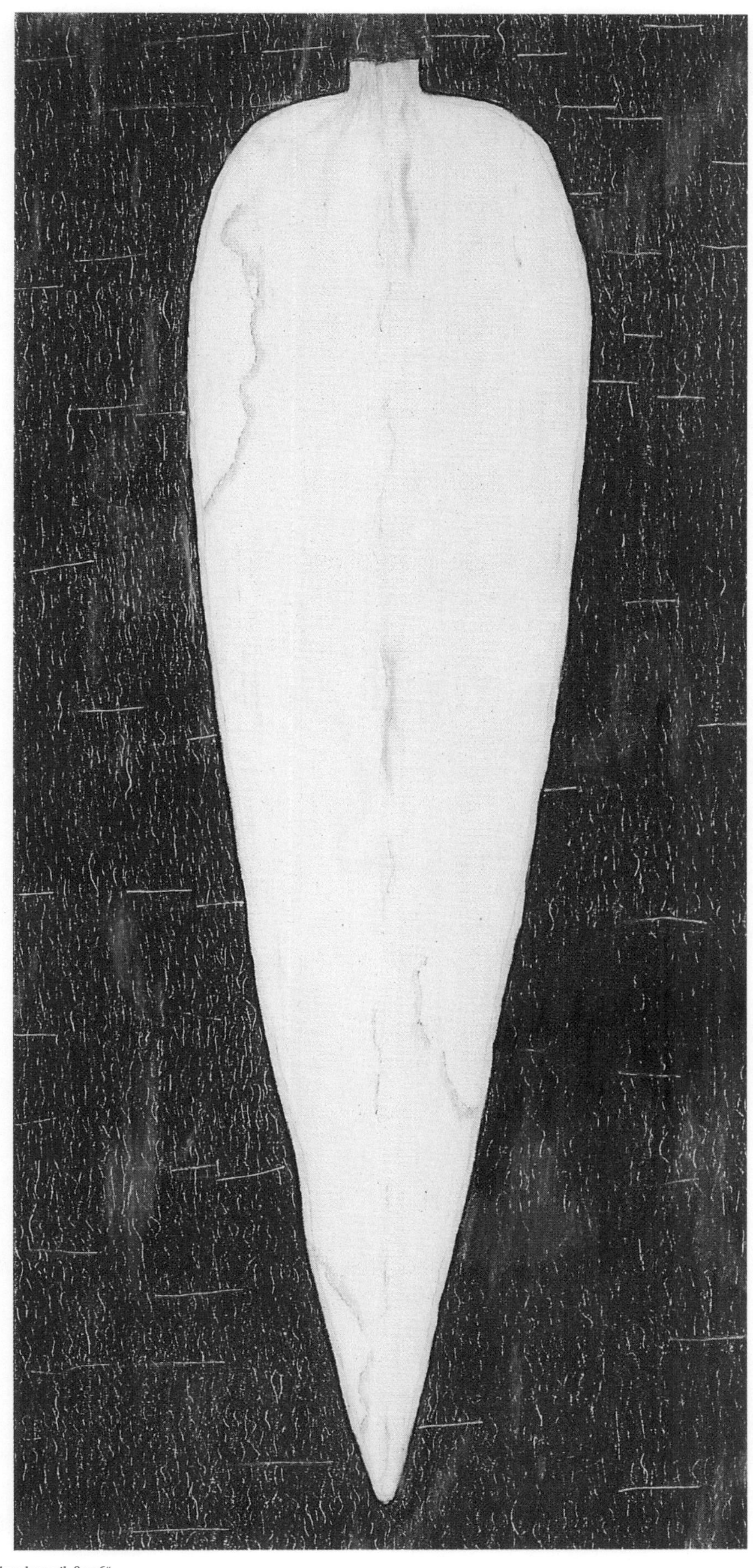

18. Mauricio Candela. **Yuca,** 1991. Colored pencil, 8 x 16"

19. Viki Byke. **Yucatan turkey,** 1991. Colored pencil, 36 x 24"

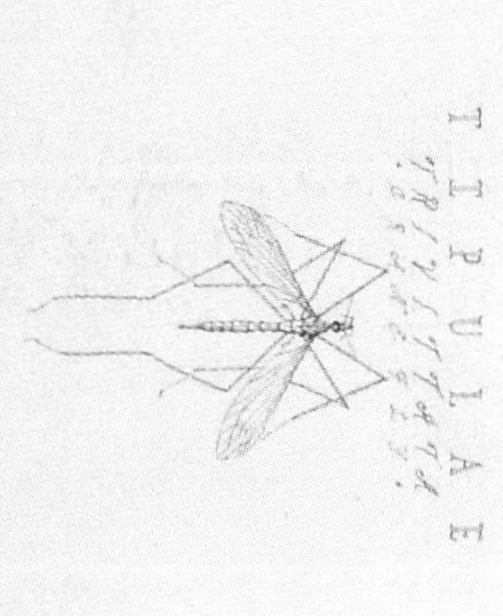

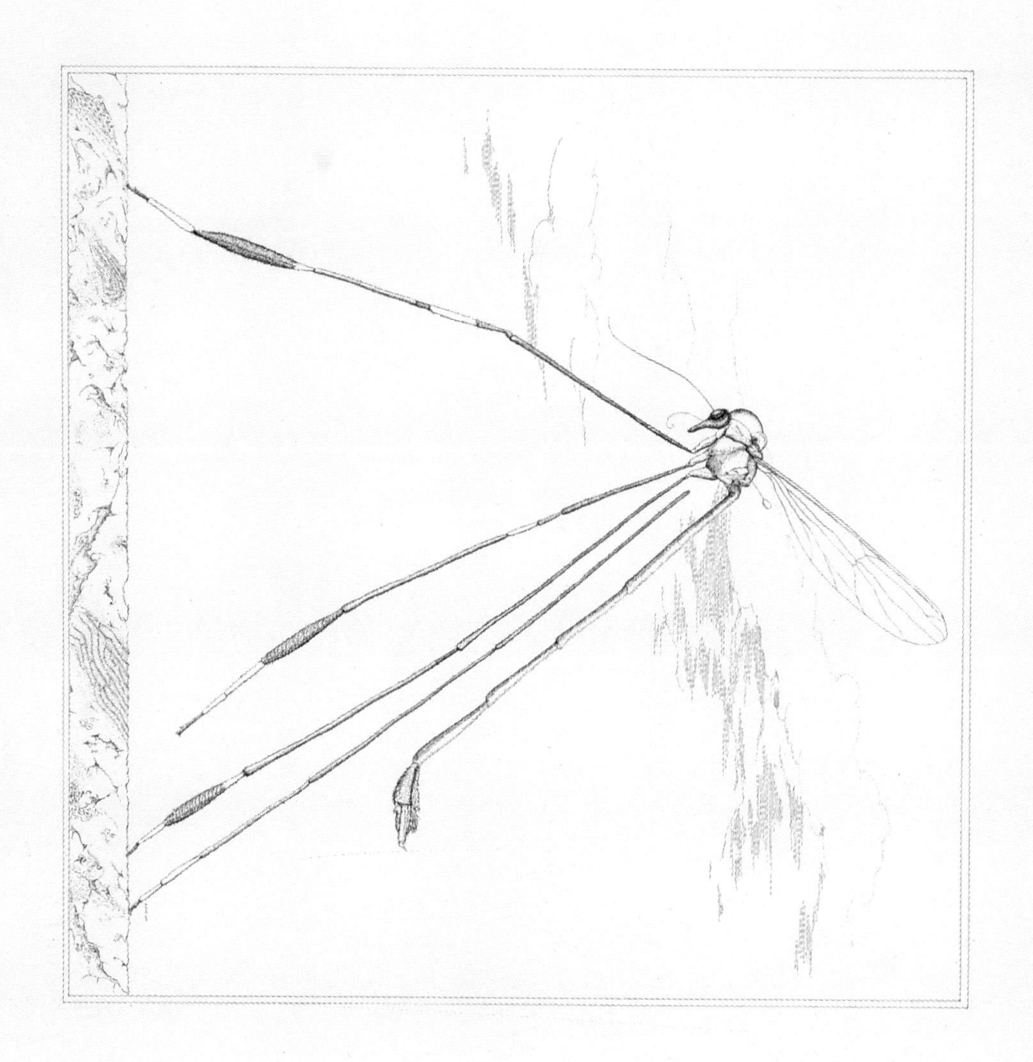

20. Ana Alvarez. **Mosquito,** 1992. ink on paper, 22 x 30"

21. Flavio Barney. **Red Mangrove,** 1990. Ink on mylar, 13 x 21"

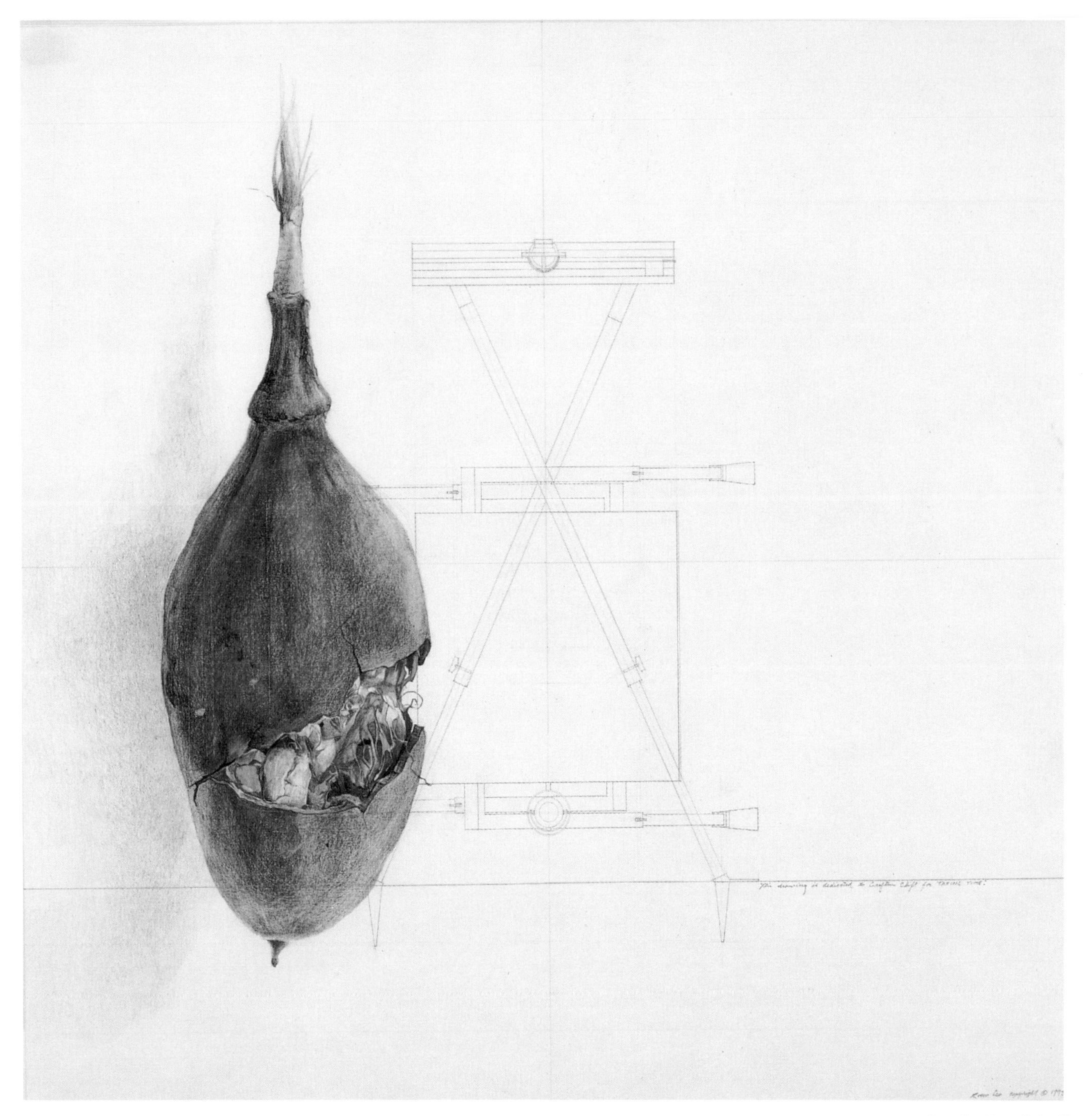

22. Rocco Ceo. **Naturalist's table and baobob seed,** 1993. Colored pencil, 19 x 19"

23. Rocco Ceo. **Traveler's Palm,** 1990. Colored pencil, 14 x 15″

24. Rocco Ceo. **Balsa Tree,** 1990. Colored pencil, 24 x 18″

25. Graciela Torres. **Conch,** 1994. Colored pencil, 28 x 16″

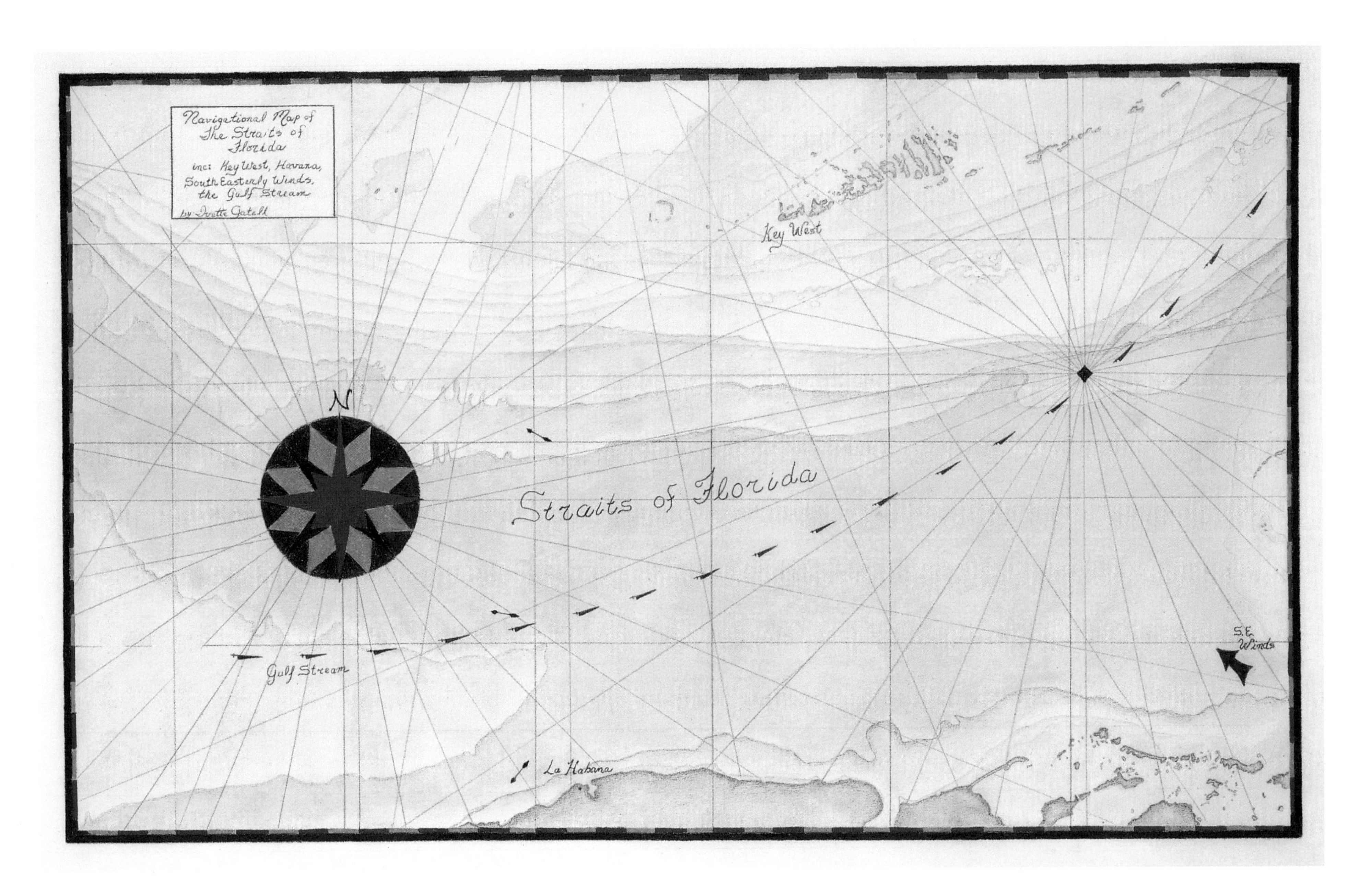

26. Ivette Gatell. **Mapa del Balsero (Map of the Cuban Rafter),** 1994. Colored pencil, 36 x 24"

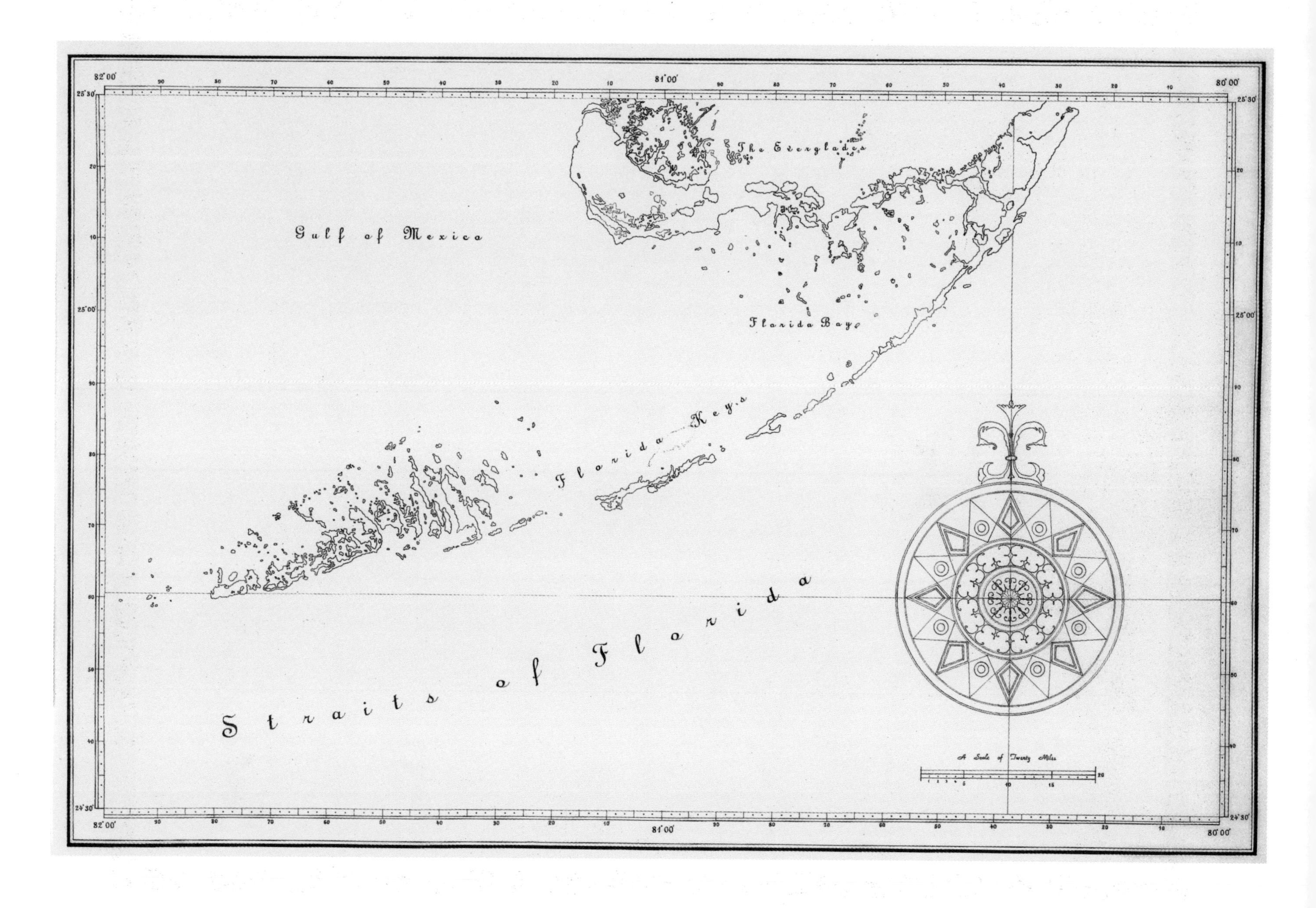

27. Antonio Fuentes. **Florida Keys,** 1994. Ink on mylar, 36 x 24″

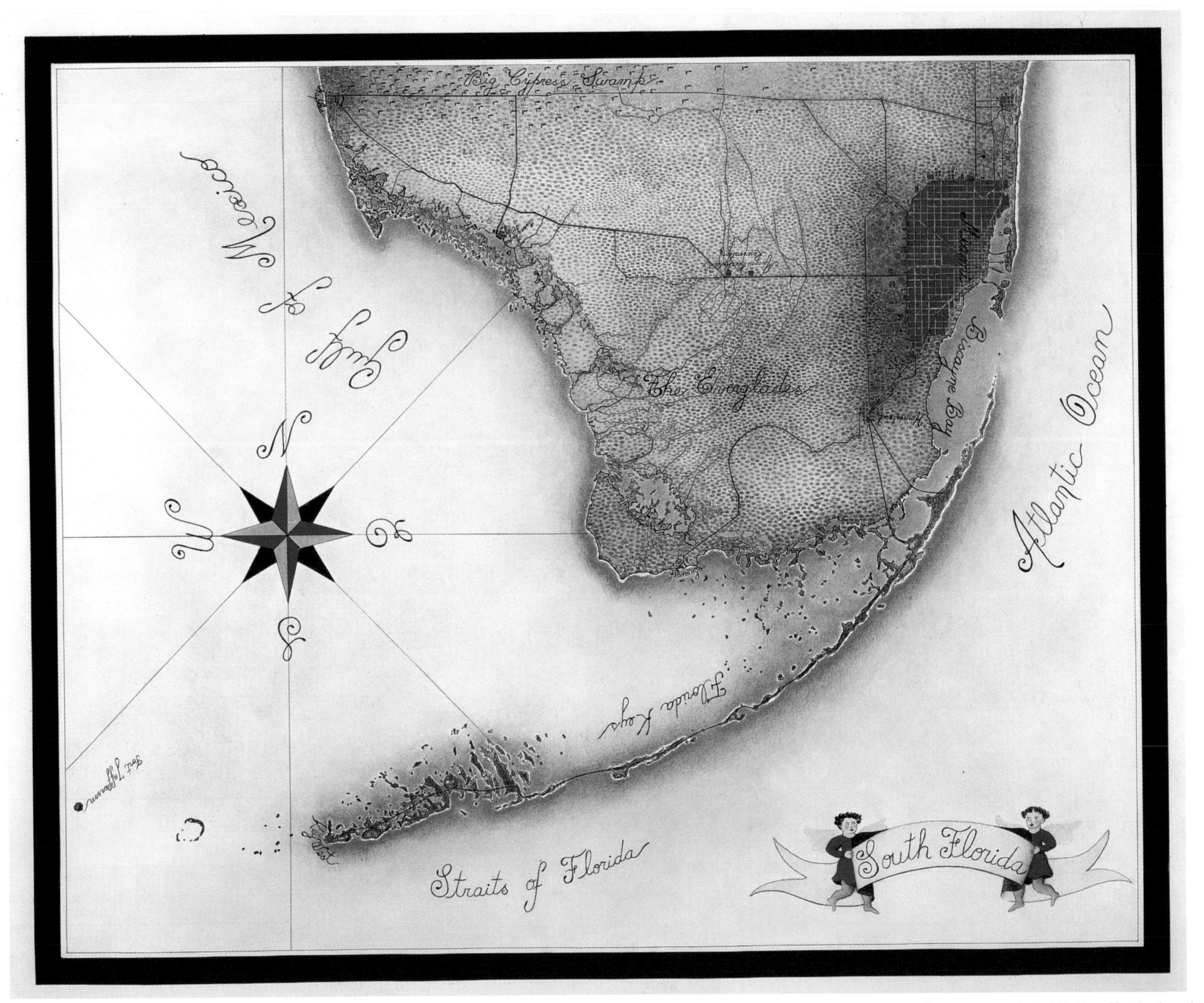

28. Rosario Marquardt. **South Florida,** 1988. Colored pencil, 38 x 30″

29. Ruth Durant, Ivette Gatell, Nicole Renee Henry, and Arthur Infeld. **McKee's Jungle Gardens,** 1994. Ink on mylar, 36 x 48″

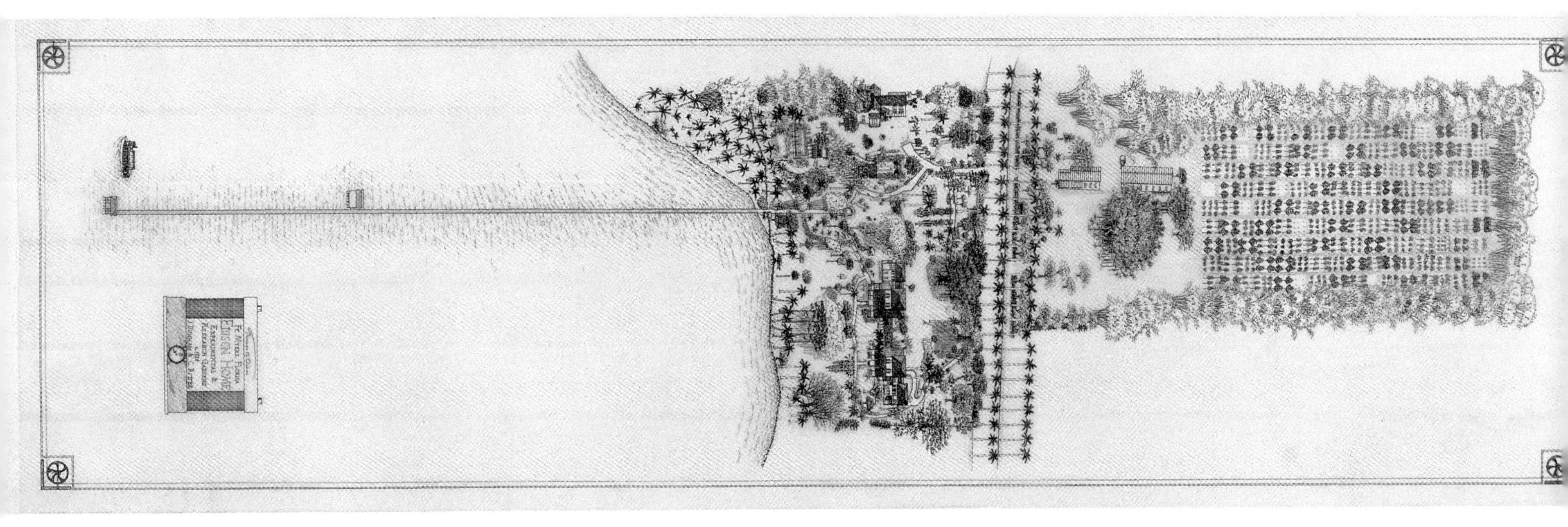
Ft. Myers Florida
Edison Home
Experimental &
Research Gardens

30. Jason Dunham and Chris Ritter. **Edison Home, Fort Meyers,** 1994. Ink on mylar, 32 x 70″

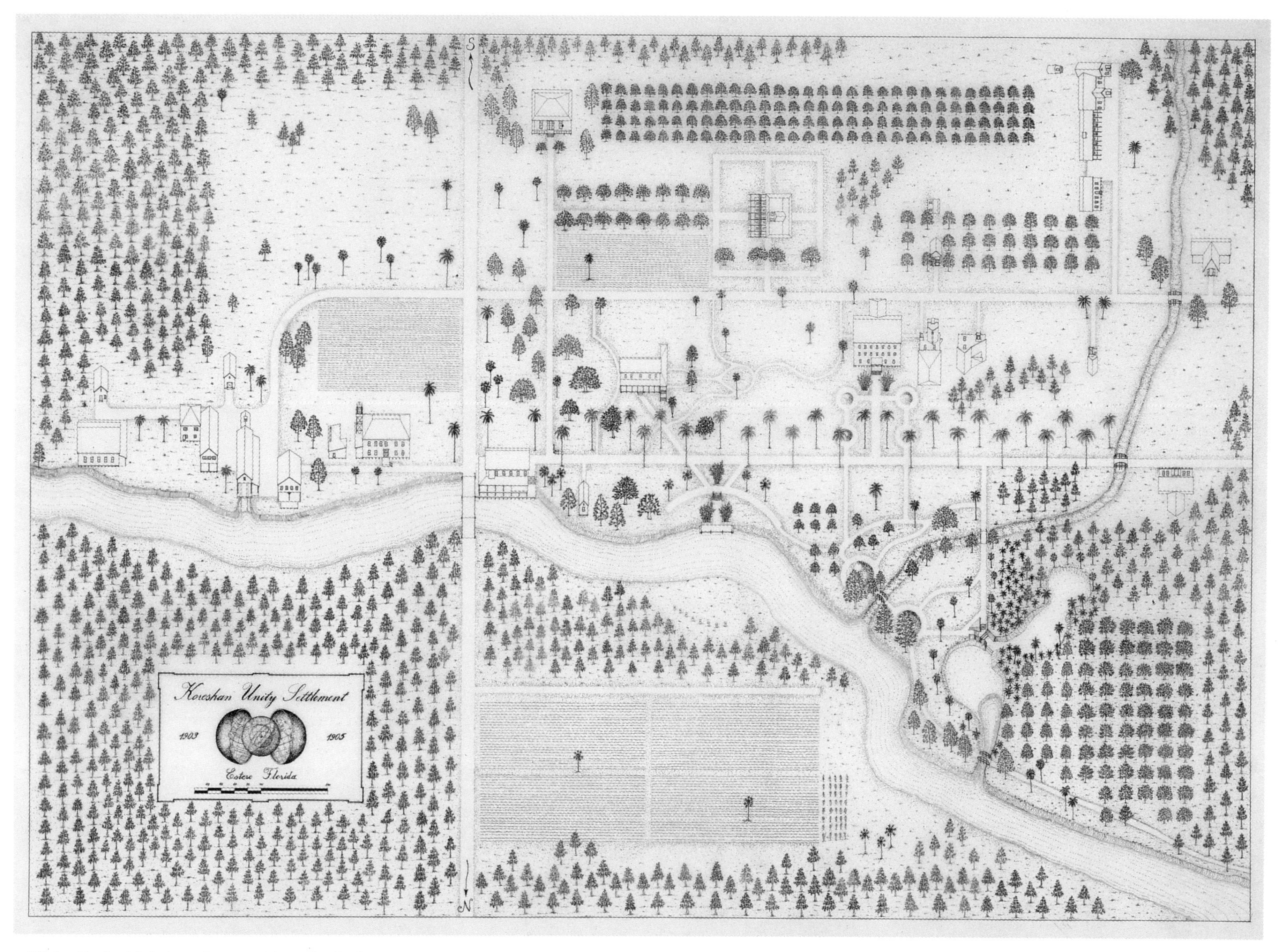

31. Adib Cure. **Koreshan Unity Settlement, Estero,** 1994. Ink on mylar, 48 x 36″

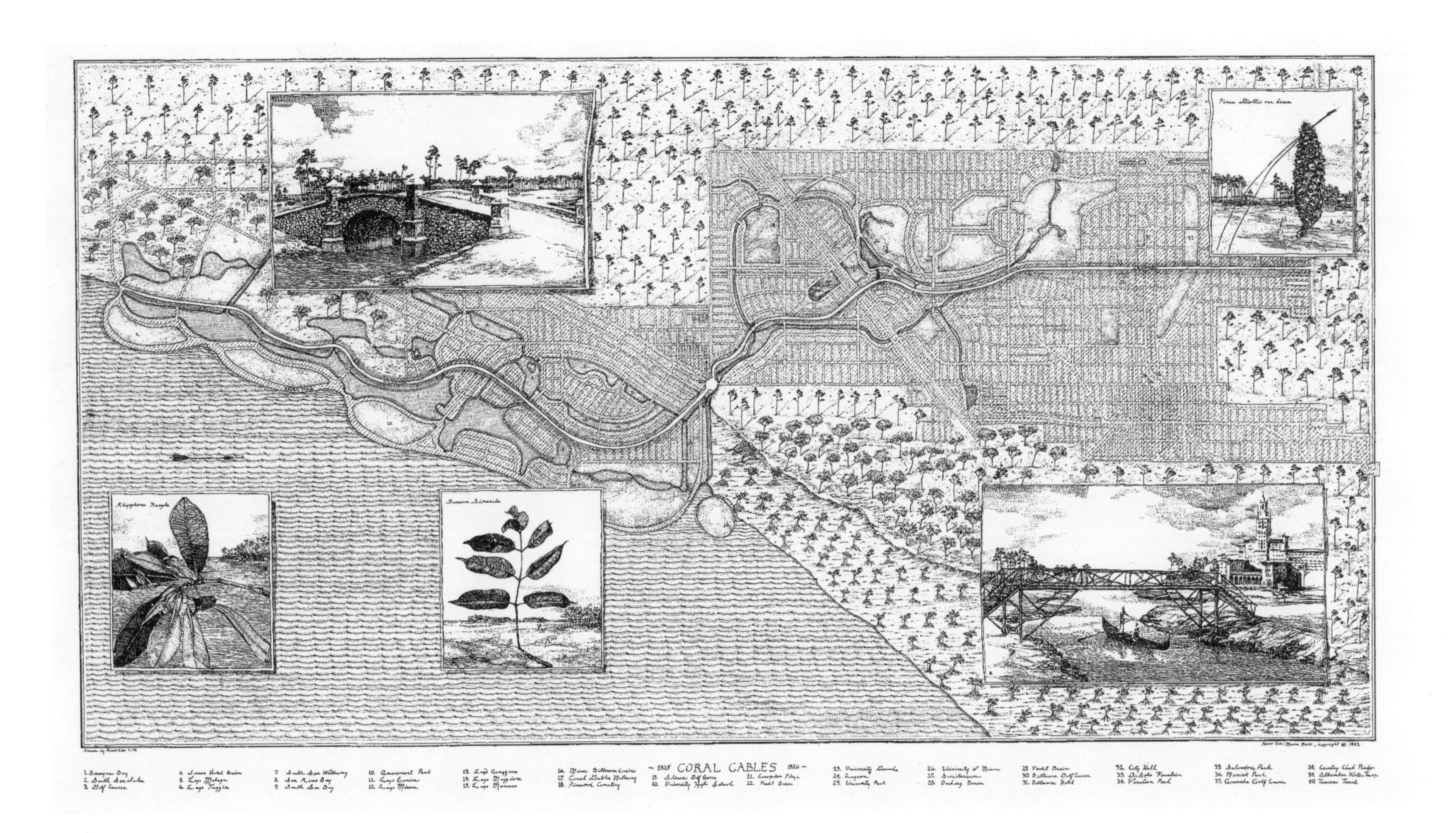

32. Rocco Ceo, Maria Nardi, and Kevin Young. **Map of Coral Gables,** 1992. Ink on paper, 46 x 24"

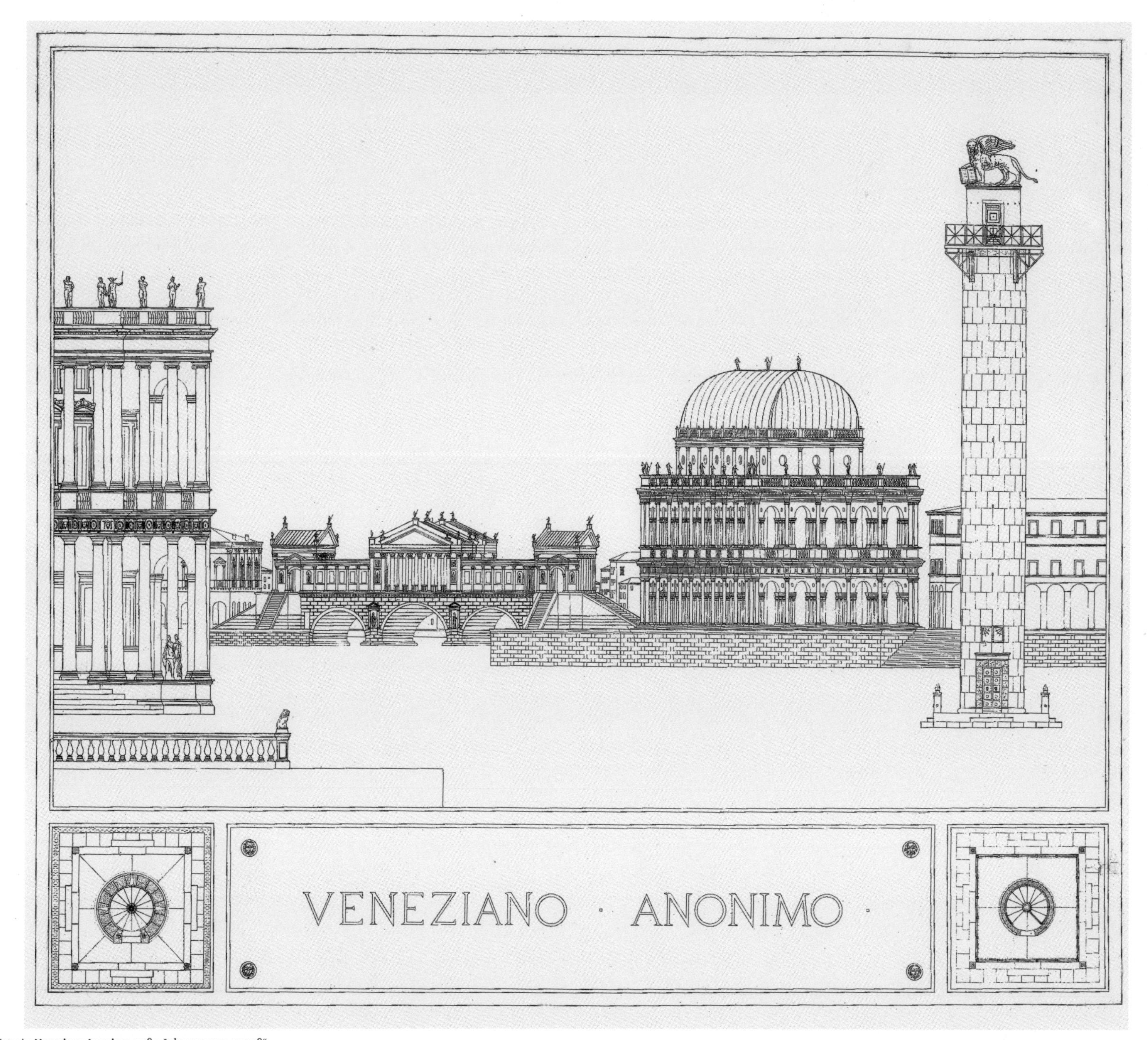

33. Roberto M. Behar and Teofilo Victoria. **Veneziano Anonimo,** 1985. Ink on paper, 42 x 38″

34. Joe Minicozzi. **Campidoglio, Rome,** 1991. Pencil, 20 x 14″

35. Thomas Spain. **Colosseum, Rome,** 1991. Pastel, 19 x 11″

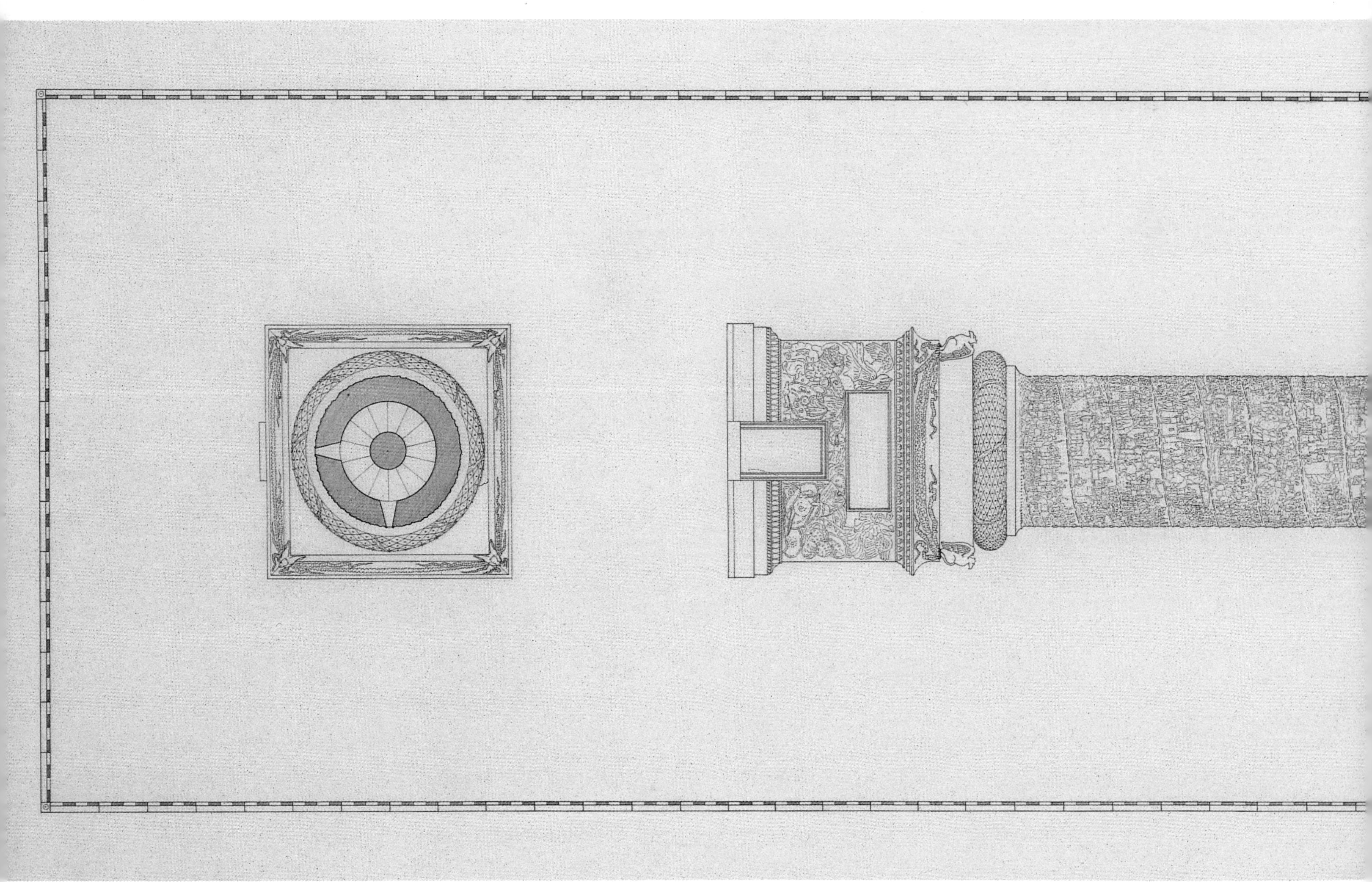

36. Eric Vogt. **Trajan's Column, Rome,** 1992. Ink on paper, 16 x 60"

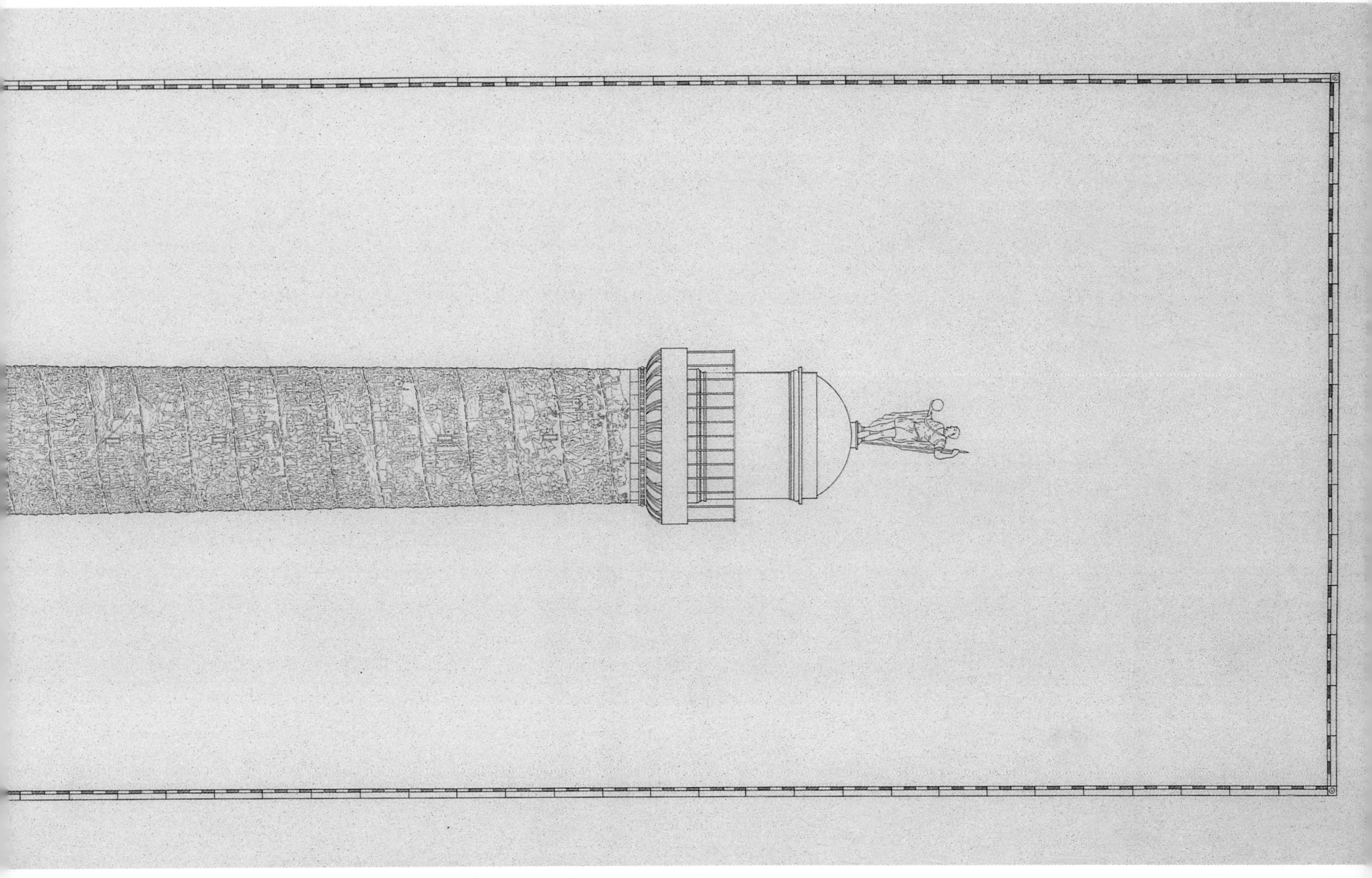

37. James Carrol. **Unfinished drawing of the New London Train Station (H. H. Richardson, architect)**, 1990. Ink on mylar, 36 x 24"

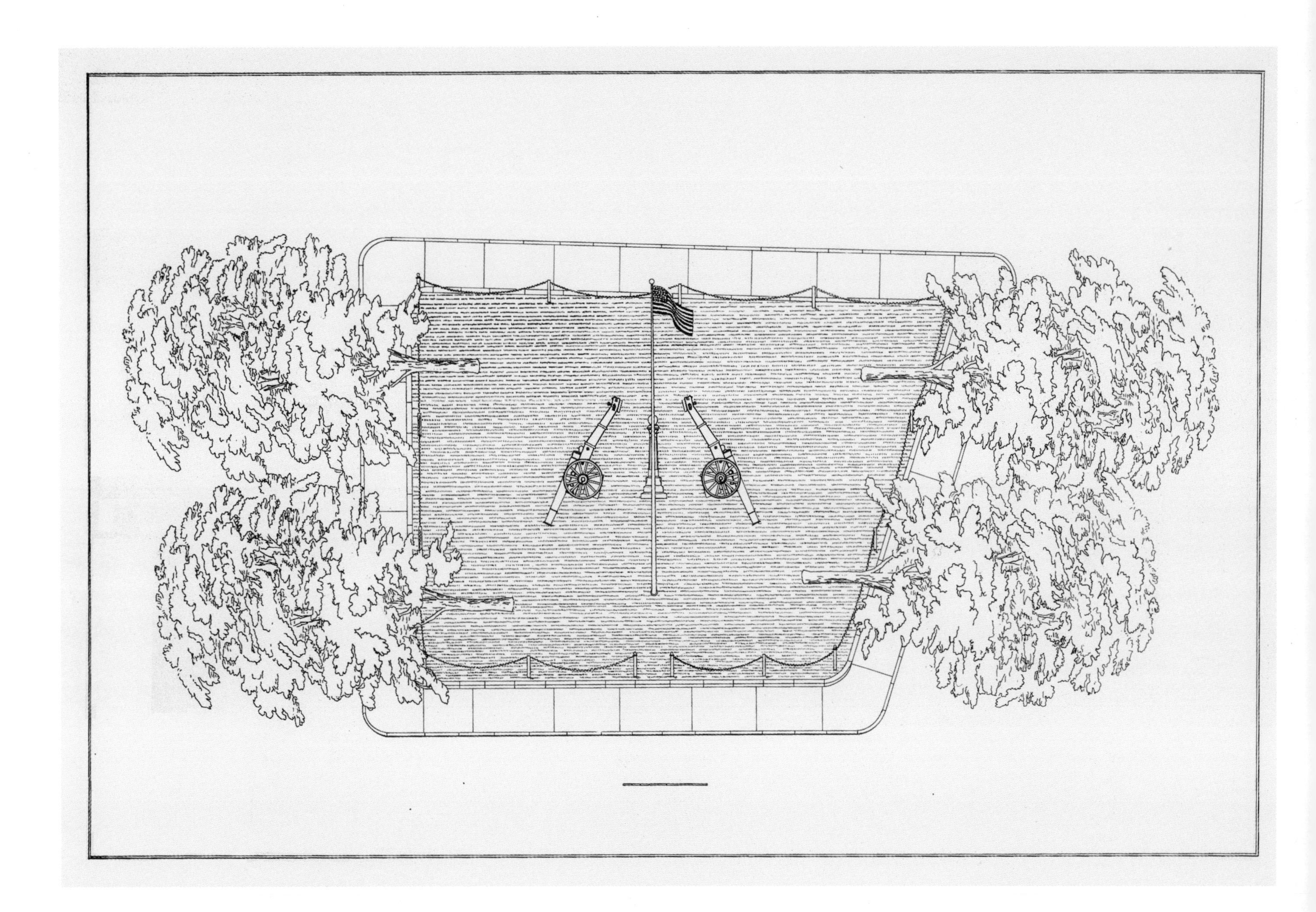

38. Robert Gray. **Stonington Green, New London,** 1990. Ink on mylar, 36 x 24″

39. Ana Alvarez. **Obelisk Churchyard, New London,** 1990. Ink on mylar, 24 x 36"

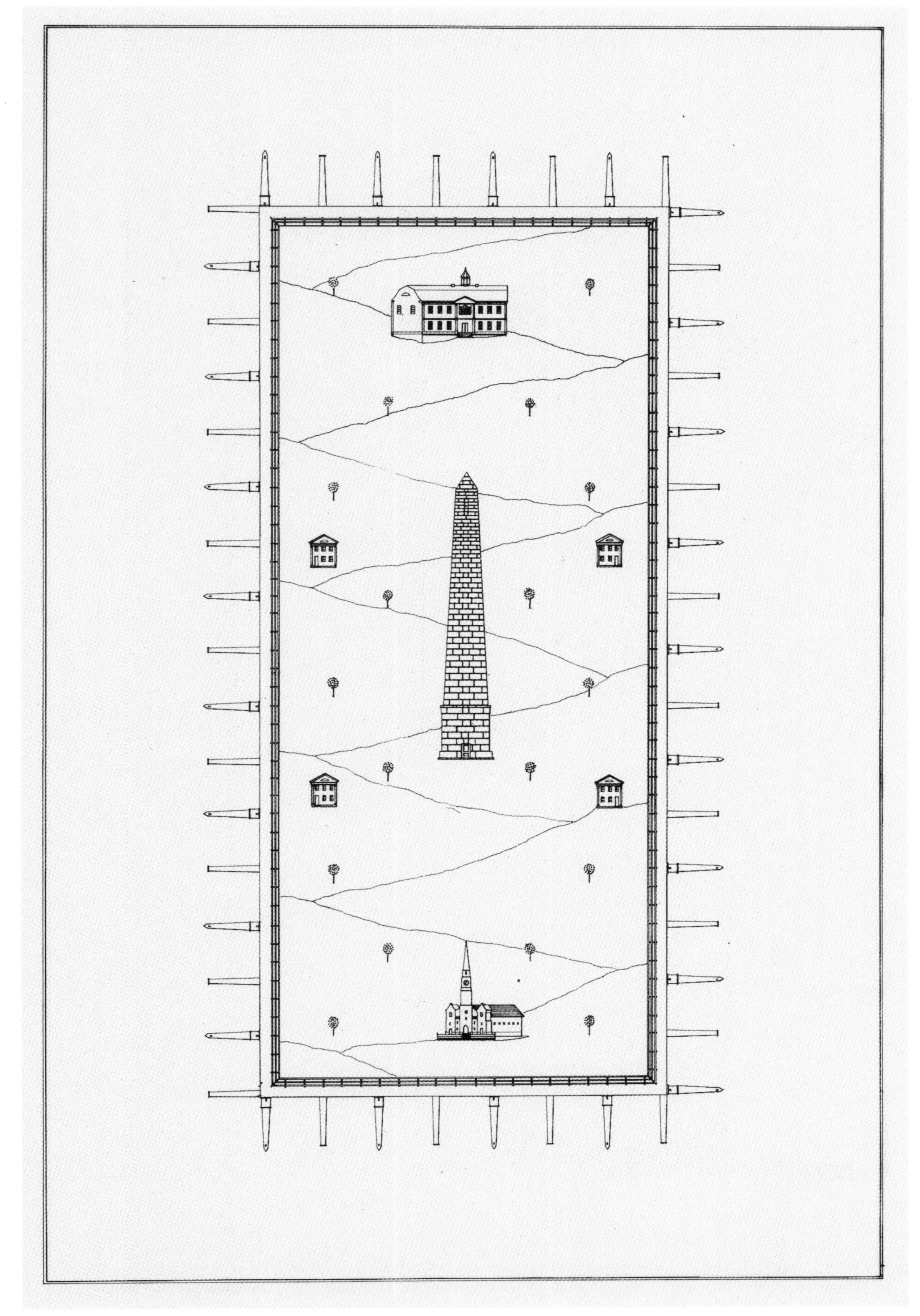

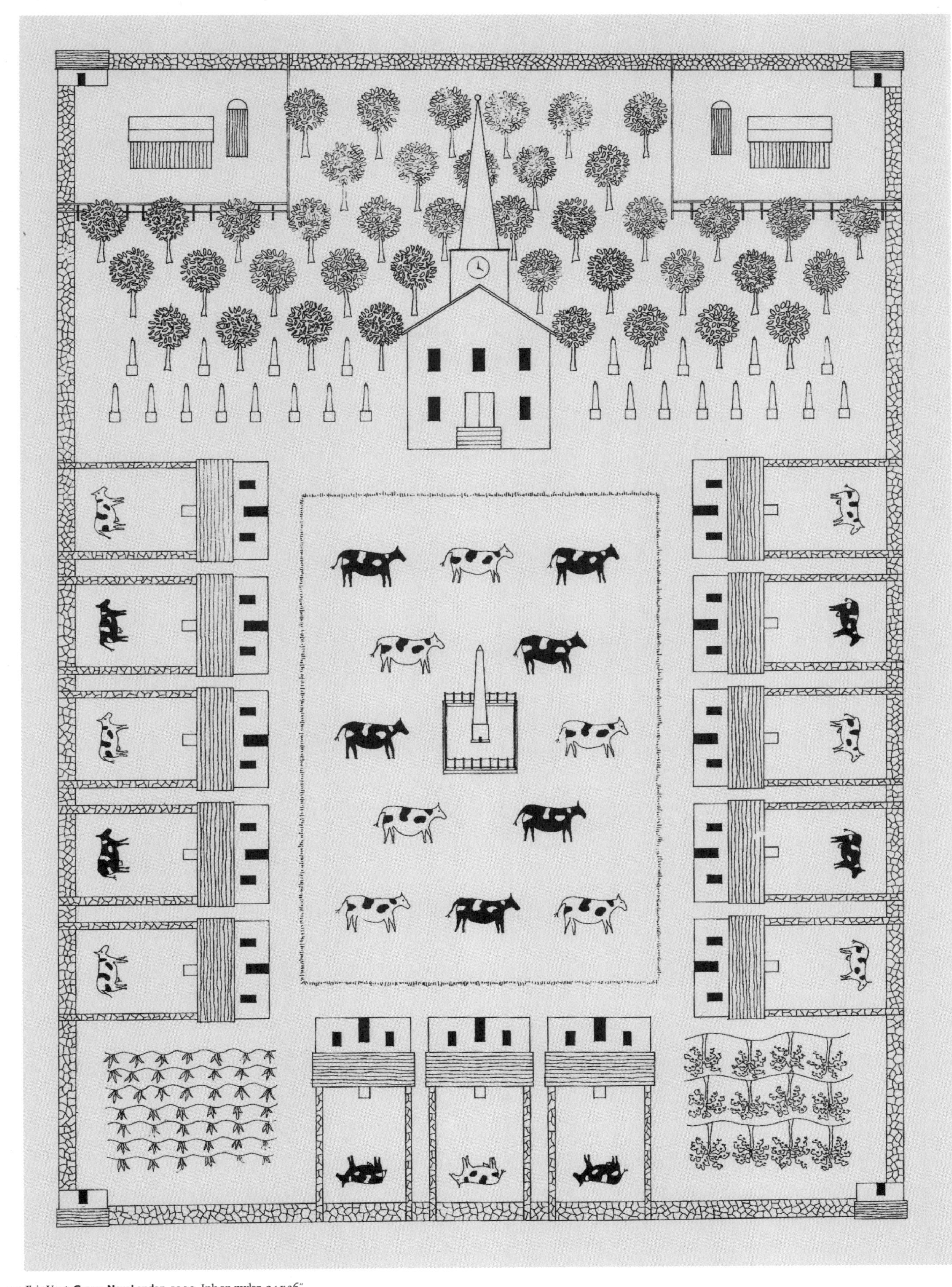

40. Eric Vogt. **Green, New London,** 1990. Ink on mylar, 24 x 36"

42. Eric Vogt. **Roman door,** 1992. Charcoal, 50 x 136″

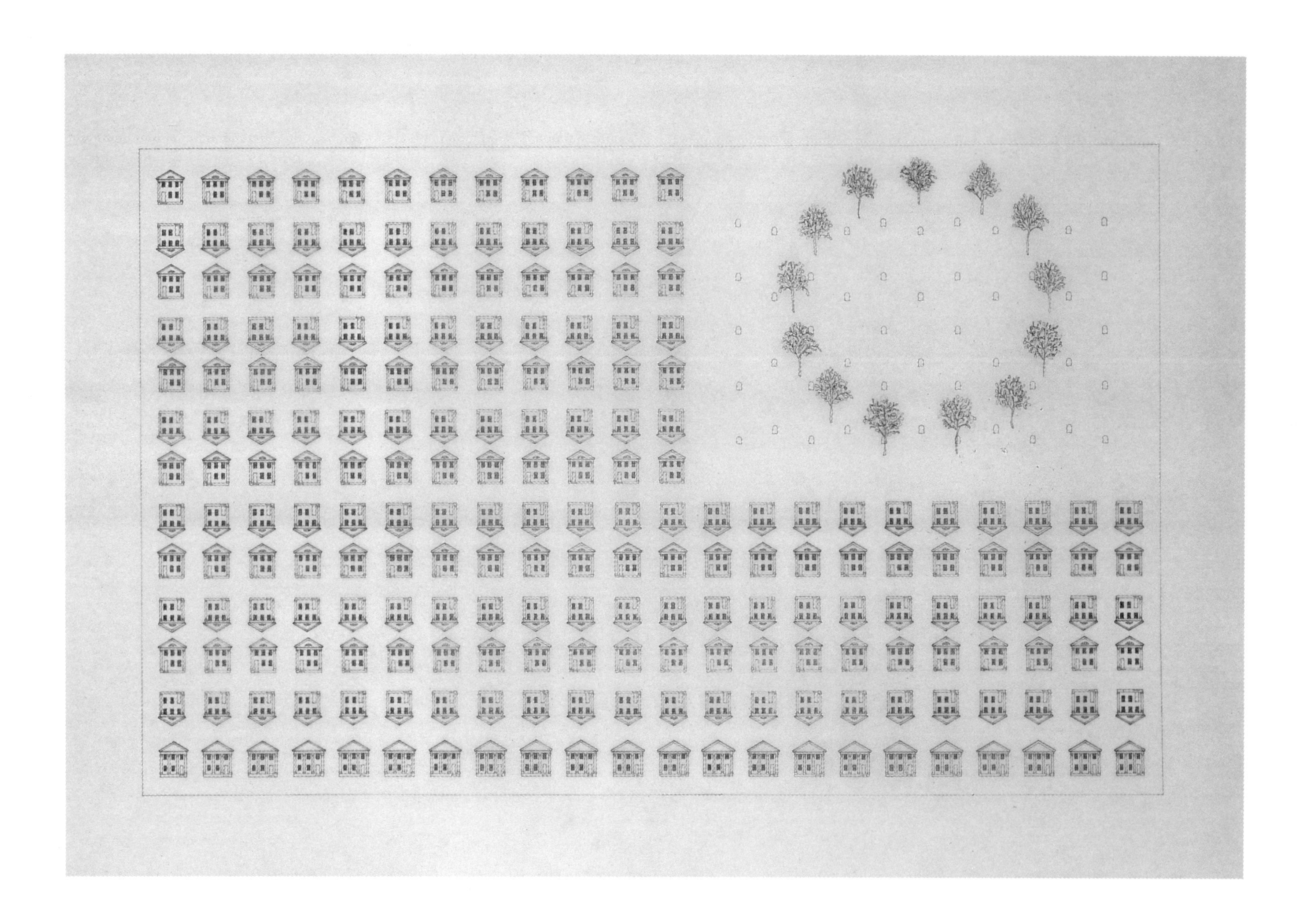

41. Chris Whittaker. **Old Glory, New London,** 1990. Ink on mylar, 36 x 24″

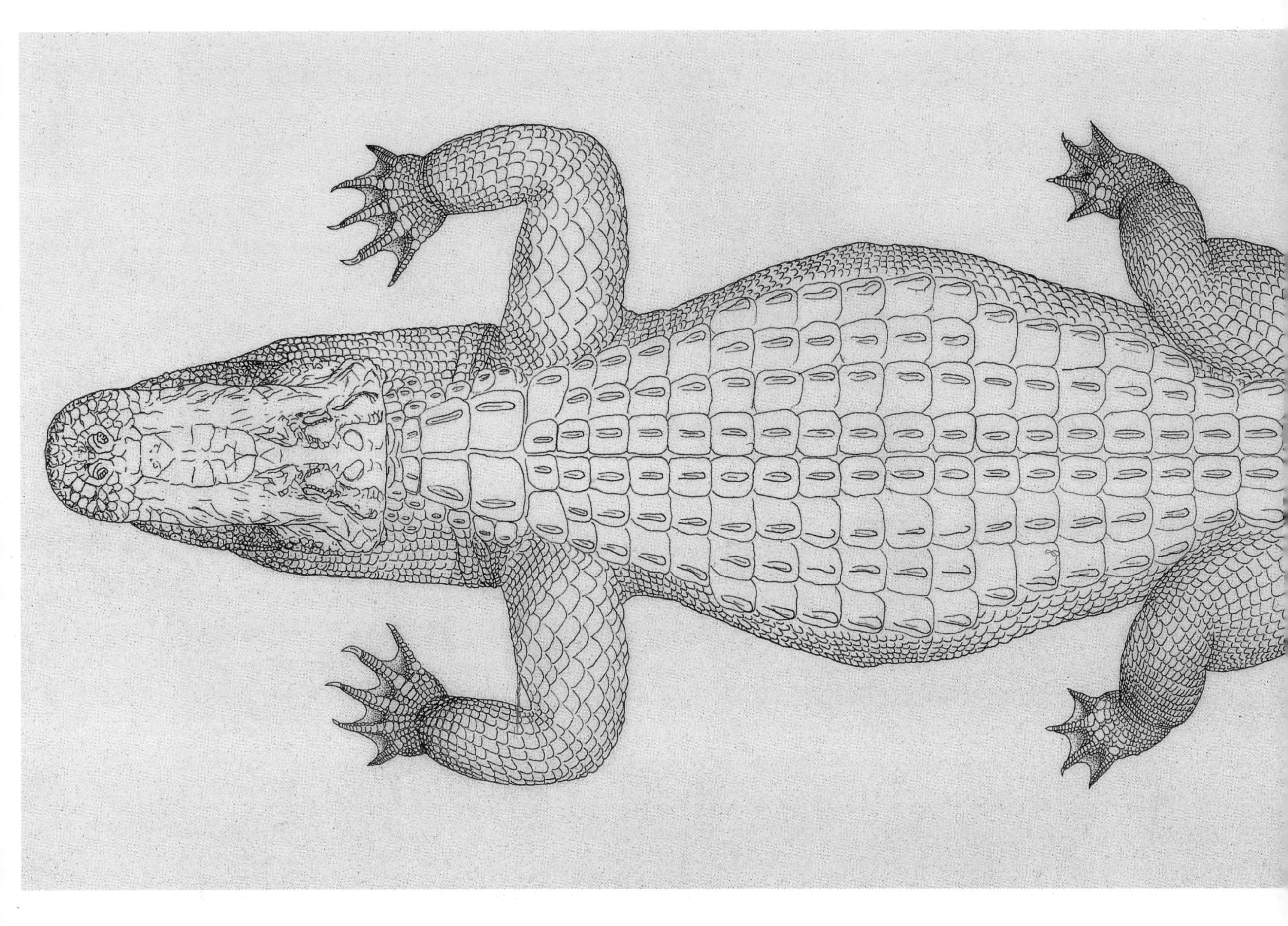

44. Robert Gray. **Alligator,** 1992. Ink on mylar, 36 x 13"

Plate 43

43. Eric Vogt. **I-95, New London,** 1990. Colored pencil, 32 x 14"

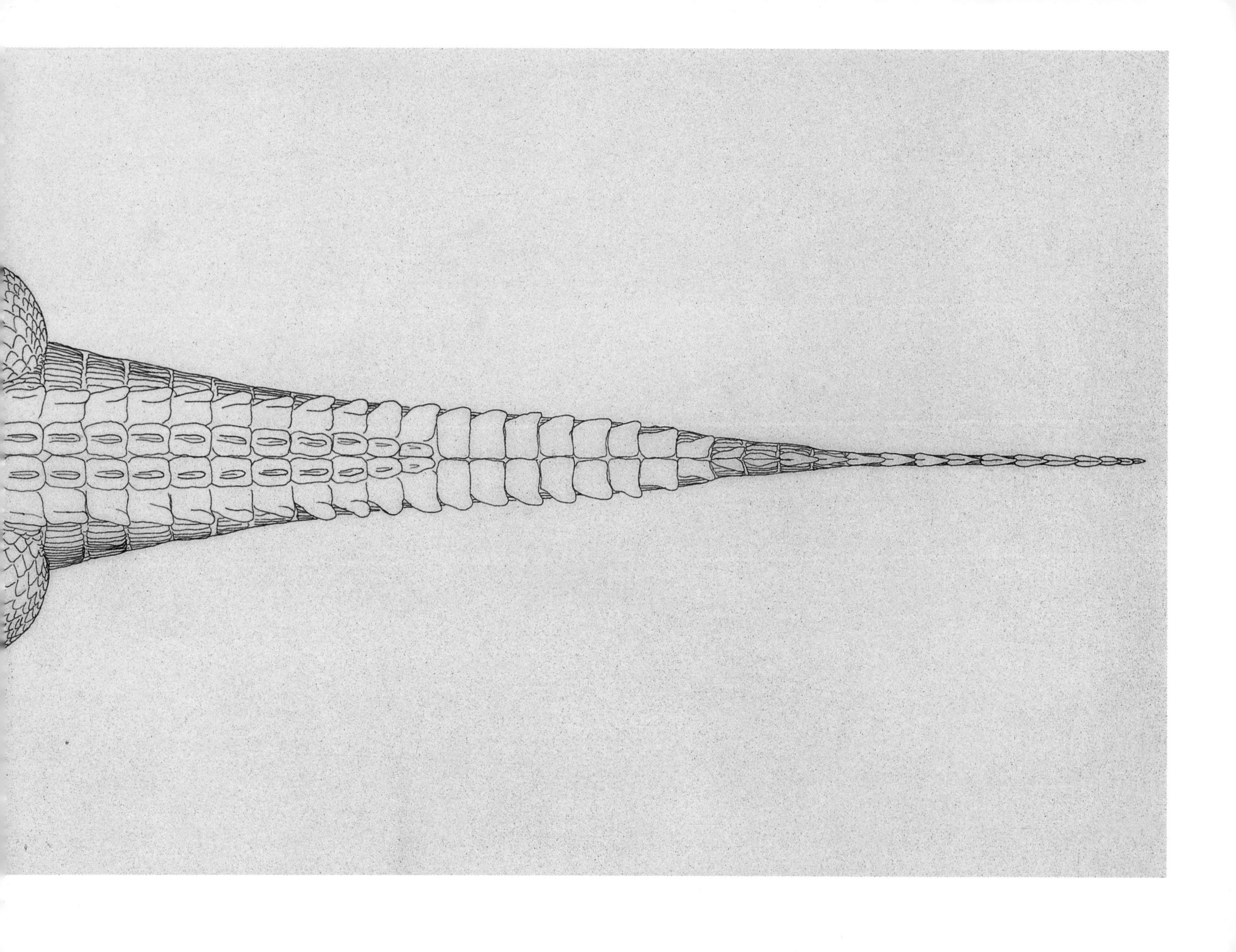

45. Ana Alvarez. **Groton Obelisk, New London,** 1990. Ink on mylar, 24 x 36″

46. James Carrol. **Harbor, New London,** 1990. Ink on mylar, 24 x 36″

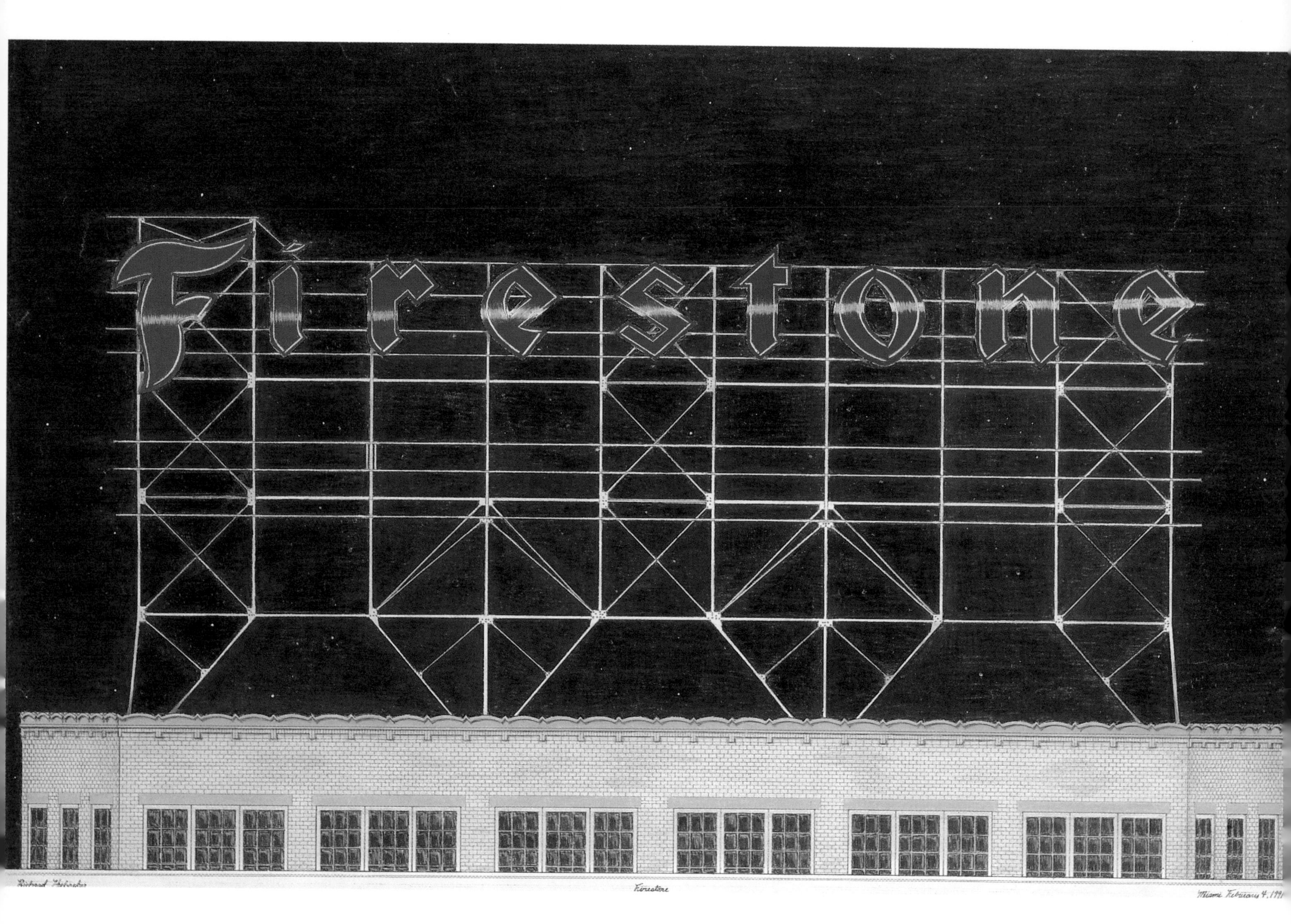

47. Richard Hubacker. **Firestone, Miami,** 1991. Colored pencil, 36 x 24"

48. Jose R. Vasquez. **Miami International Airport,** 1991. Colored pencil, 32 x 20″

Plate 49

49. Carol Dufresne. **Seminole Sampler,** 1991. Colored pencil, 24 x 36″

50. William Caldwell. **Domes of Miami,** 1991. Colored pencil, 34 x 22″

51. Jorge Trelles and Luis Trelles. **Brickell Bridge competition entry, Miami,** 1991. Colored pencil, 30 x 40"

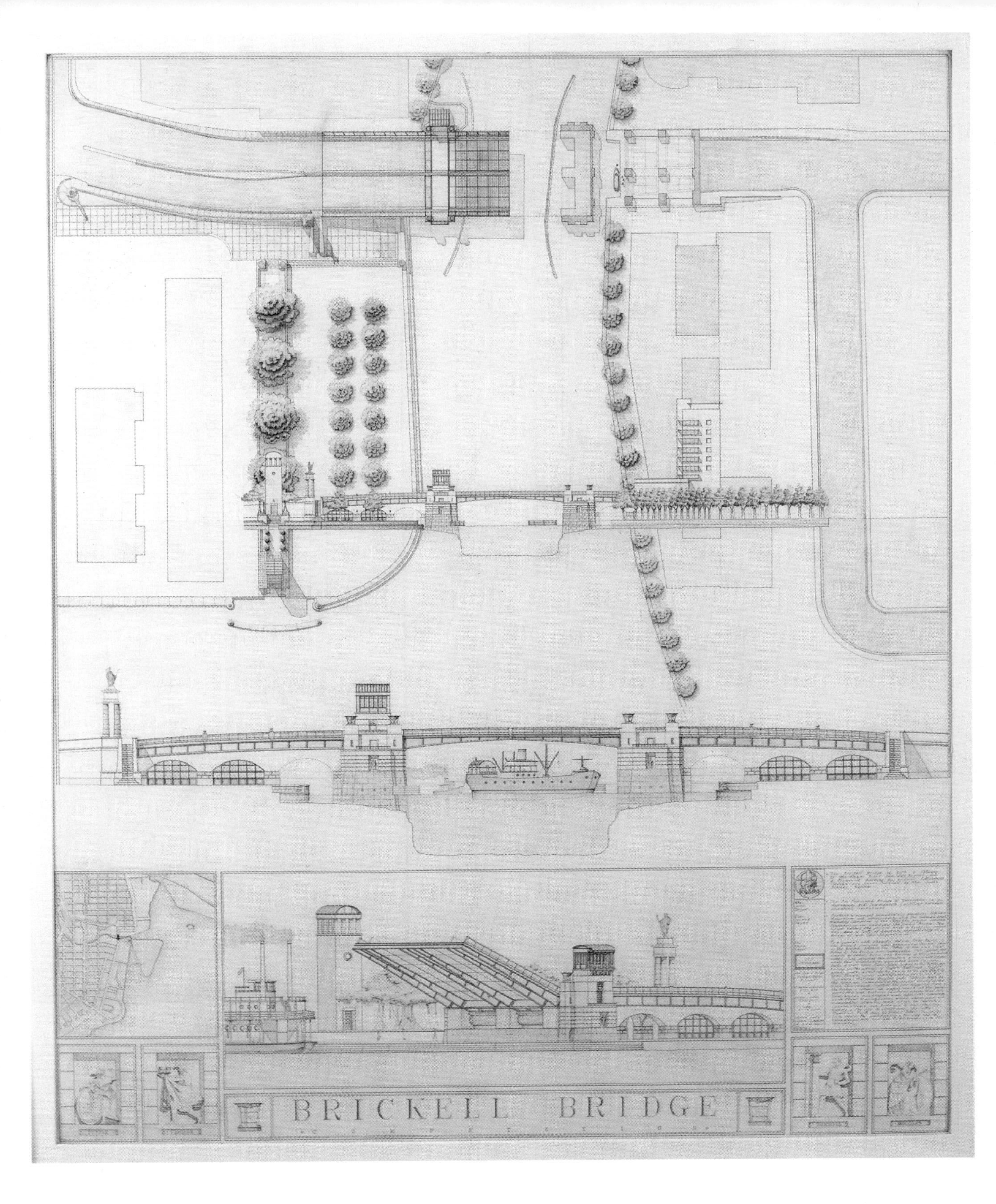

52. Jorge Hernandez, Raphael Portuondo, and Miguel Sardinas. **Brickell Bridge competition entry, Miami,** 1991. Colored pencil, 30 x 40"

53. Roberto M. Behar, Tomas Lopez-Gottardi, and Teofilo Victoria. **Brickell Bridge competition entry, Miami,** 1991. Colored pencil, 30 x 40"

54. Lourdes Luaces. **Everglades boat, elevation,** 1991. Colored pencil, 36 x 24″

55. Lourdes Luaces. **Everglades boat, sections,** 1991. Colored pencil, 36 x 24″

56. Lourdes Luaces. **Everglades boat, plan,** 1991. Colored pencil, 36 x 24″

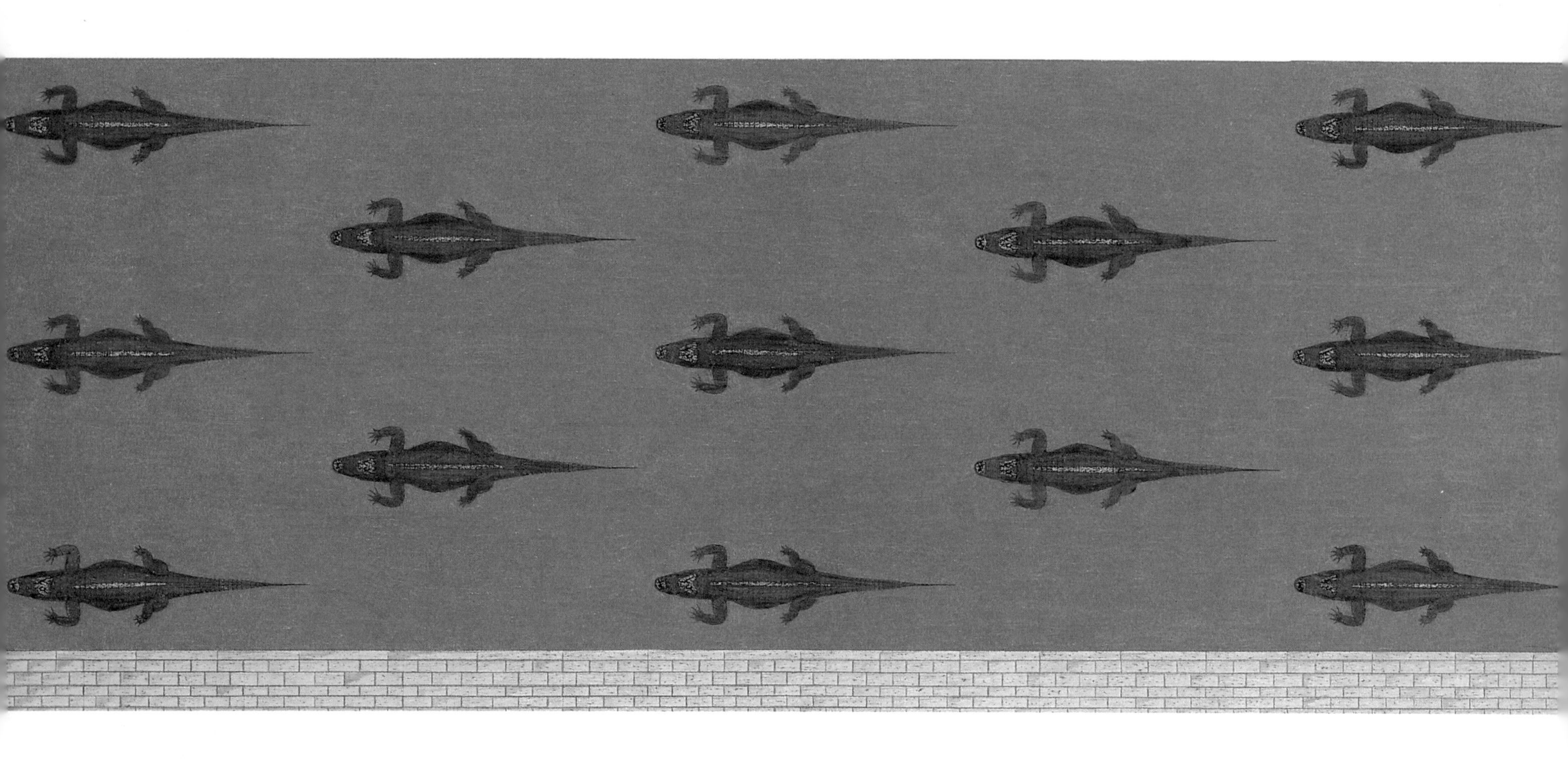

57. Robert Gray. **Alligator plaza,** 1991. Colored pencil, 36 x 24"

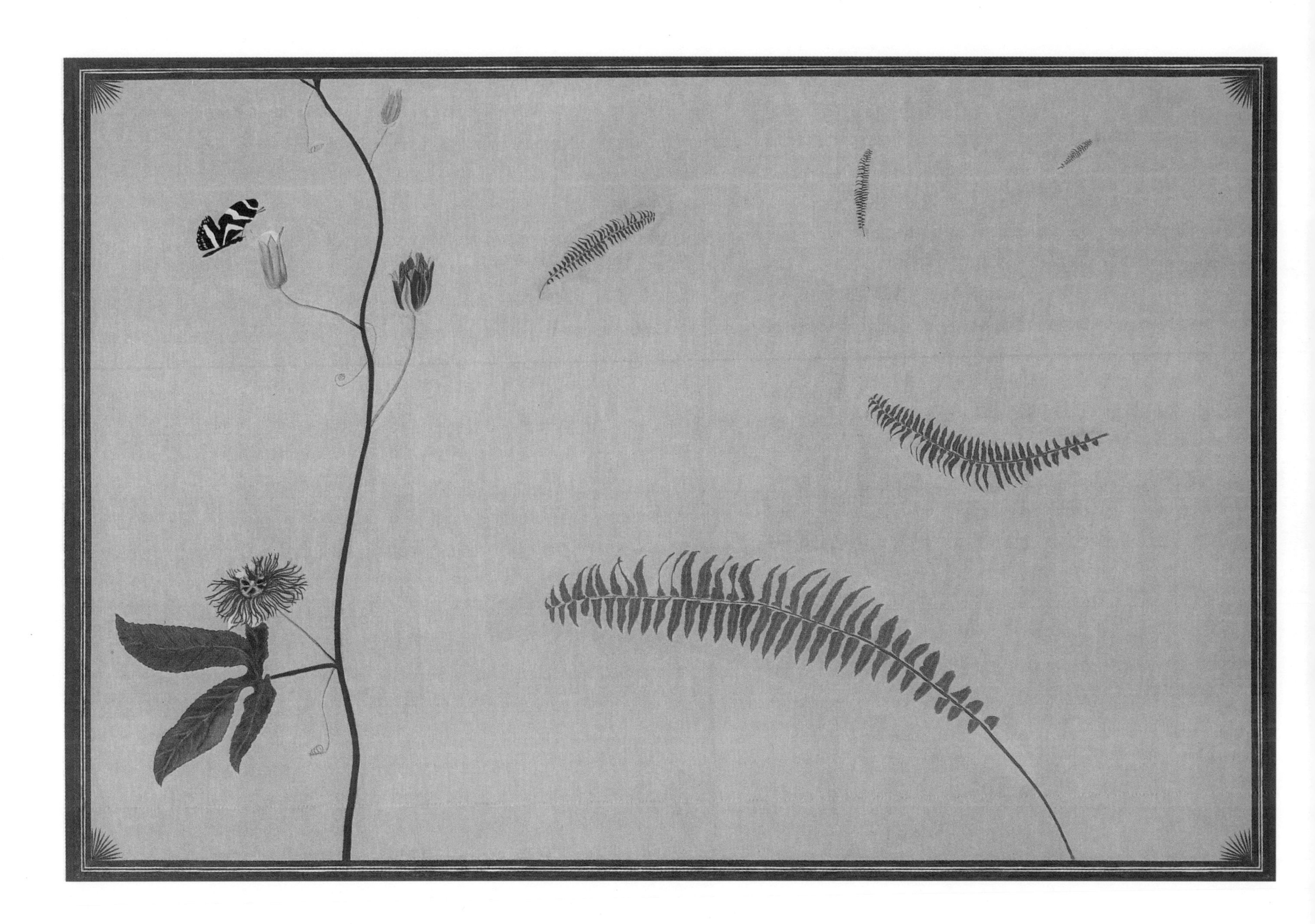

58. Jim Lawson. **Beach towel,** 1991. Colored pencil, 38 x 25″

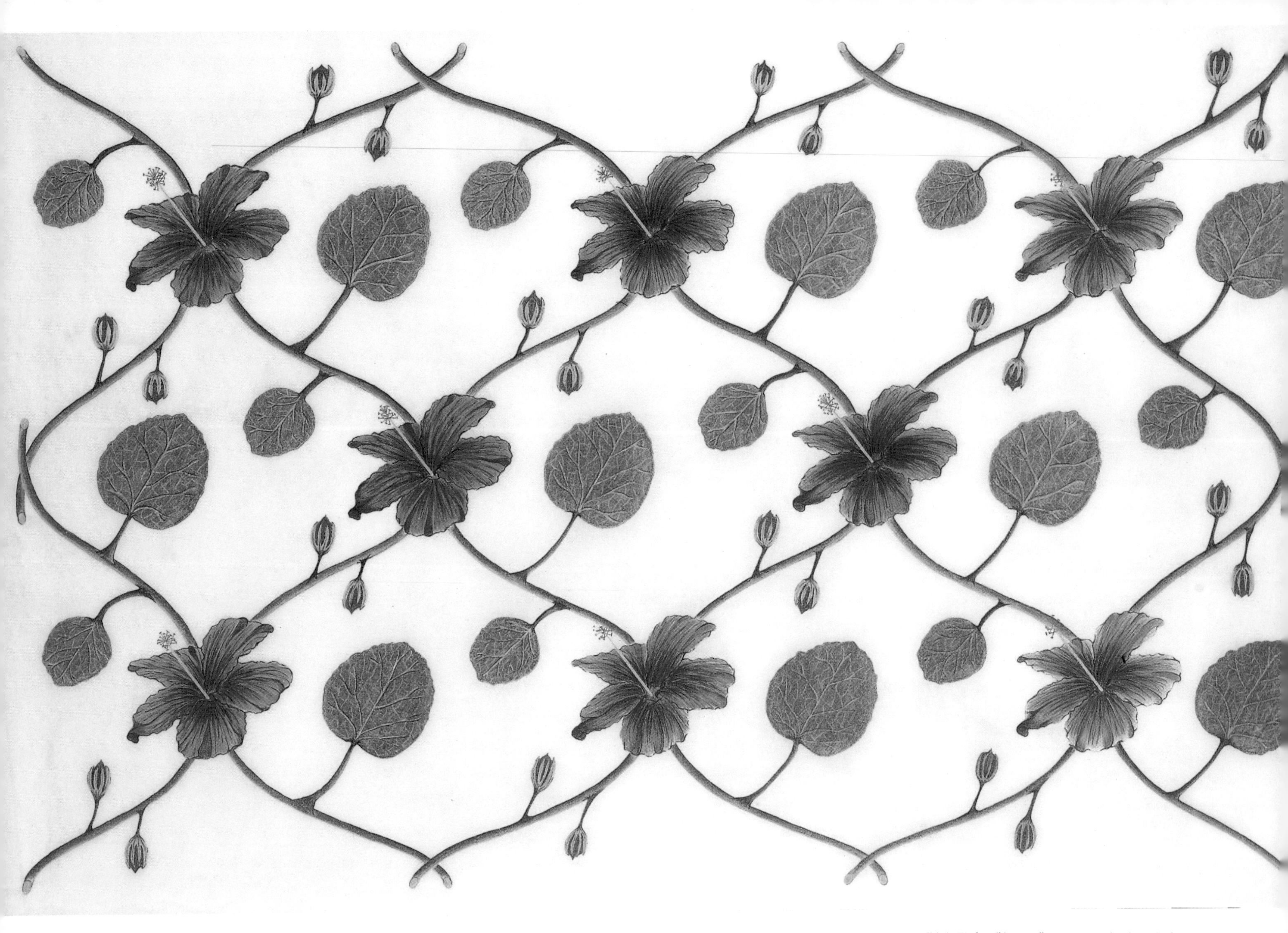

59. Kristin Wazlo. **Hibiscus wallpaper,** 1994. Colored pencil, 36 x 24"

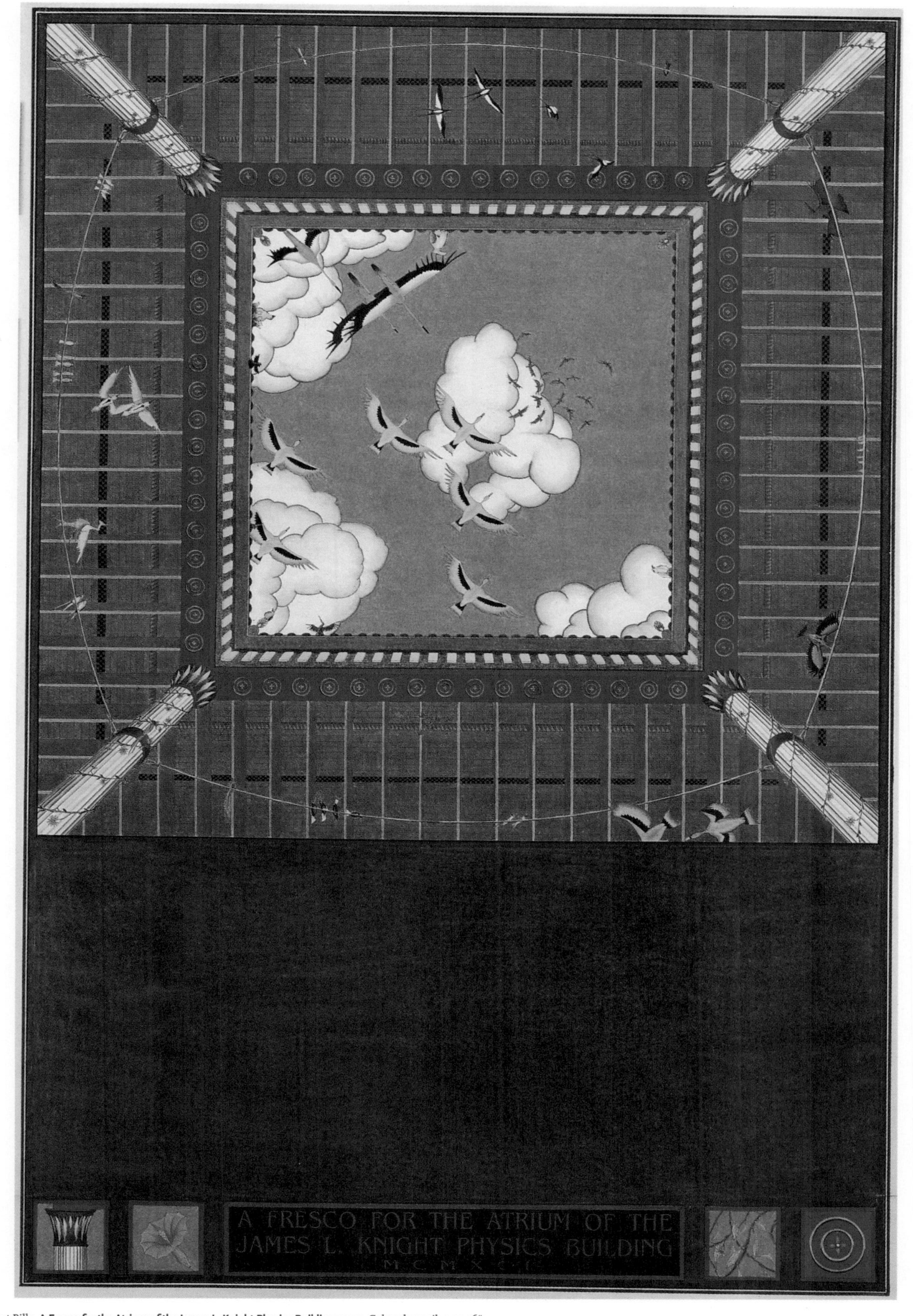

60. Robert Pilla. **A Fresco for the Atrium of the James L. Knight Physics Building,** 1991. Colored pencil, 24 x 36"

Plate 61

61. Marcelino Marrero. **Gallo Fino,** 1991. Colored pencil, 16 x 31″

62. William Real. **Town for migrant workers, Florida City,** 1991. Colored pencil, 38 x 12″

63. Nelson Bean. **A Maya Christmas Card,** 1991. Tempera on wood, 13 x 13"

64. Roger Gramm. **Yucatan,** 1991. Tempera on wood, 18 x 24"

65. Miriam Tropp. **Maya plinth,** 1993. Colored pencil, 23 x 23″

66. Roger Gramm. **Castillo, Chichen Itzá,** 1991. Ink on paper, 48 x 24″

67. Eric Vogt. **Cemetery, Yucatan,** 1991. Colored pencil, 16 x 24"

OSARIO
FAMILIA
M. LOPENZA
OSARIO
BARRERA
VICTORIA
MANUEL
RECUERDO
OSARIO
FAMILIA
CABALLERO.TZAB

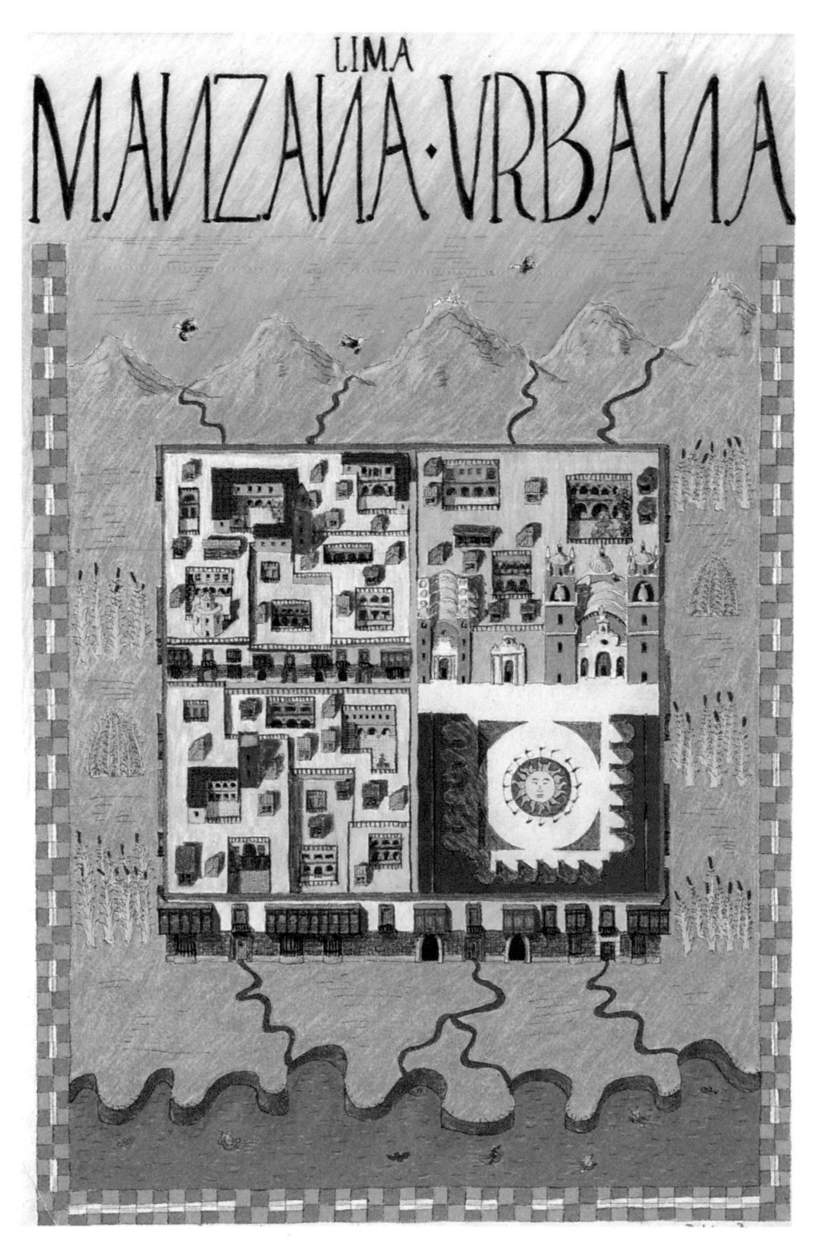

68. Rodrigo Reyes. **Lima Manzana Urbana (Lima Urban Block),** 1994. Colored pencil, 13 x 19″

69. Juan Carlos Rosas. **Lima, Plazoleta,** 1994. Colored pencil, 13 x 19″

70. Fernando Castillo. **Lima, Plaza Mayor,** 1994. Colored pencil, 13 x 19"

71. Liliana Bringas. **Casa Picoaga, Cuzco,** 1994. Ink on paper, 36 x 24"

72. Juan Carlos Rosas. **Calle Suyt'Uqhatu, Cuzco,** 1994. Ink on paper, 24 x 36"

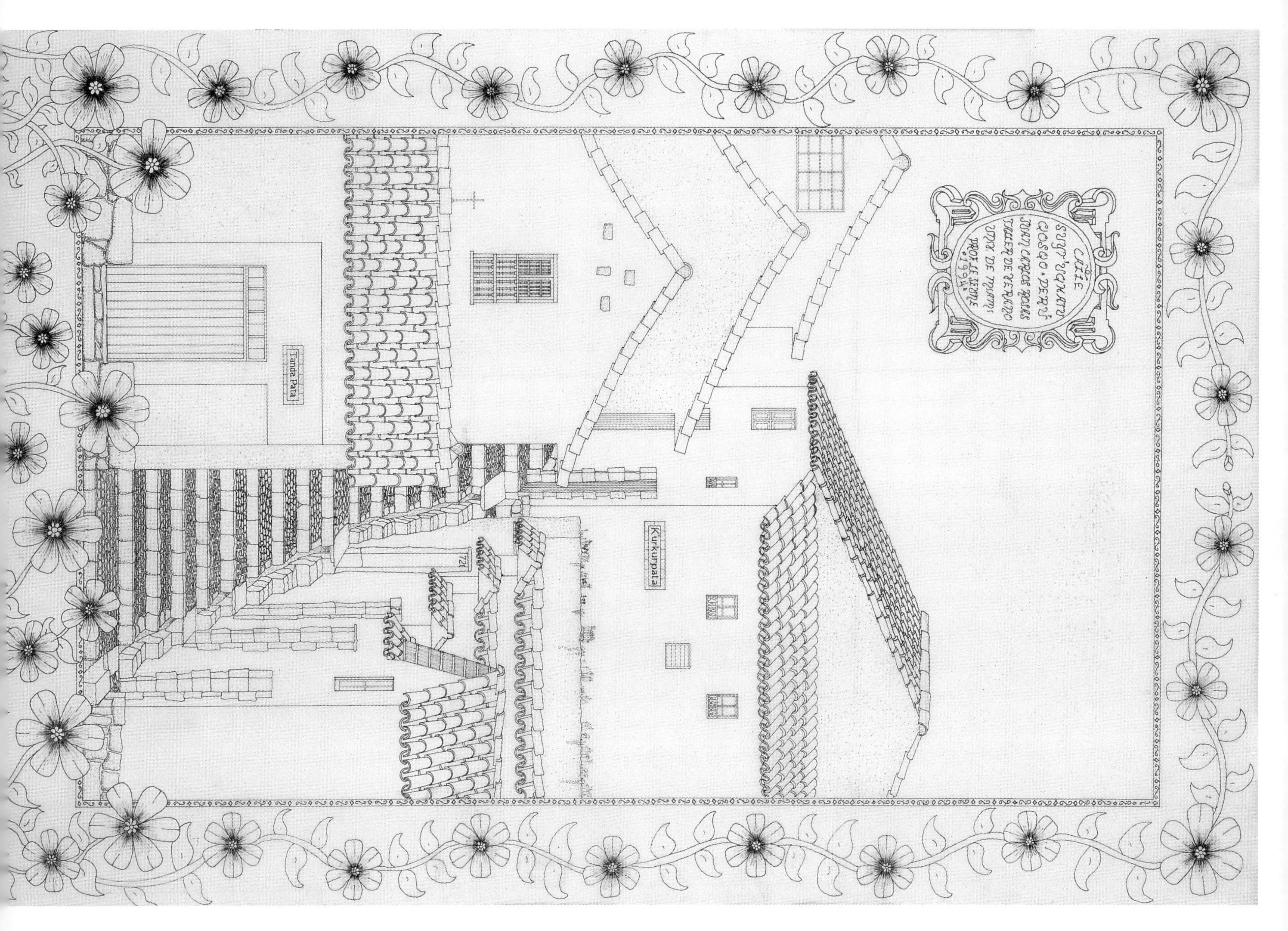
Tanda Pata
Kurkurpata

73. Claudia Bancalari. **Water Plaza,** 1994. Colored pencil, 24 x 17"

74. David Celis. **Camaroneros,** 1994. Colored pencil, 18 x 27"

Al bajar el sol iban llegando, y al salir la luna una
memoria lejana empezó a cantar "... mira como vienen
los camaroneros a encender luceros en el litoral..."

75. Trent Greenan. **Iglesia de Santa Domingo, Cuzco,** 1994. Ink on paper, 36 x 24″

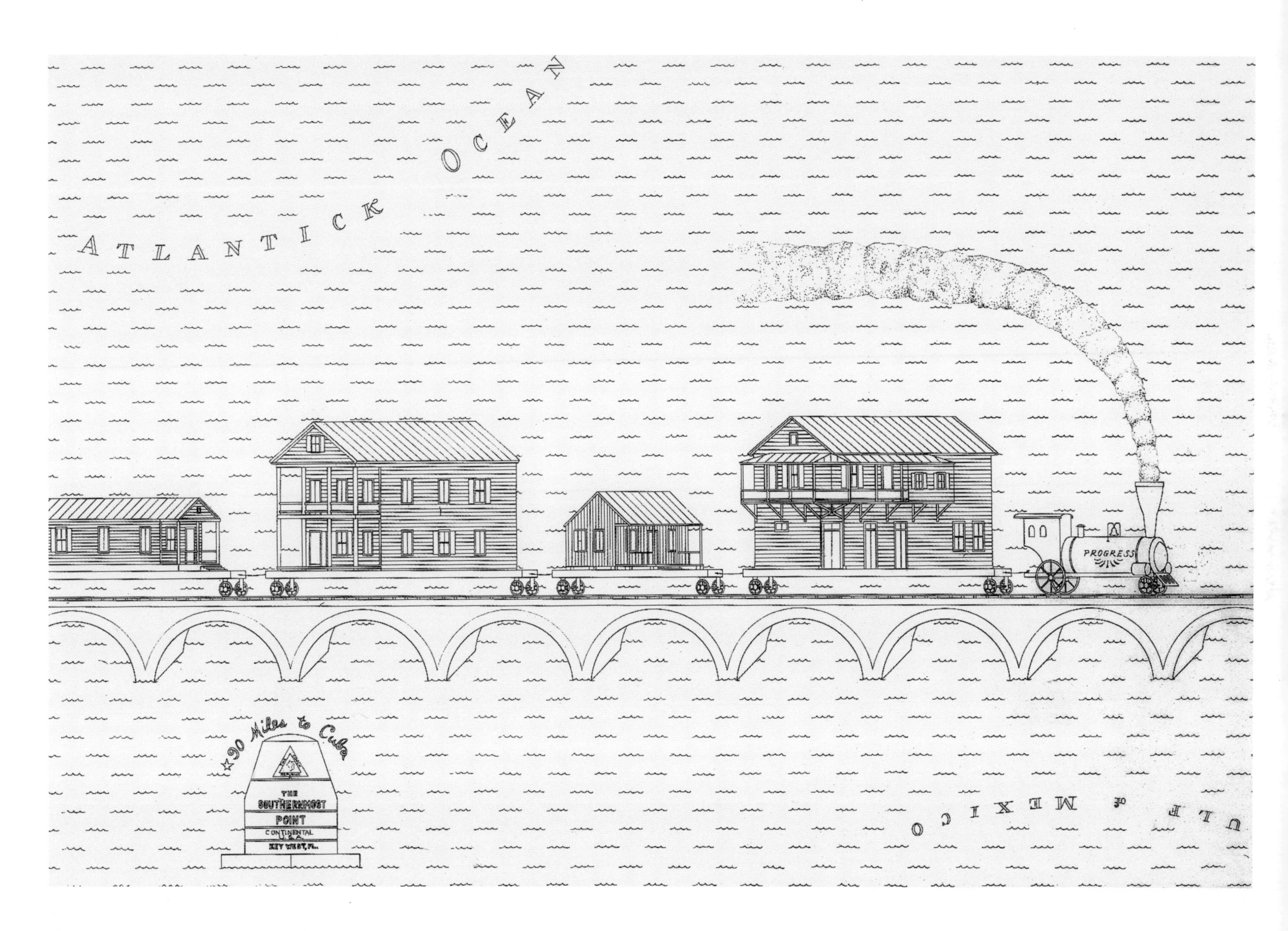

76. Kevin Storm. **Overseas Highway,** 1994. Ink on paper, 28 x 19"

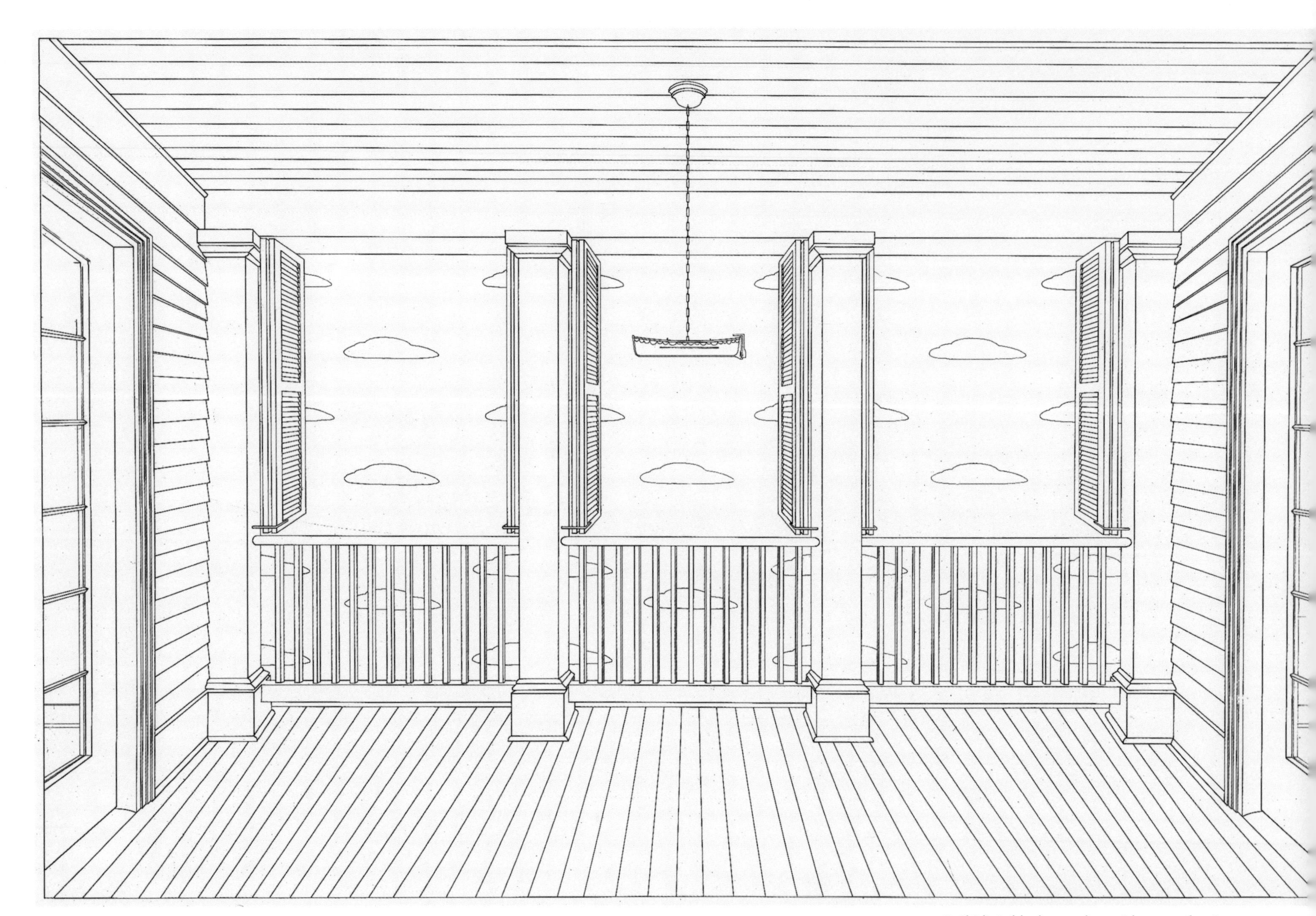

77. David Celis. **Audubon house porch,** 1994. Ink on paper, 36 x 24″

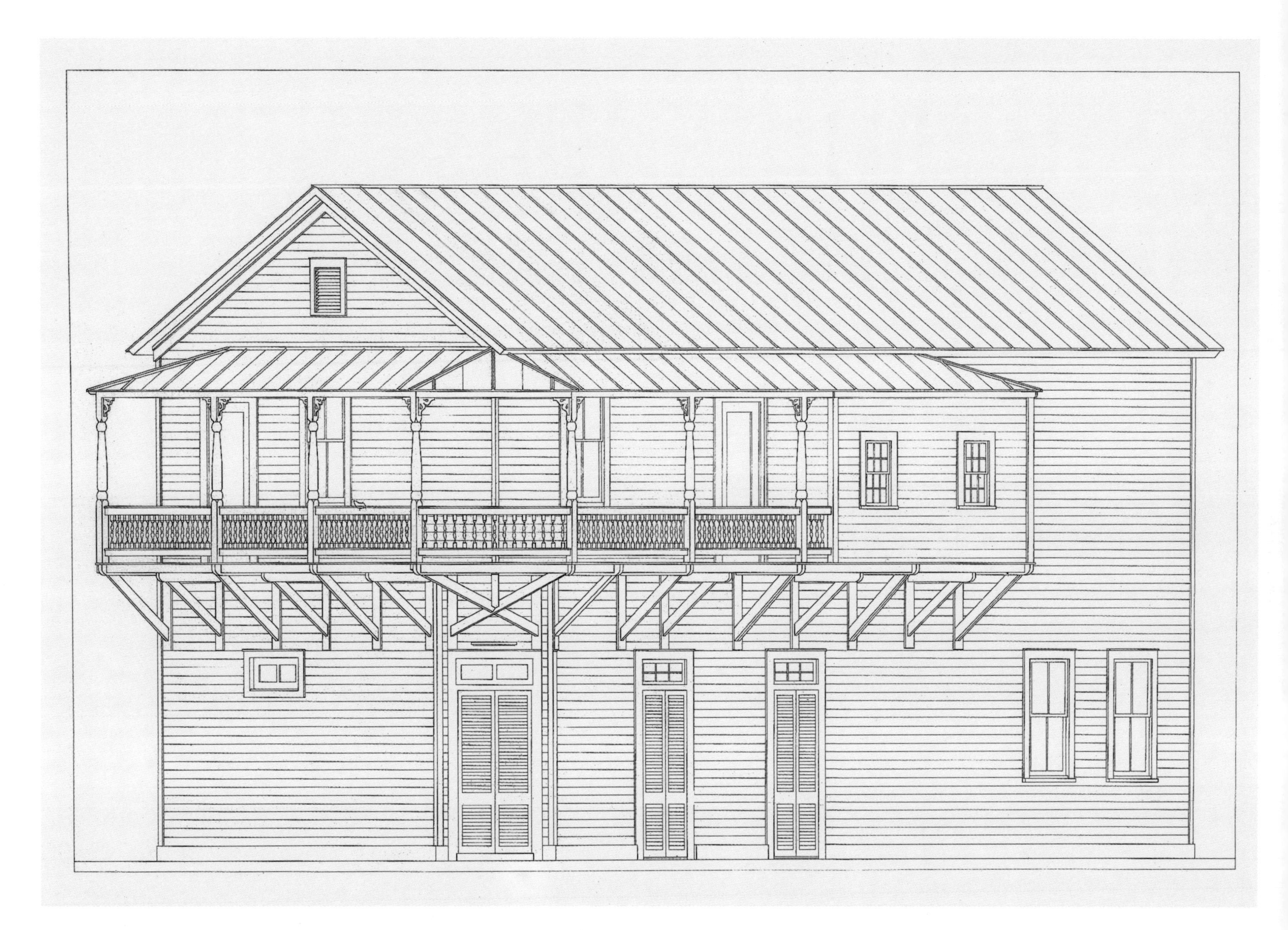

78. Kevin Storm. **Corner House, Key West,** 1994. Ink on paper, 36 x 24″

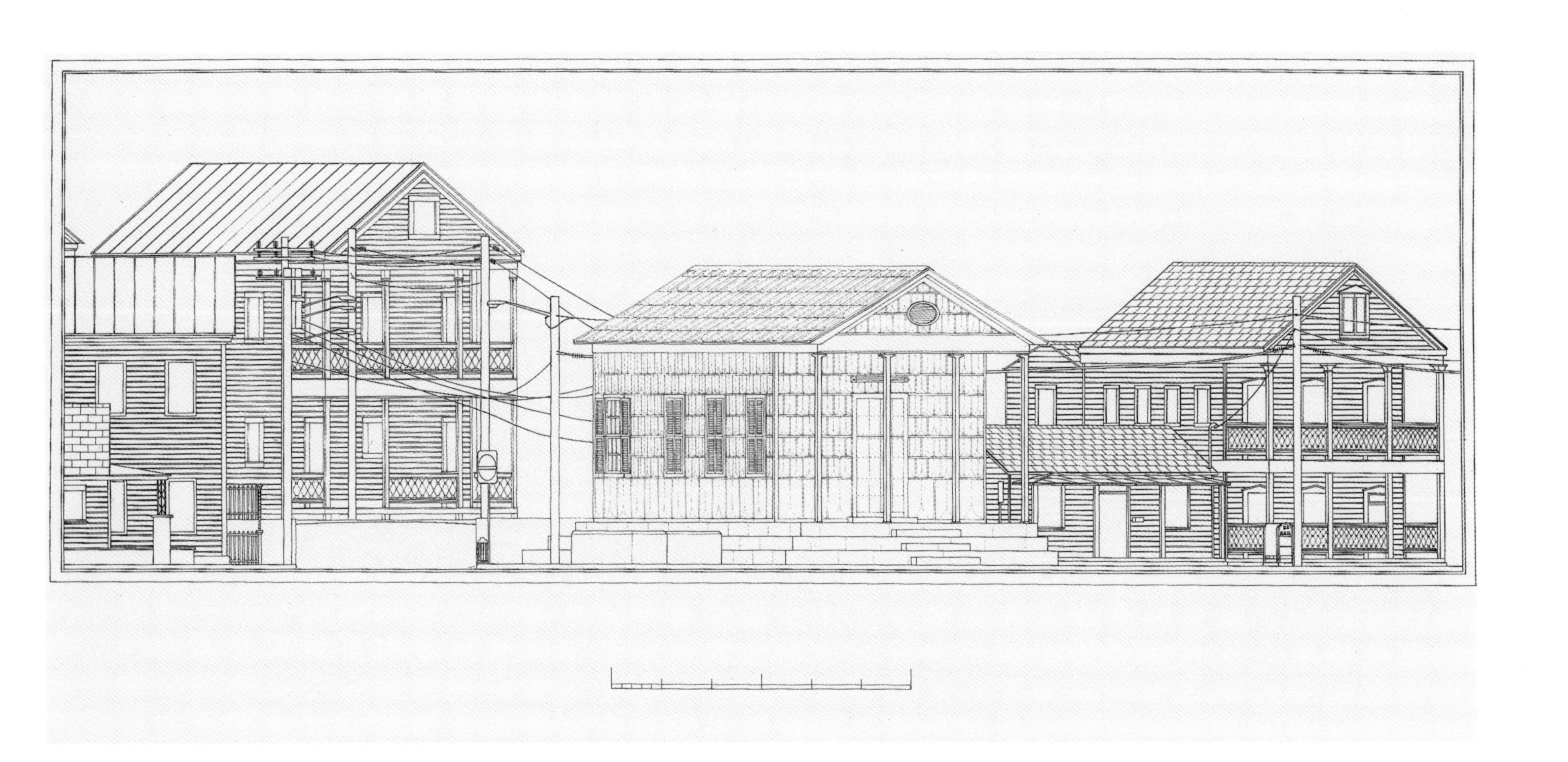

79. Claudia Bancalari. **Casa del Balsero, street view,** 1994. Ink on paper, 36 x 17"

80. Claudia Bancalari. **Casa del Balsero, interior,** 1994. Ink on mylar, 18 x 12″

81. Jose Jaen. **Houses of the Tobacco Rollers,** 1994. Colored pencil, 30 x 18"

82. Kristin Wazlo. **The Sinking of the Maine,** 1994. Colored pencil, 24 x 36″

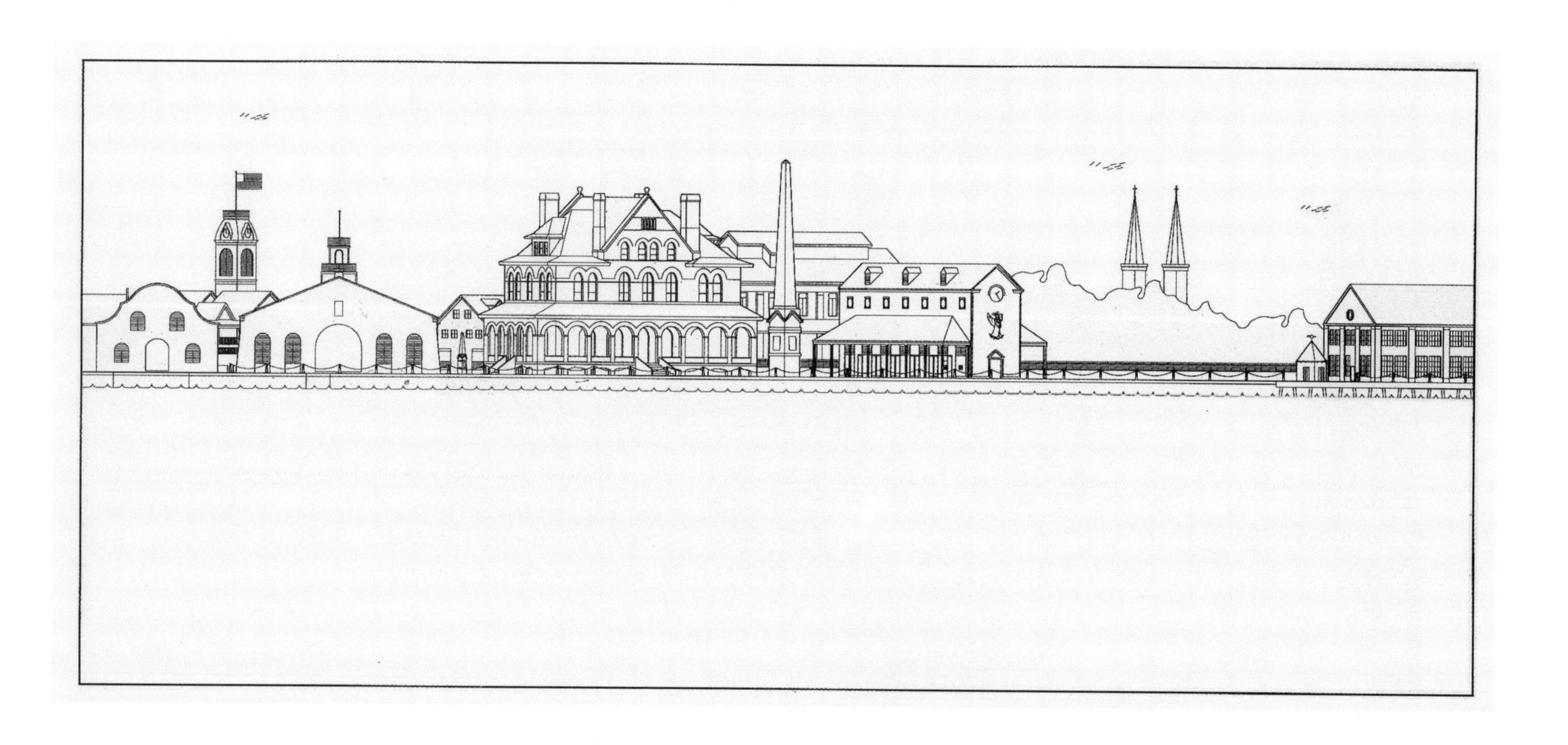

83. John White. **Ferry Station, ferry to La Habana, elevation from waterfront,** 1994. Ink on mylar, 36 x 24″

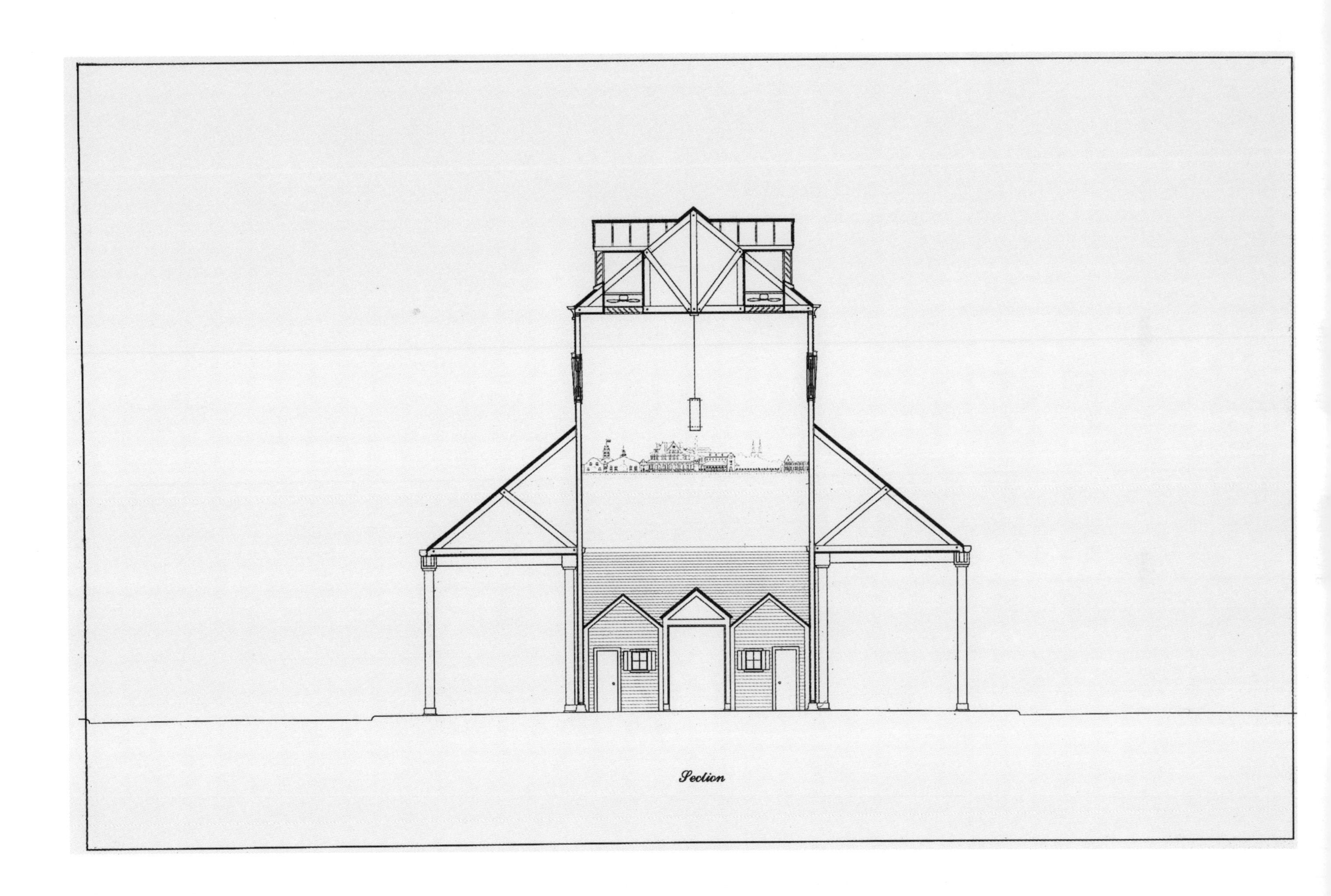

84. John White. **Ferry Station, ferry to La Habana, section,** 1994. Ink on mylar, 36 x 24″

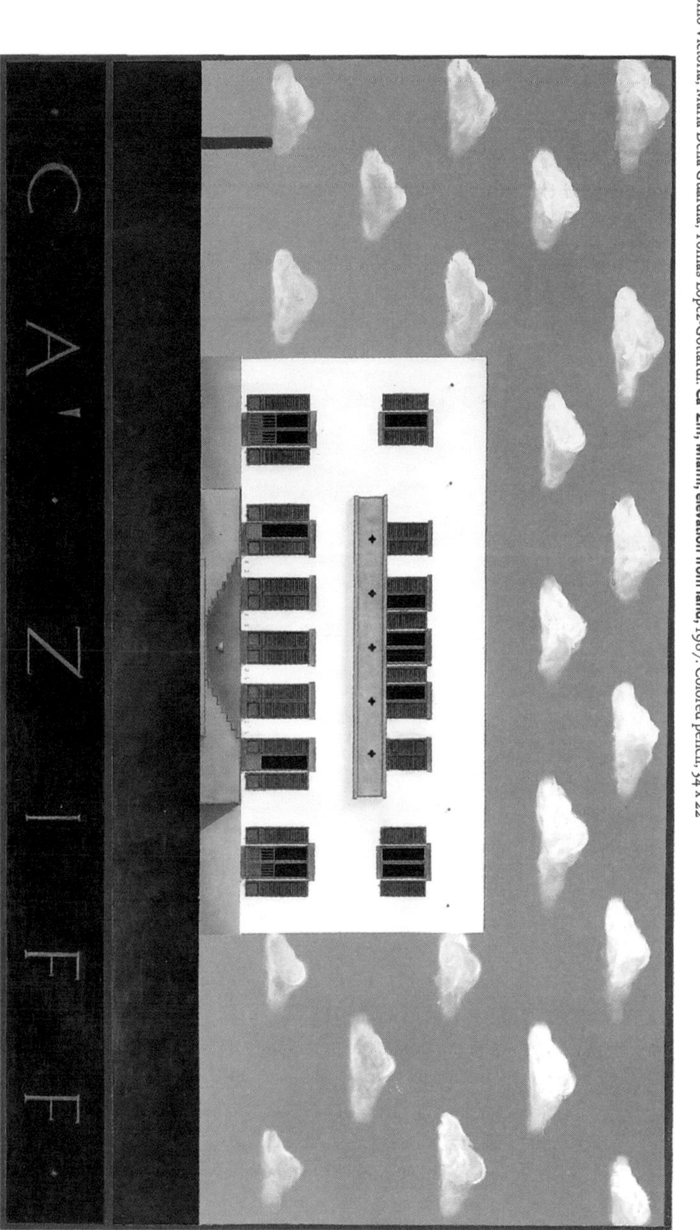

85. Teofilo Victoria, Maria Della Guardia, Tomas Lopez-Gottardi. **Ca' Ziff, Miami, elevation from land,** 1987. Colored pencil, 34 x 22"

86. Teofilo Victoria, Maria Della Guardia, Tomas Lopez-Gottardi. **Ca' Ziff, Miami, view from Biscayne Bay,** 1987. Ink on mylar, 48 x 36"

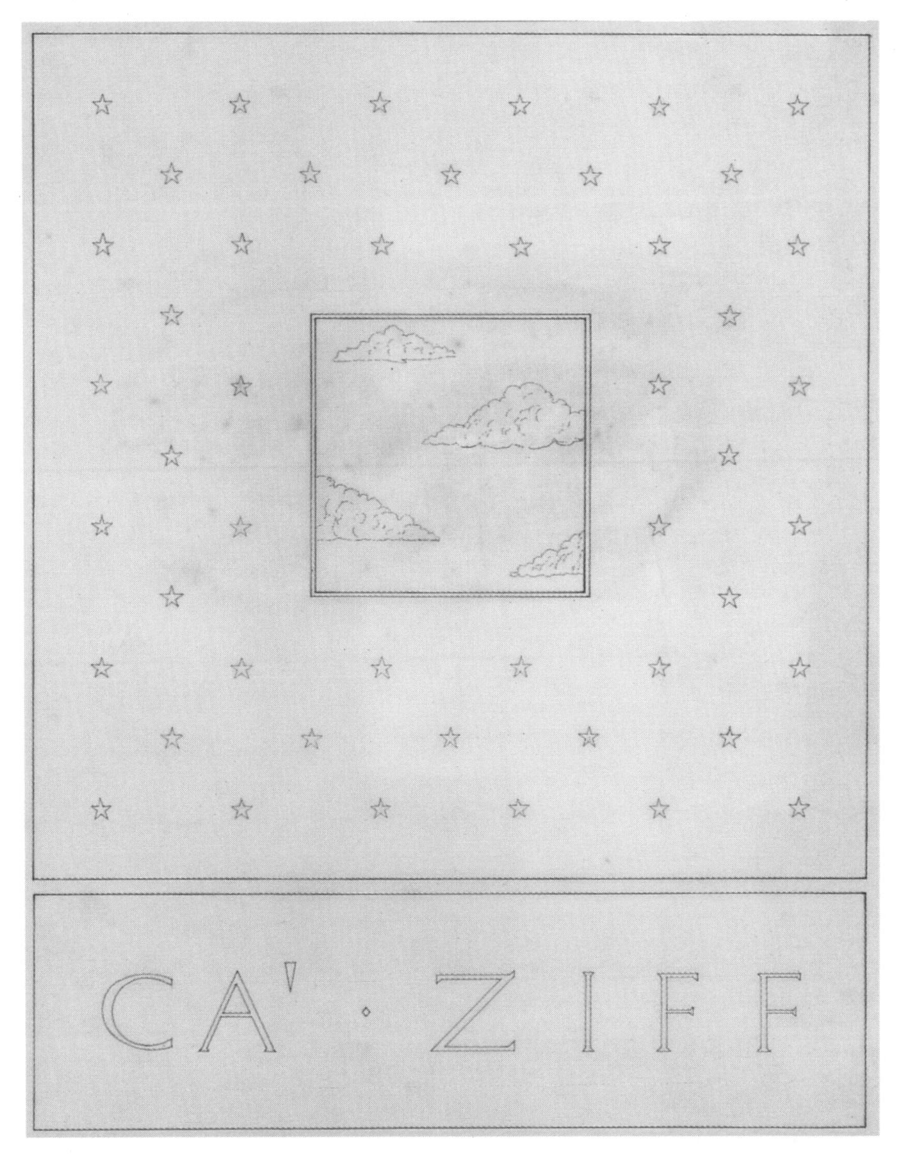

87 (left). Teofilo Victoria, Maria Della Guardia, Tomas Lopez-Gottardi. **Ca' Ziff, Miami, atrium floor, 1987.** Colored pencil, 13 x 16″

88 (right). Teofilo Victoria, Maria Della Guardia, Tomas Lopez-Gottardi. **Ca' Ziff, Miami, atrium ceiling,** 1987. Ink, 13 x 16″

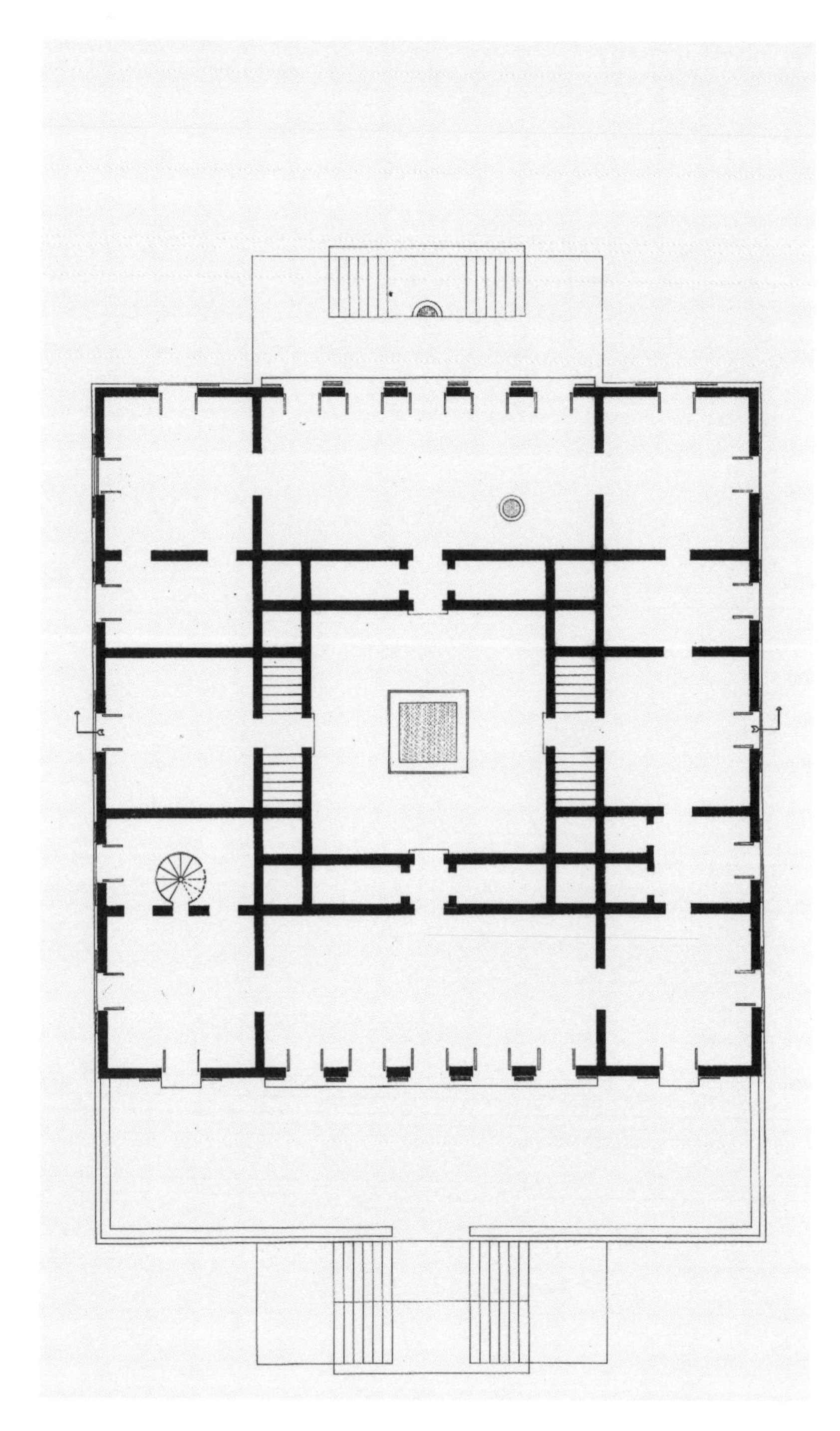

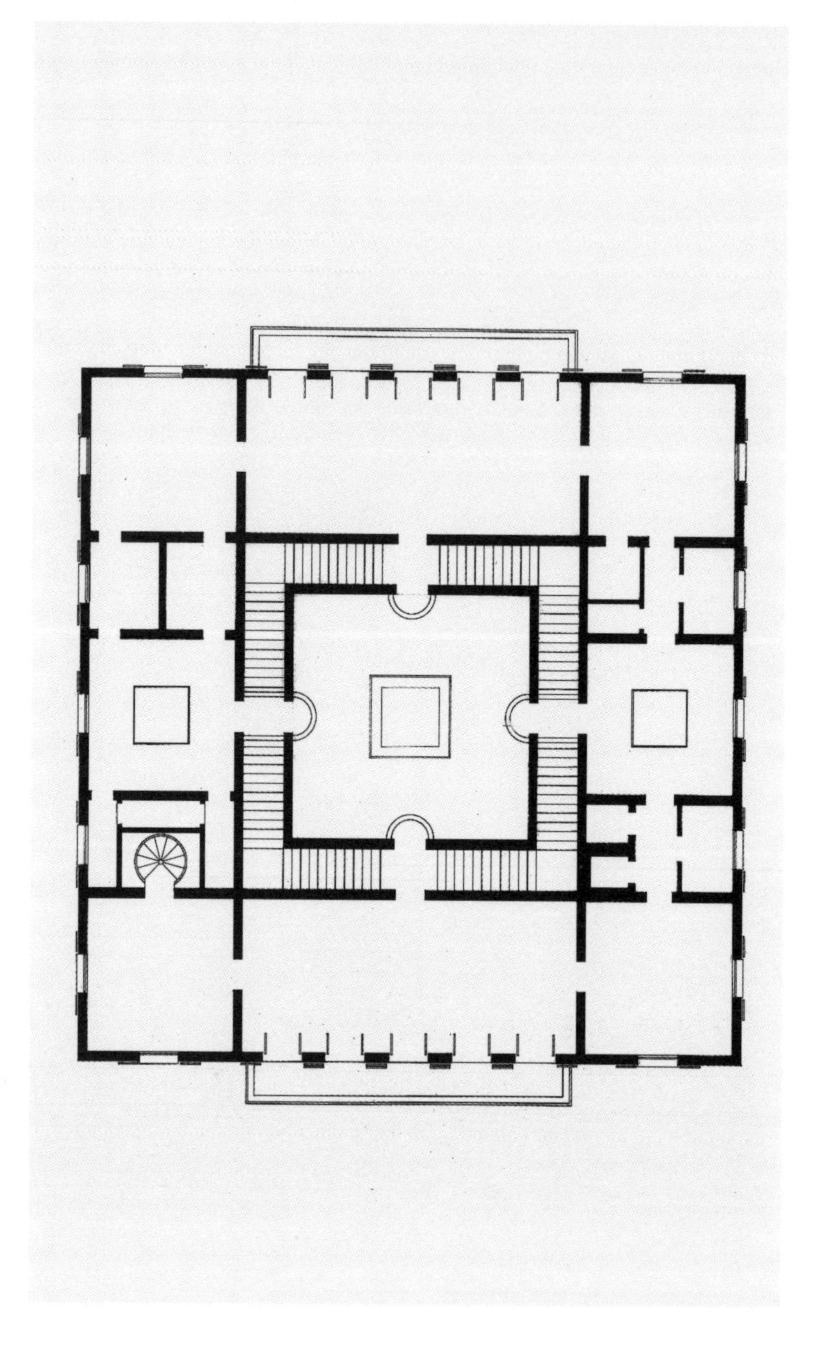

89 (left). Teofilo Victoria, Maria Della Guardia, Tomas Lopez-Gottardi. **Ca' Ziff, Miami, first floor plan,** 1987. Ink on mylar, 24 x 36″

90 (right). Teofilo Victoria, Maria Della Guardia, Tomas Lopez-Gottardi. **Ca' Ziff, Miami, second floor plan,** 1987. Ink on mylar, 24 x 36″

91 (left). Teofilo Victoria, Maria Della Guardia, Tomas Lopez-Gottardi. **Ca' Ziff, Miami, atrium elevation,** 1987. Colored pencil, 13 x 16″

92 (right). Teofilo Victoria, Maria Della Guardia, Tomas Lopez-Gottardi. **Ca' Ziff, Miami, Jania's drawing room,** 1987. Colored pencil, 11 x 9″

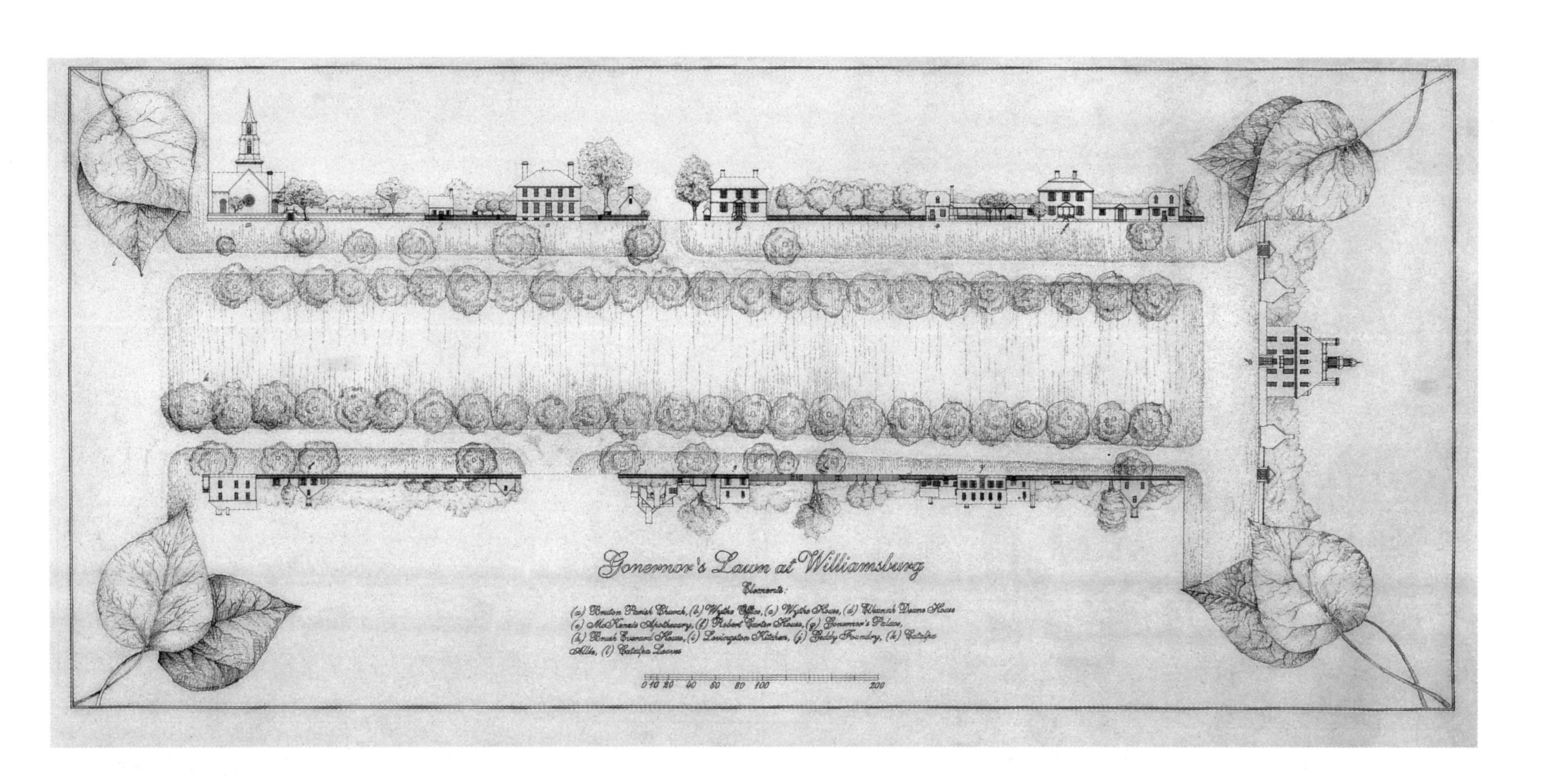

93. Jorge Hernandez, Francis Lyn. **Governor's Lawn at Williamsburg,** 1992. Ink on paper, 60 x 26″

94. Jorge Hernandez. **Tres Villas,** 1991. Colored pencil, 48 x 24"

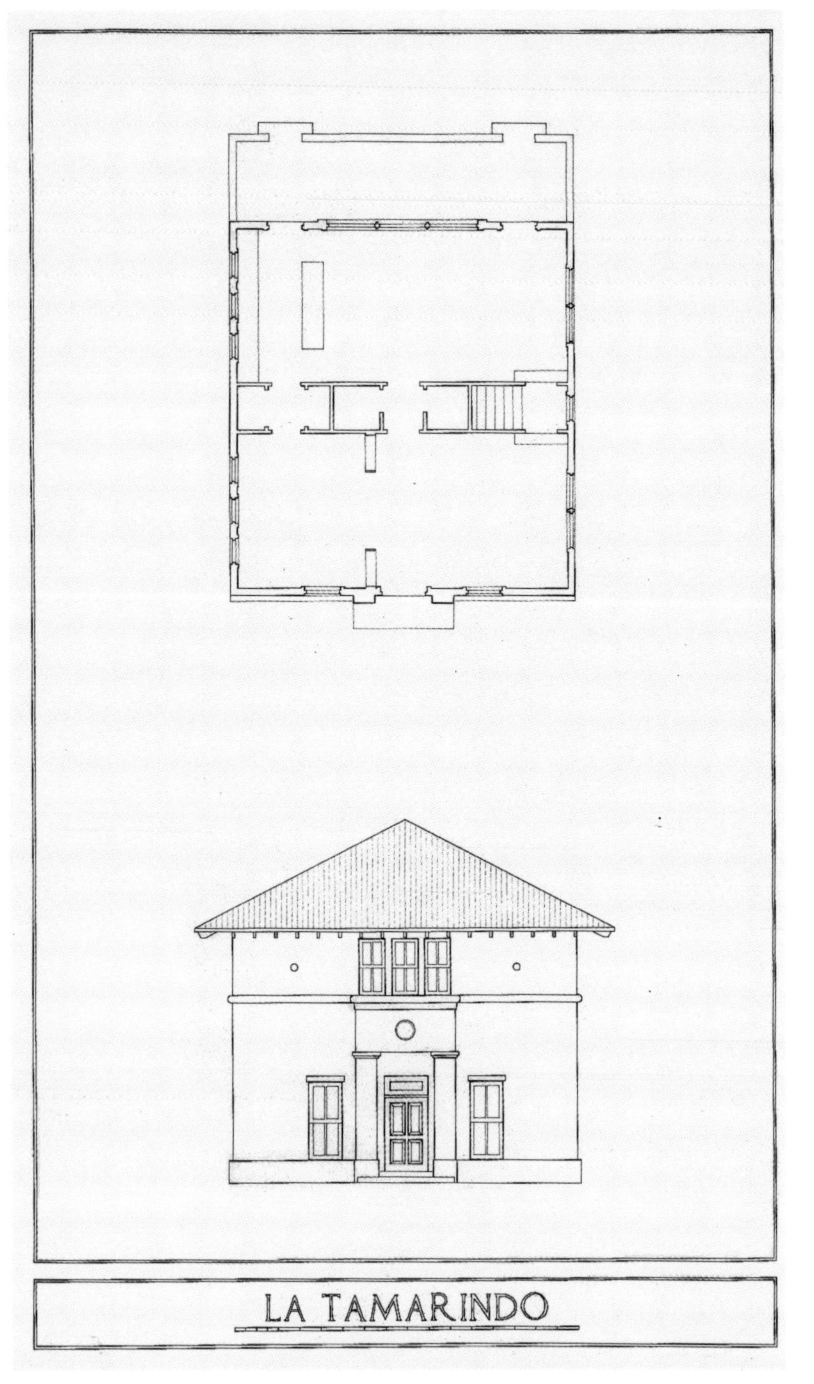

95. Jorge Hernandez. **La Tamarindo (Hernandez House),** 1992. Ink on paper, 18 x 24″

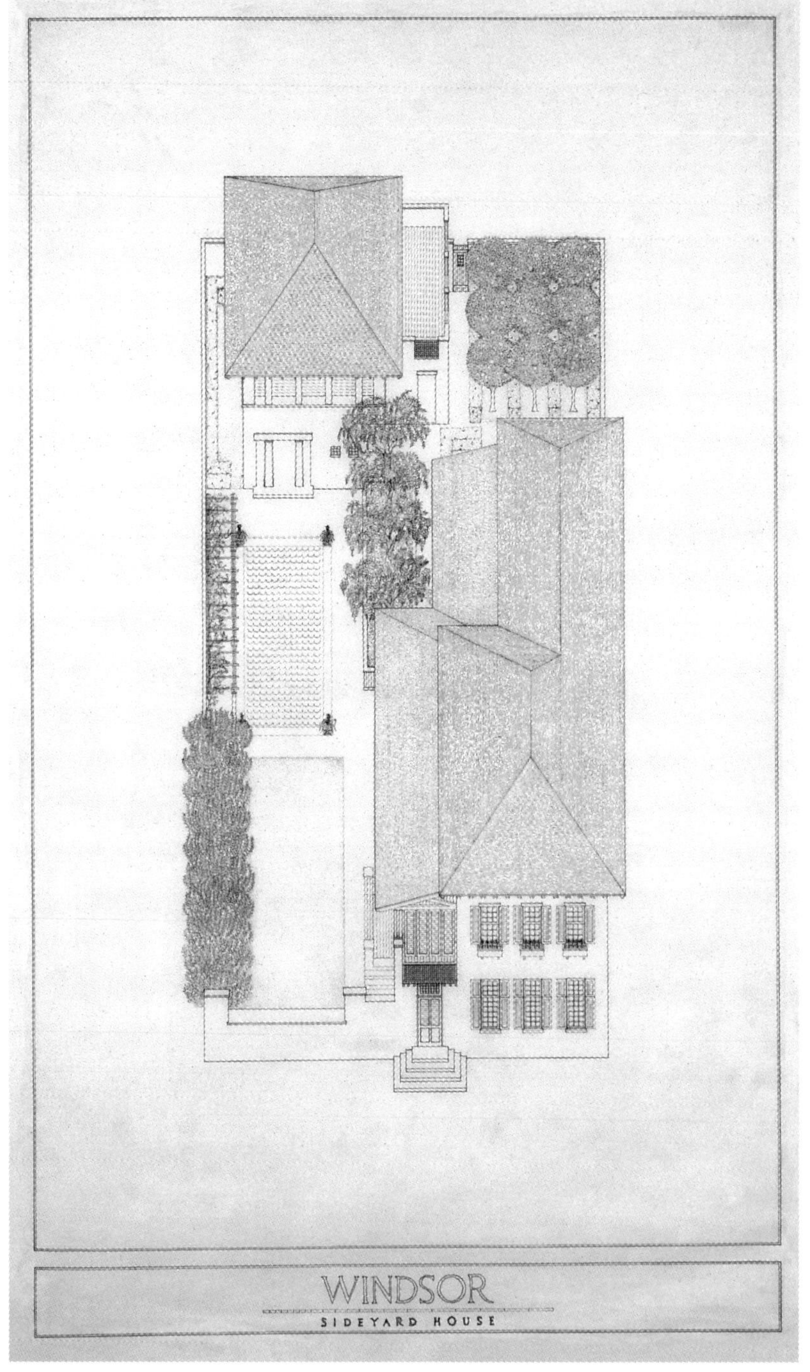

96. Dennis Hector, Jorge Hernandez, Joanna Lombard, Francis Lyn. **Side-Yard House, Windsor,** 1992. Ink on paper, 23 x 37″

97. Thomas Spain and Rolando Llanes. **Martinez Residence, Coral Gables,** 1992. Colored pencil, 20 x 36″

98. Thomas Spain. **Village Center, Windsor (Scott Merrill, architect),** 1994. pencil, 24 x 18″

99. Charles Barrett. **Belvedere House, Windsor, elevations and plan**, 1992. Ink, 15 x 29"

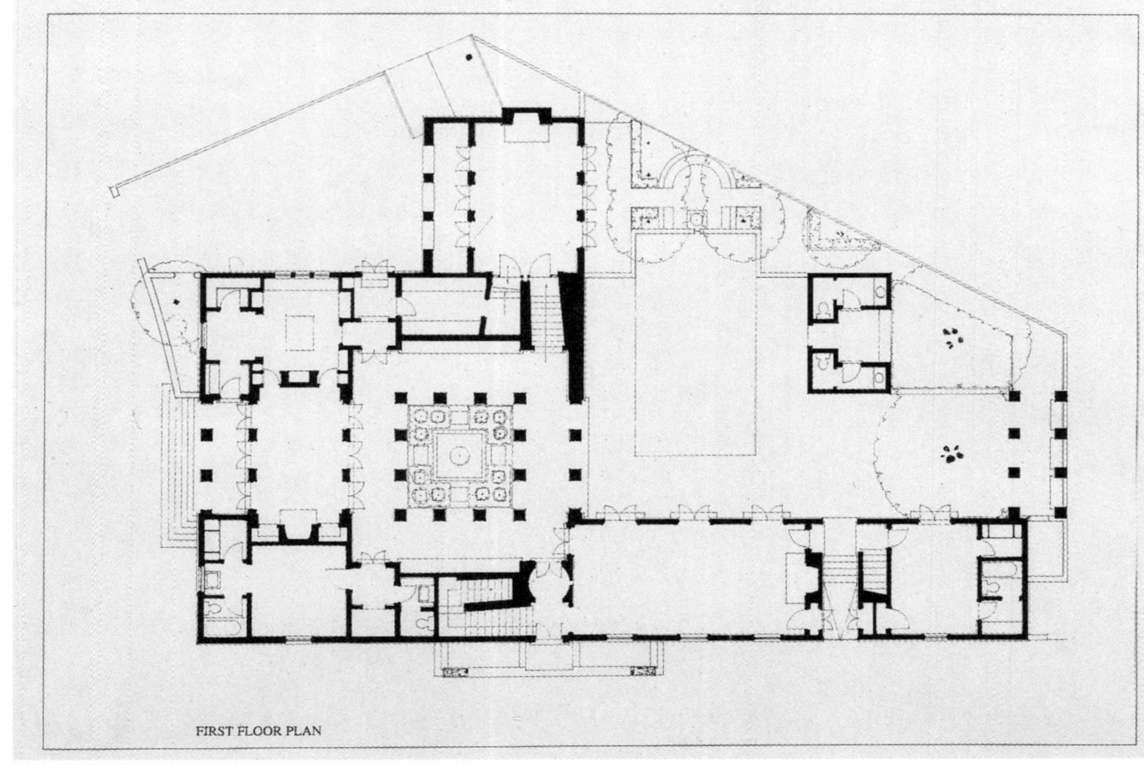

100. Charles Barrett. **Belvedere House, Windsor, perspective of atrium,** 1992. Ink on paper, 11 x 8½″

101. Charles Barrett. **Bath house, Seaside, section, elevation, plan,** 1988. Ink, 16 x 24"

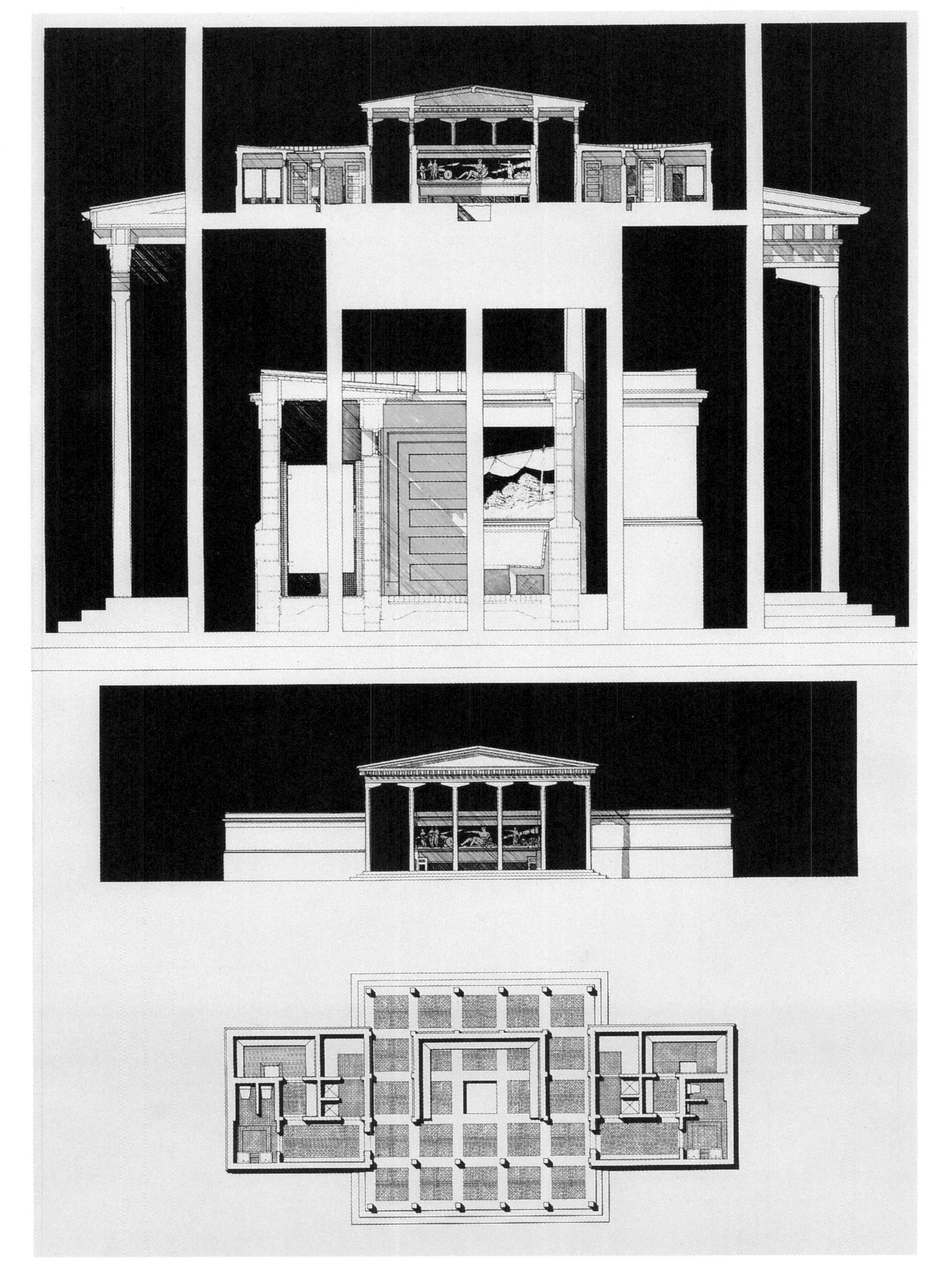

102. Charles Barrett. **Brick building, Mashpee,** 1992. Ink and pencil, 18 x 12″

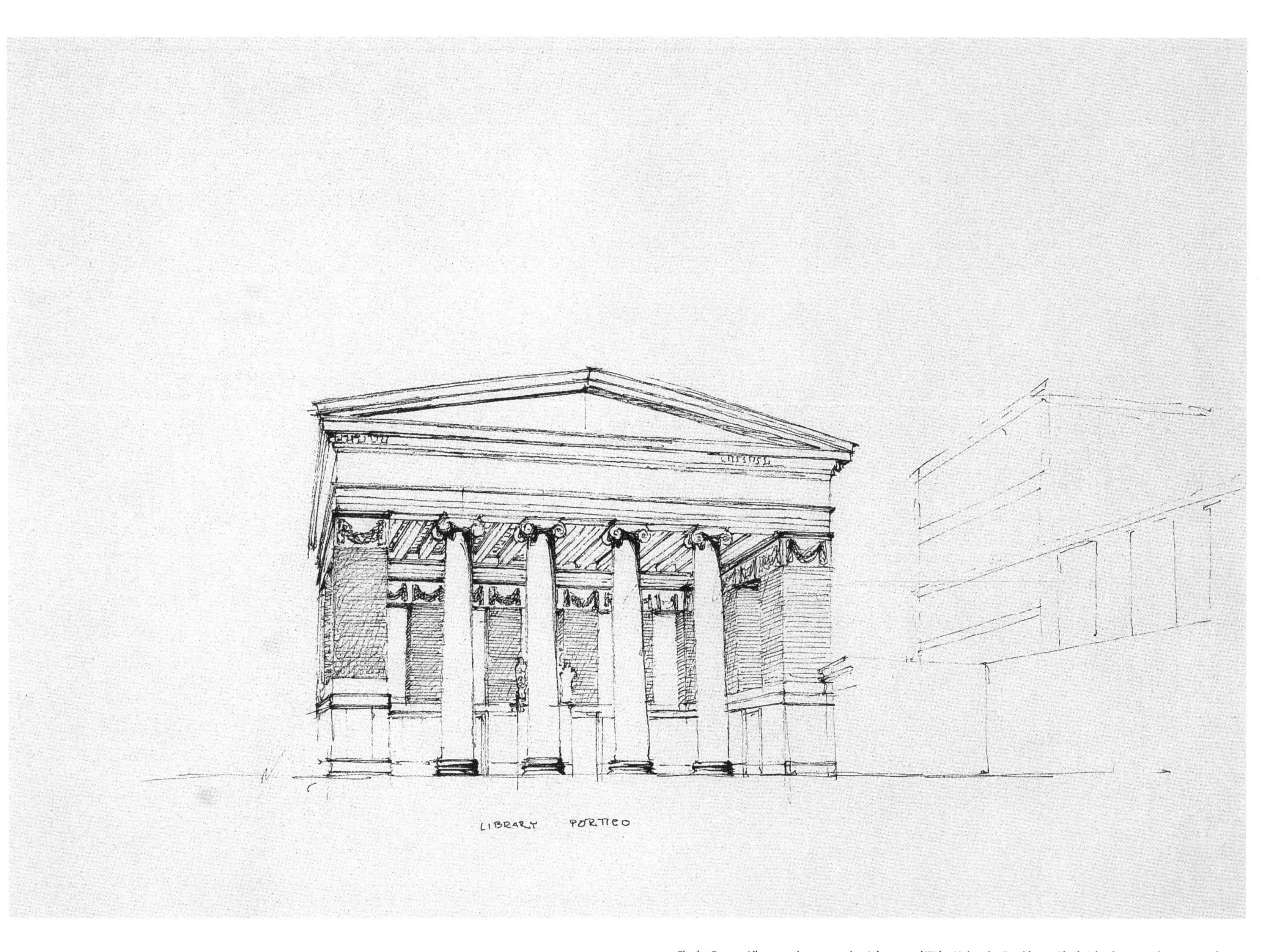

103. Charles Barrett. **Library portico perspective, Johnson and Wales University, Providence, Rhode Island,** 1992. Ink on paper, 18 x 12″

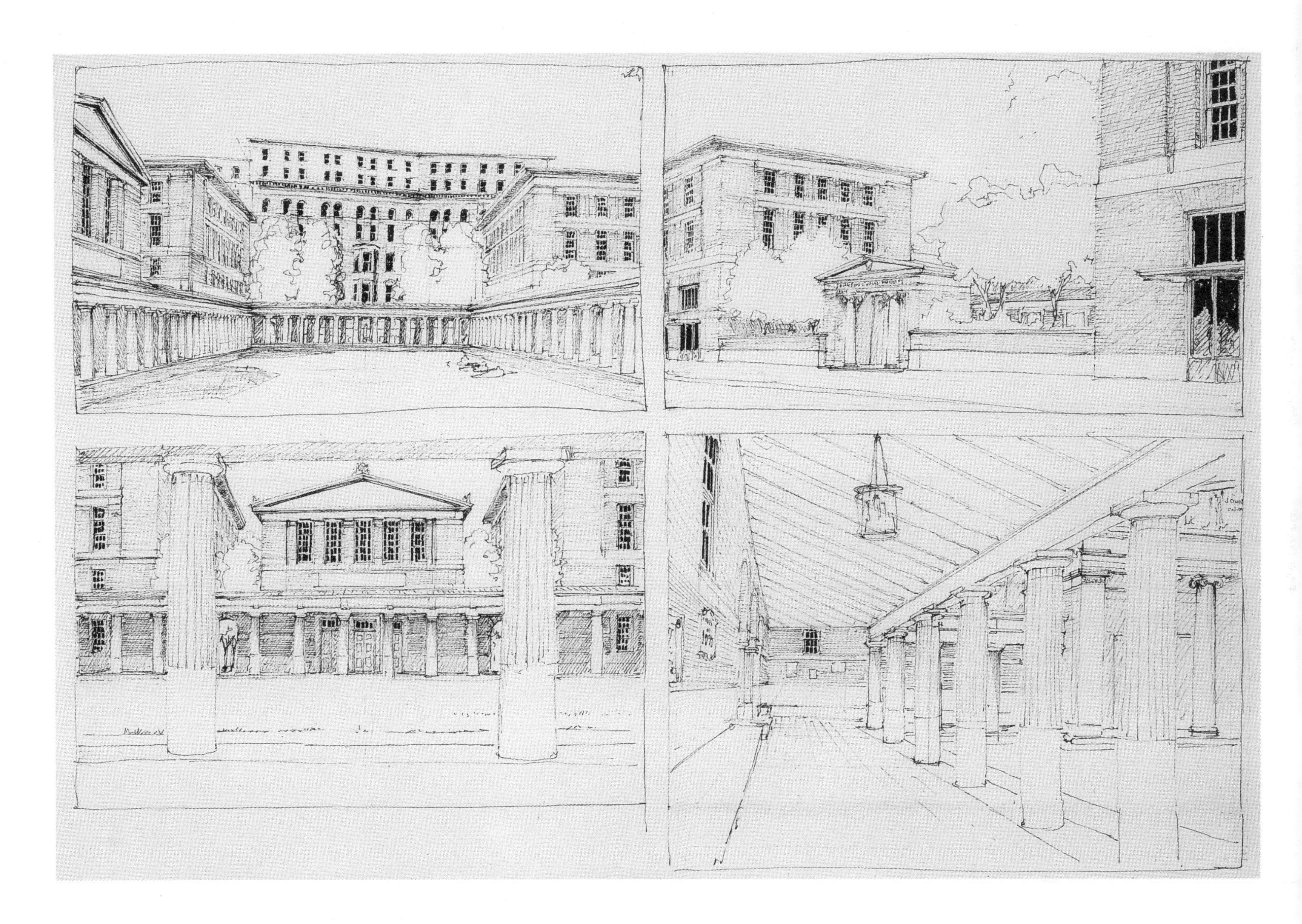

104. Charles Barrett. **Library quadrangle perspectives, Johnson and Wales University, Providence, Rhode Island,** 1992. Ink on paper, 36 x 24″

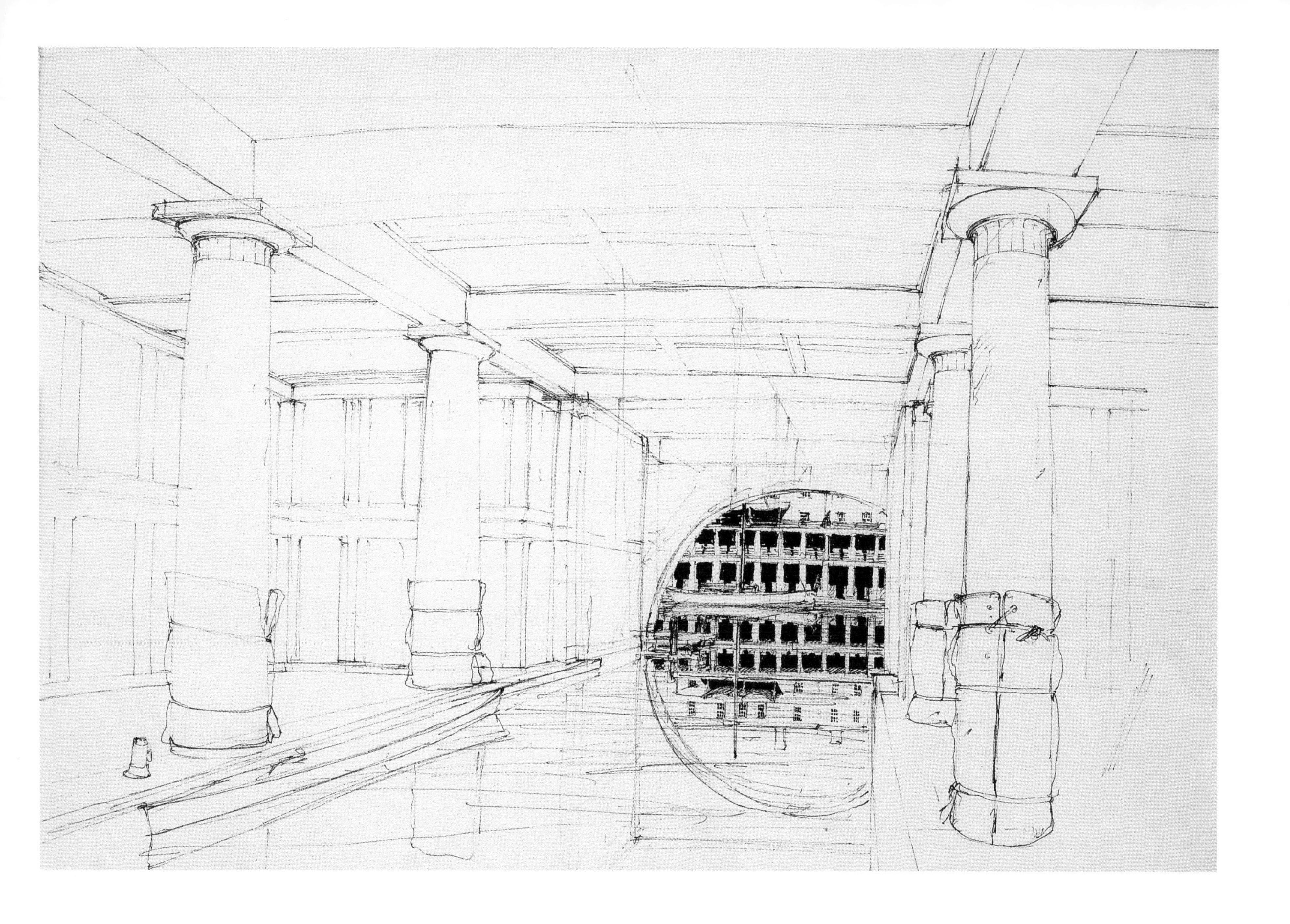

105. Charles Barrett. **Coral Gables waterway,** 1991. Ink on paper, 18 x 12"

106. Charles Barrett. **Proposed town of Treasure Island, San Francisco Bay,** 1979. Ink on paper, 36 x 24"

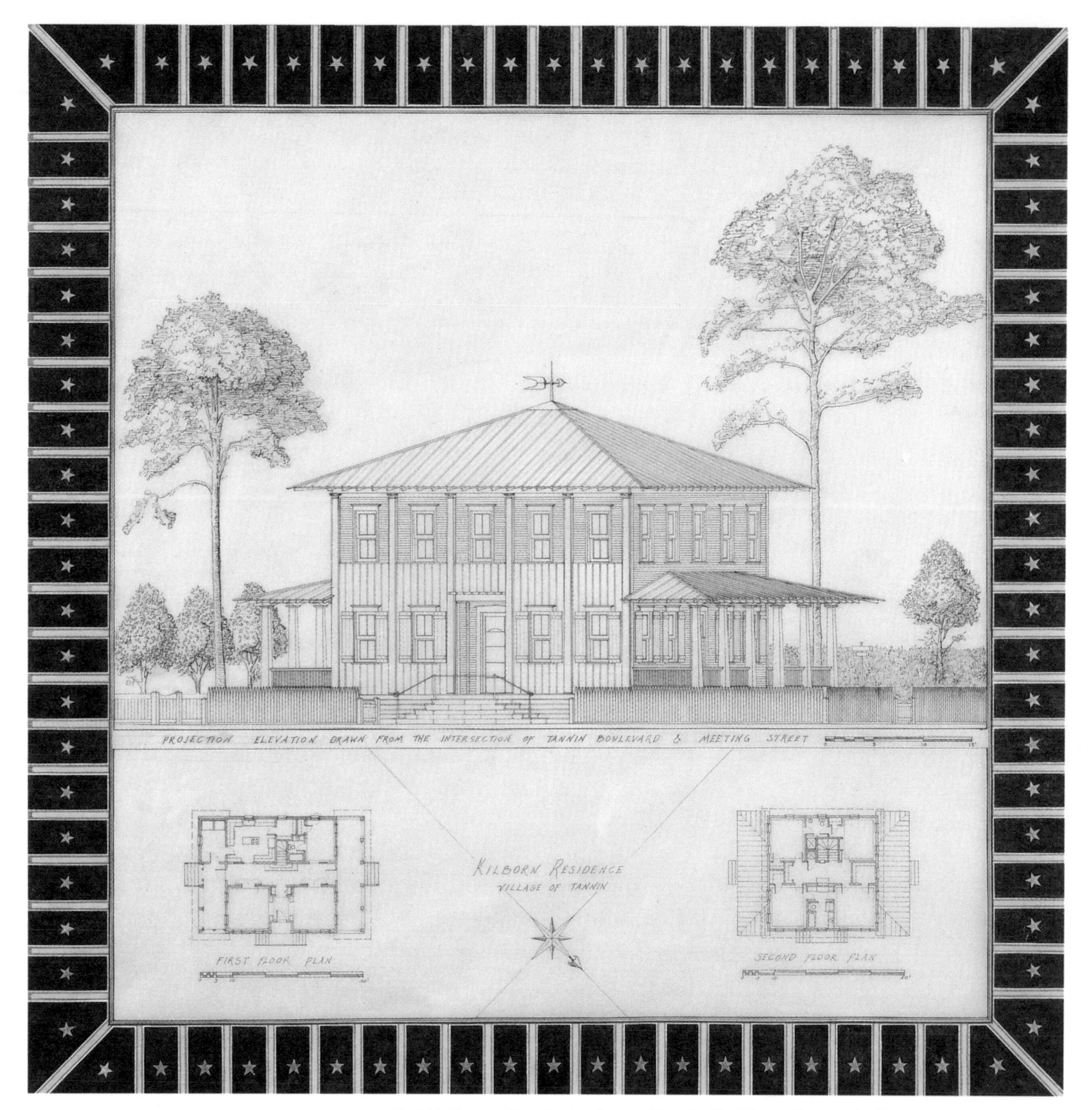

107. Frank Martinez, Juan Carruncho, Ana Alvarez, and Laura Garofalo. **Kilborn Residence, Tannin, Alabama, projection elevation and plans,** 1993. Ink and colored pencil on trace, 24 x 24"

108. Frank Martinez, Juan Carruncho, Ana Alvarez, and Marcelino Marrero. **Pool house, Tannin, Alabama,** 1994. Ink on paper, 39 x 13"

109. Eric Valle, **house types, Charleston,** 1993. Colored pencil, 120 x 10″

110. Jorge Trelles and Luis Trelles. **Rancho Camaliz stable, Redland, Florida,** 1990. Coffee wash, 34 x 12″

111. Jorge Trelles and Luis Trelles. **Tigertail House, Coconut Grove,** 1991. Coffee wash, 22 x 17"

112. Teofilo Victoria, Jorge Trelles, and Luis Trelles. **Blue House, Miami,** 1993. Colored pencil, 22 x 17″

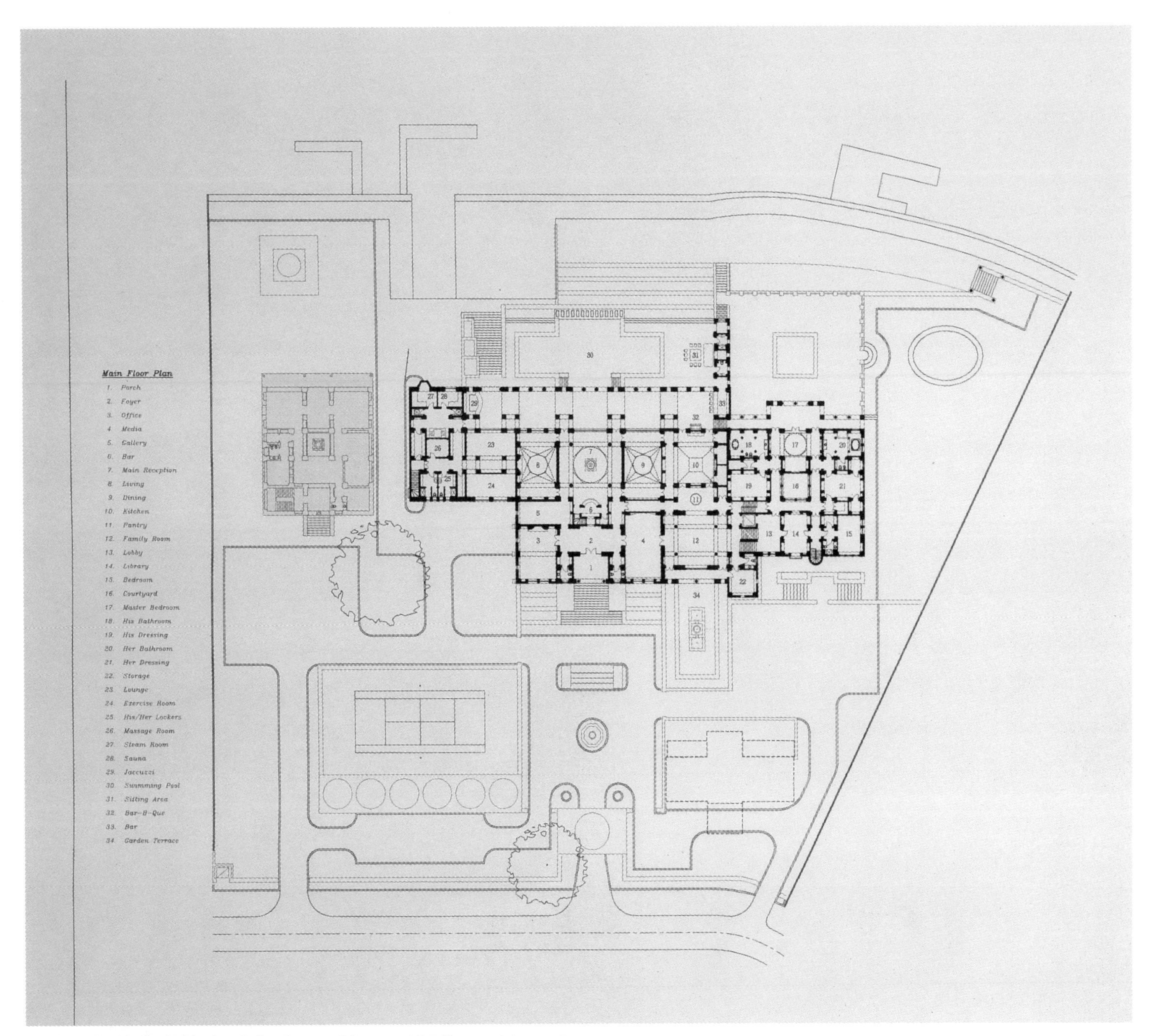

113. Abdel Wahed El Wakil. **Kramer House, Star Island, Miami Beach, main floor plan,** 1994. Ink on paper (plotted by computer), 24 x 24"

114. Roberto M. Behar. **San Diego,** 1988. Colored pencil, 17 x 24".

115. Roberto M. Behar. **Motel Room**, 1988. Colored pencil, 17 x 24"

116. Roberto M. Behar. **Table Clock,** 1987. Colored pencil, 30 x 20"

117. Roberto M. Behar. **Temple for Seaside,** 1987. Colored pencil, 30 x 20″

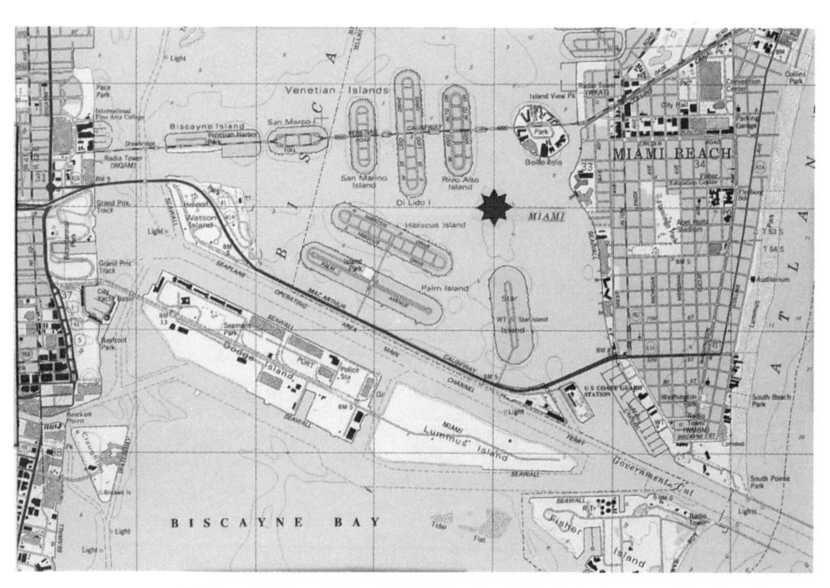

118. Roberto M. Behar with Fauziah Ab-Rahim. **Star of Miami, site plan,** 1992. Colored pencil, 10 x 7″

119. Roberto M. Behar with Fauziah Ab-Rahim. **Star of Miami, plan,** 1992. Pastel and pencil, 24 x 36″

120. Roberto M. Behar and Rosario Marquardt. **Star of Miami, hammock entrance,** 1992. Pastel and pencil, 27 x 10″

121. Roberto M. Behar and Rosario Marquardt. **Jungle Cab, Metro Project, Miami,** 1994. Pastel and pencil, 34 x 15"

122. Roberto M. Behar and Rosario Marquardt. **Star of Miami, blue bench and hammock,** 1992. Pastel and pencil, 13 x 10″

123. Rosario Marquardt. **Stories of the Conquest,** 1992. Oil on canvas, 18 x 24"

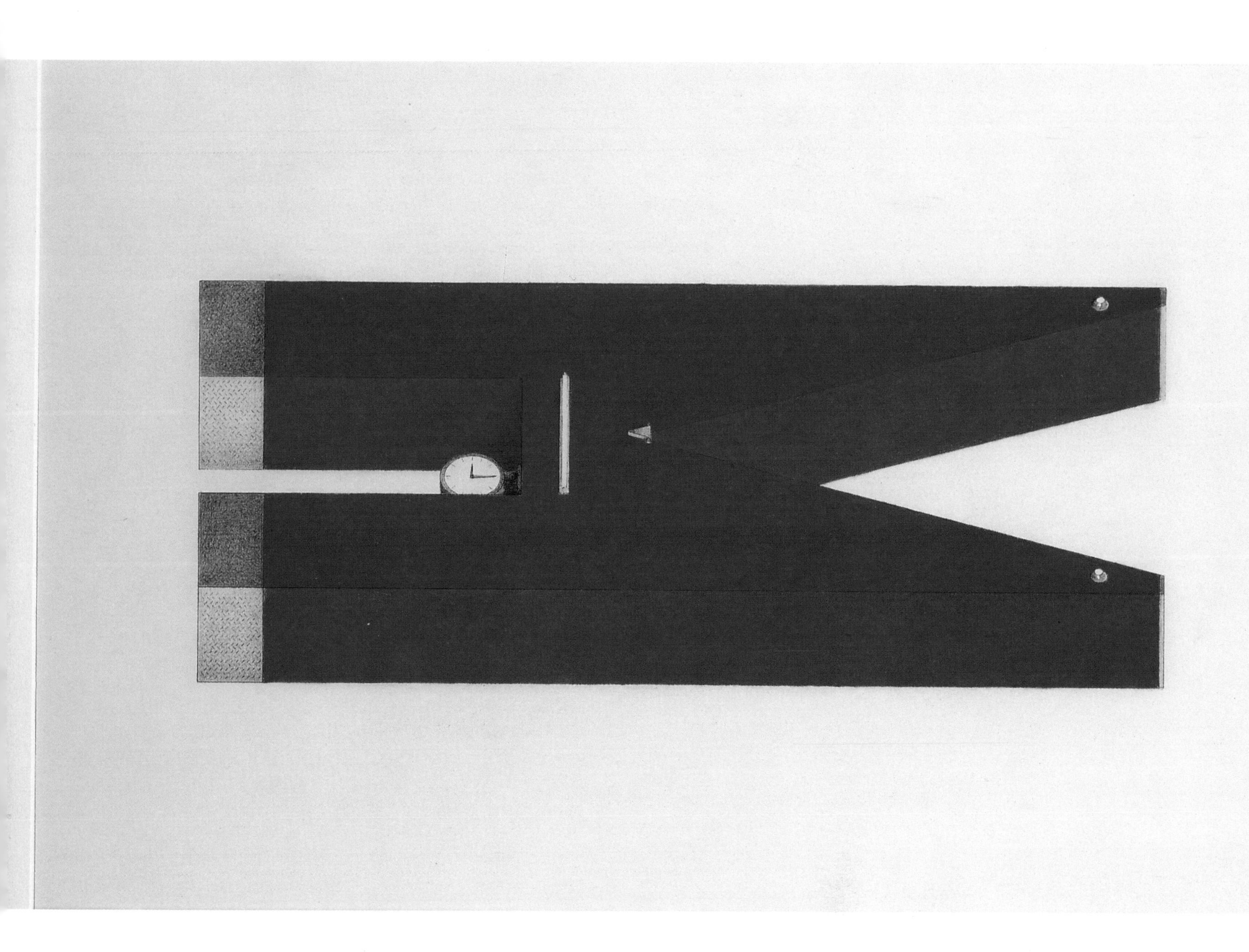

Plate 124

124. Roberto M. Behar and Rosario Marquardt. **An M for Miami,** 1994. Colored pencil, 14 x 24″

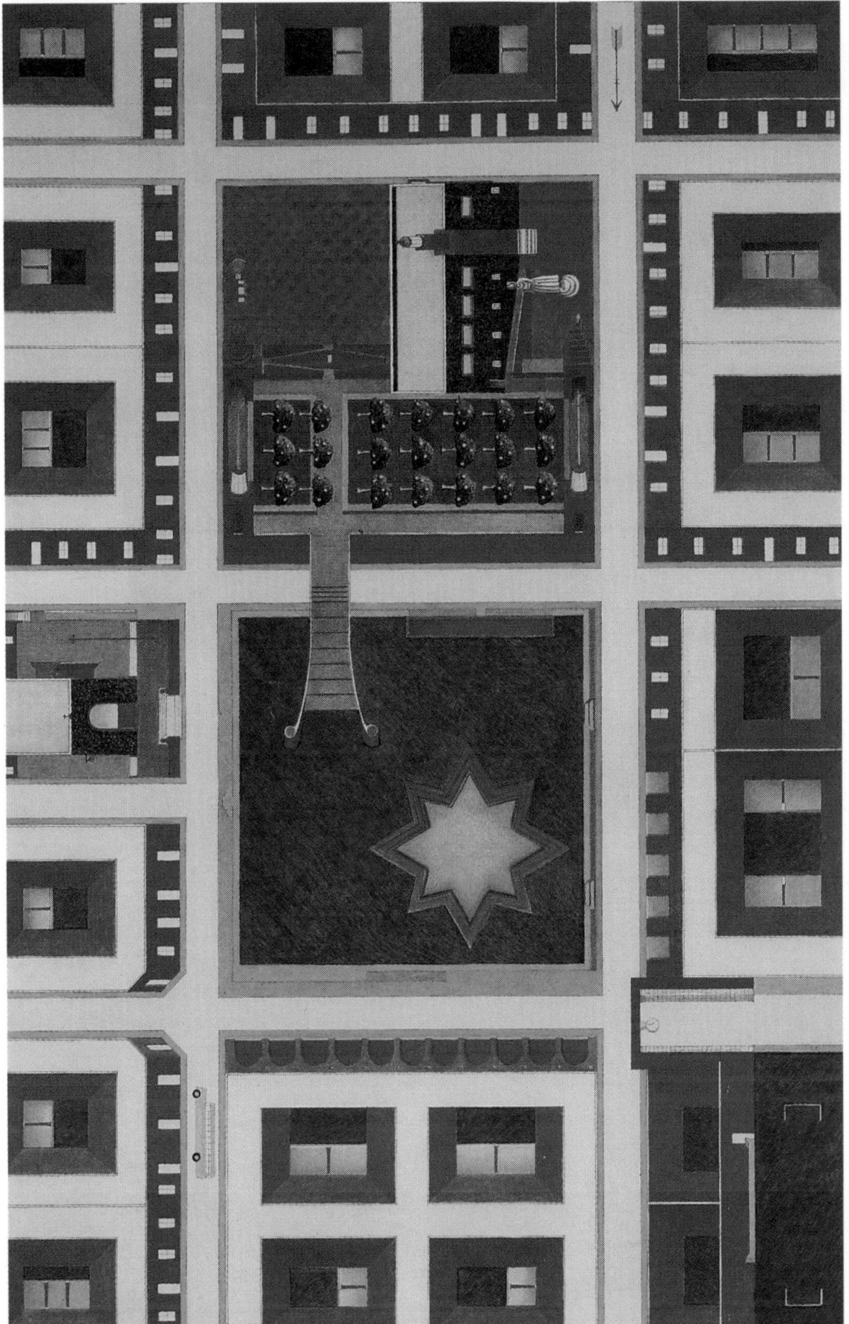

125 (left). Roberto M. Behar. **Little Guatemala: Central Area, South Dade,** 1992. Pastel and pencil, 24 x 36″

126 (right). Roberto M. Behar. **Little Guatemala: Town Plan, South Dade,** 1992. Ink on paper, 24 x 36″

127. Roberto M. Behar. **Little Guatemala: Arriving to Little Guatemala, South Dade,** 1992. Colored pencil, 25 x 12"

128. Roberto M. Behar. **Little Guatemala: View of Lateral Plaza Meetinghouse and Public Terrace, South Dade,** 1992. Pastel and pencil, 36 x 12″

129. Rolando Llanes. **Habitat for Humanity housing (Armando Montero, architect), South Dade,** 1992. Colored pencil, 18 x 12"

130. Jaime Correa. **Dorfplatz, Vockerode,** 1992. Colored pencil, 6 x 7″

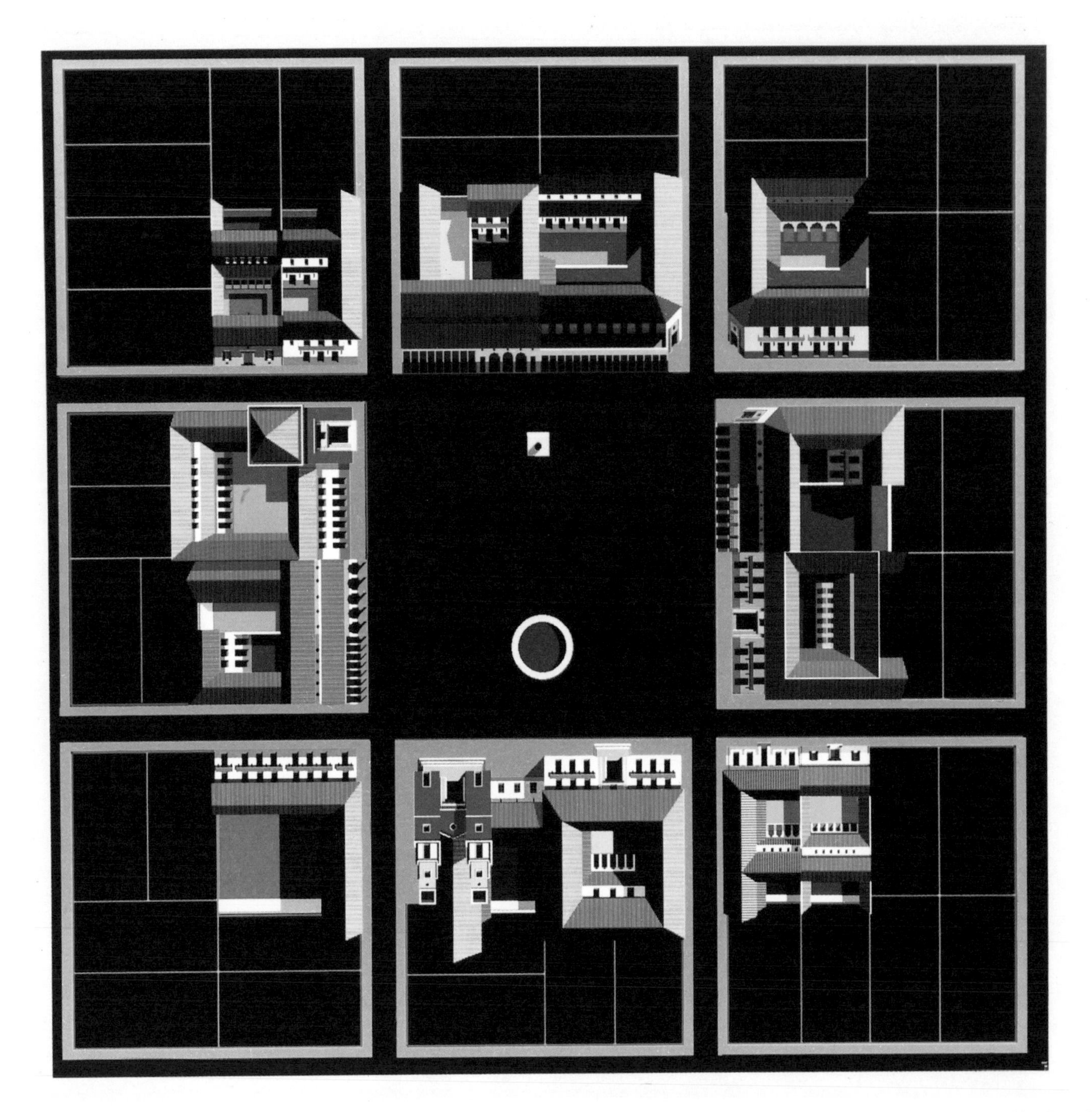

131. Jaime Correa. **Colonial city plan,** 1992. Digital image, 40 x 40"

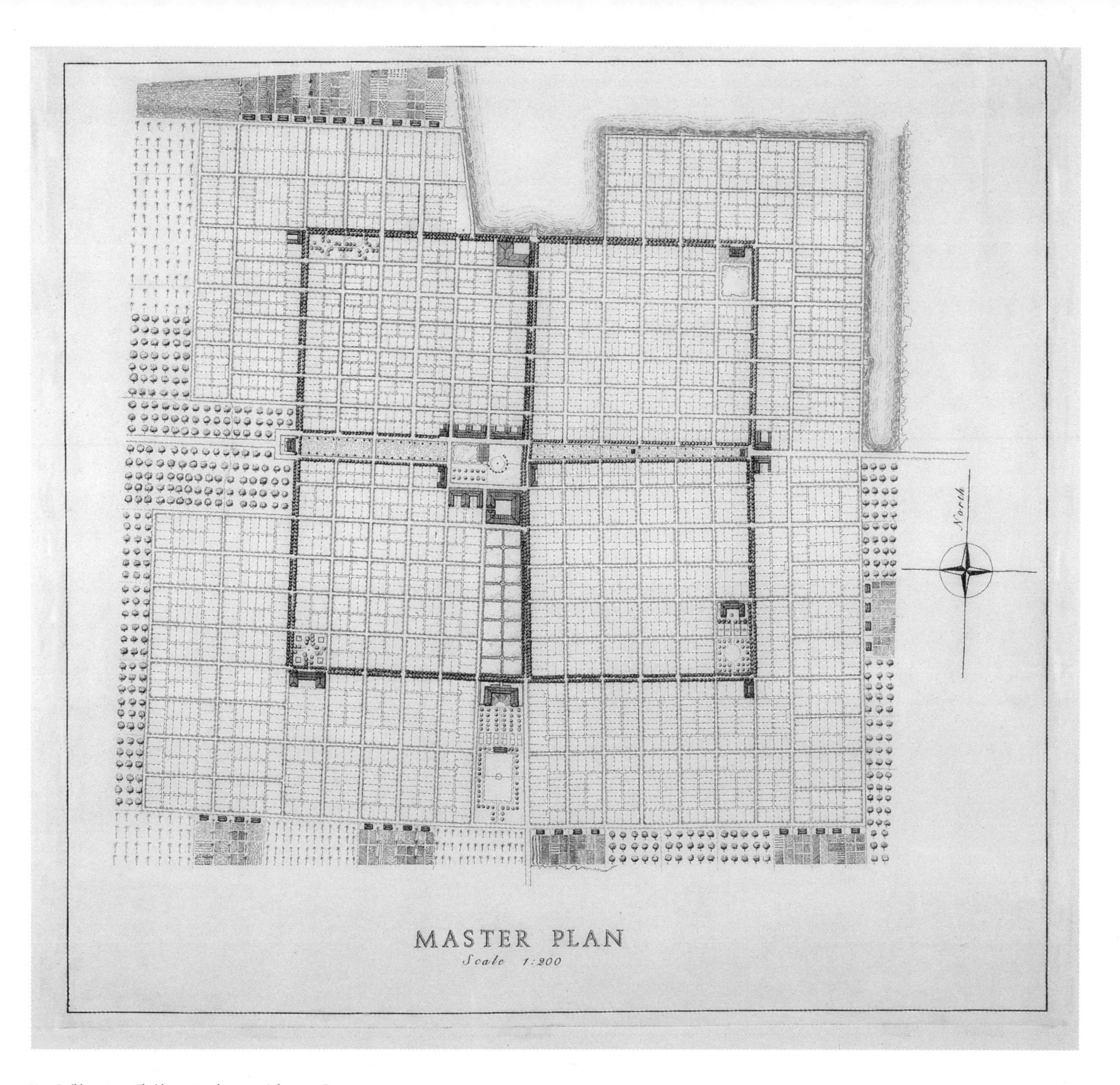

132. Adriana Veras and Jaime Correa. **New Caribbean town, Florida, master plan,** 1993. Ink, 24 x 24″

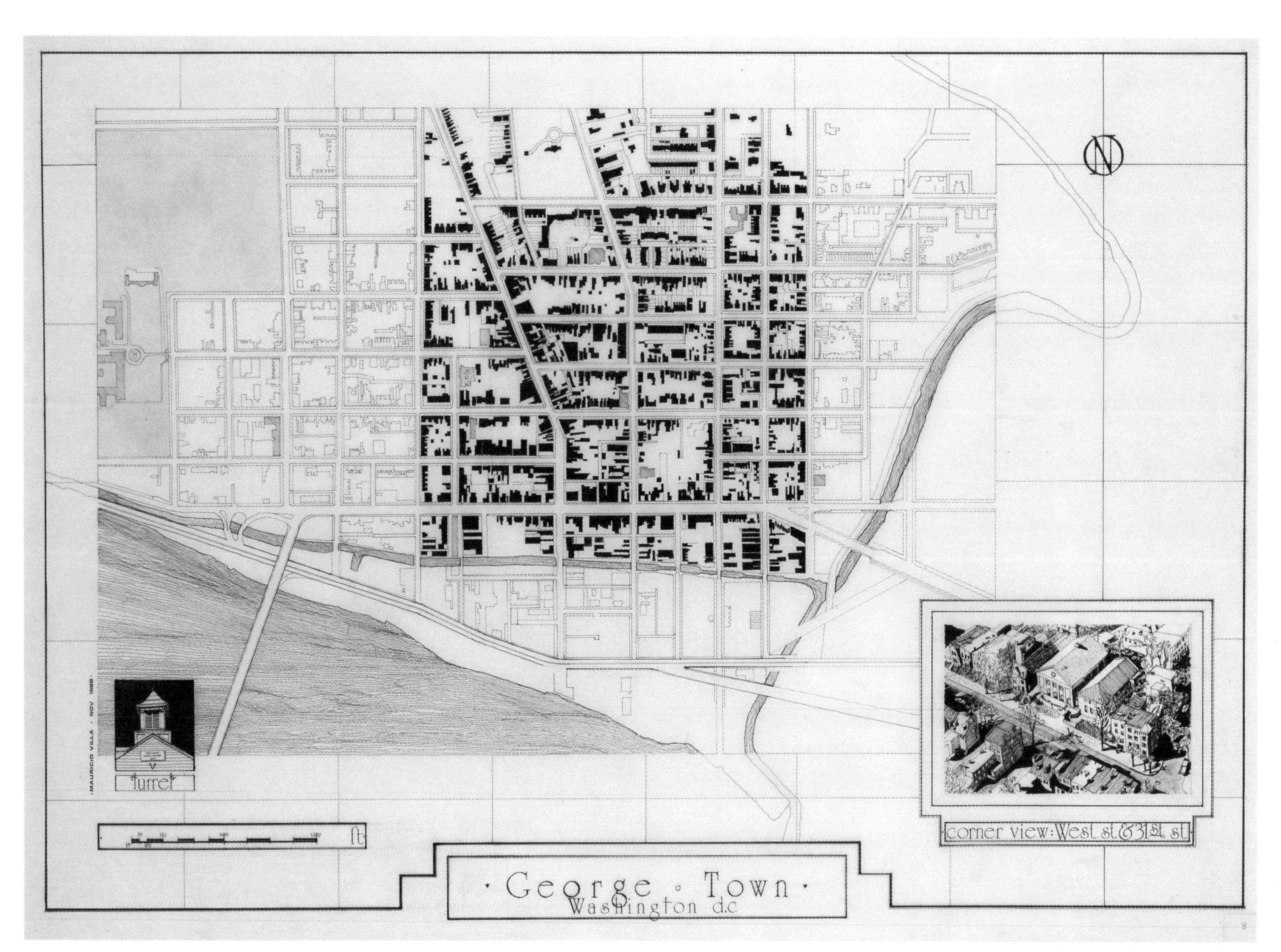

133. Mauricio Villa. **Georgetown,** 1988. Ink on mylar, 39 x 27″

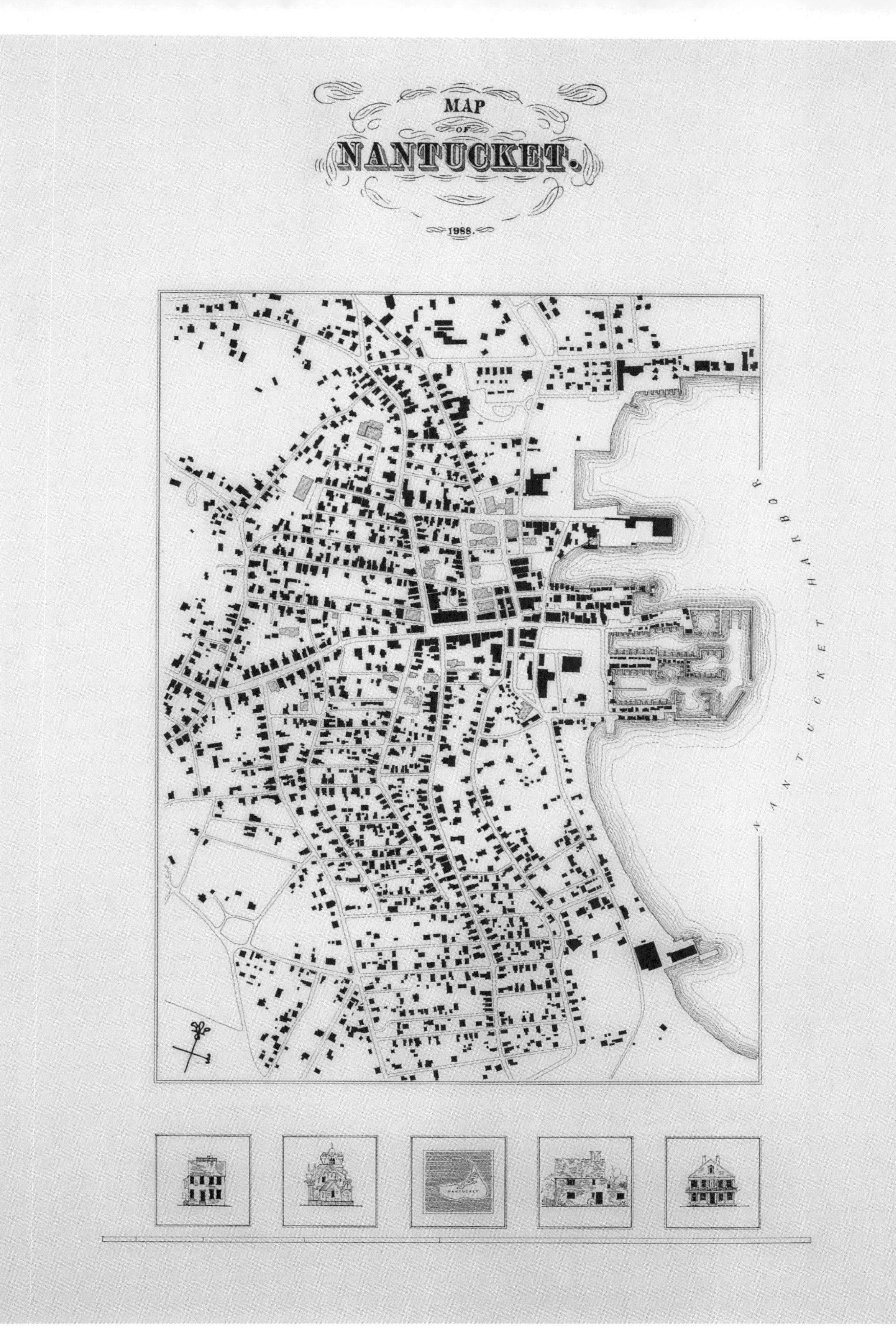

134. Grace Perdomo. **Nantucket,** 1988. Ink on mylar, 28 x 40"

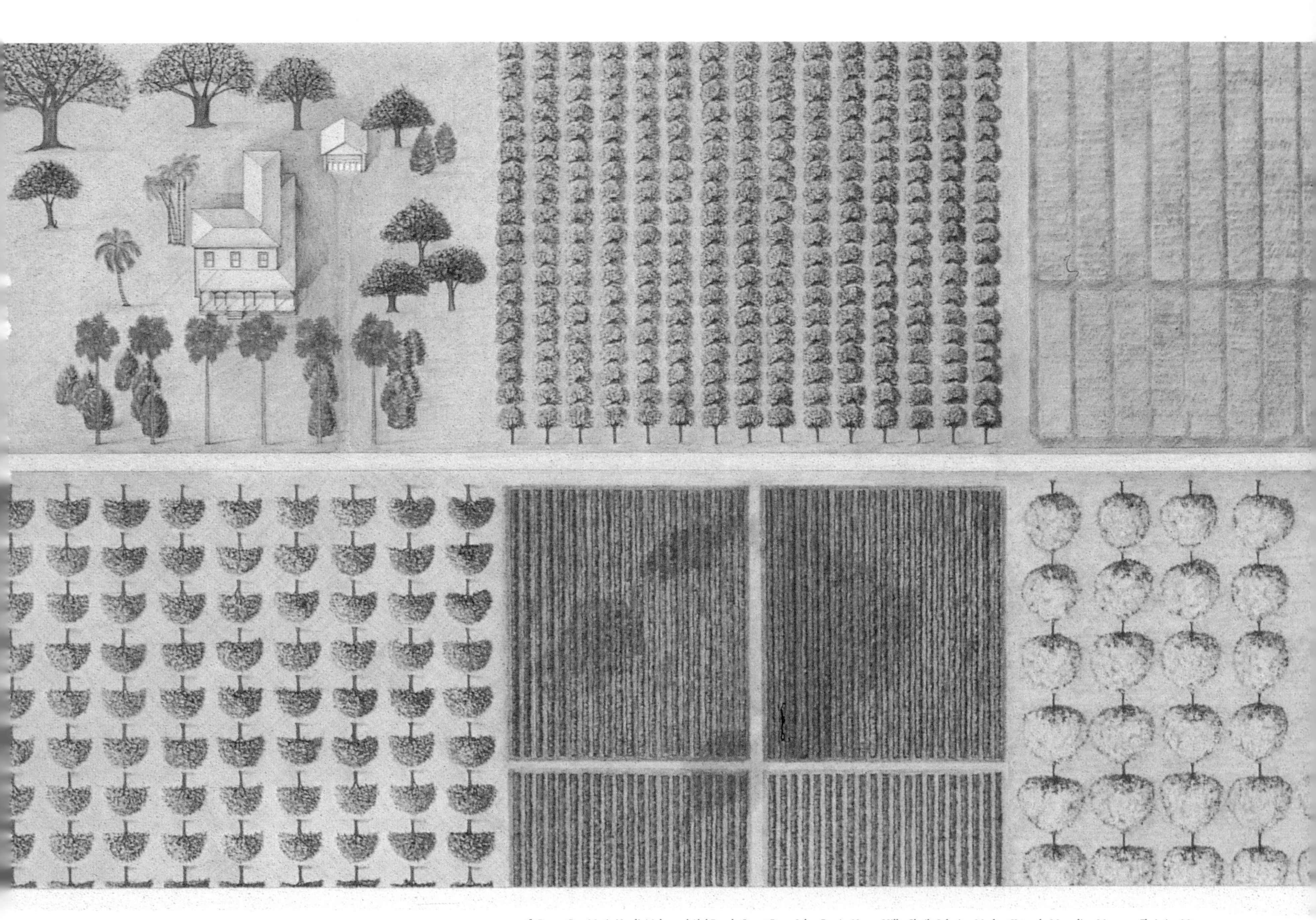

136. Rocco Ceo, Maria Nardi, Mohamed Abd Razak, Stuart Baur, John Garcia, Nancy Hills, Sheila Iglesias, Markus Ketnath, Marcelino Marrero, Christine Marzouca, Dan Negas, Jorge Planas, Albert Rodriguez, David Rosenblum, Miriam Tropp. **Silver Palm, Redland,** 1992. Colored pencil, 121 x 18"

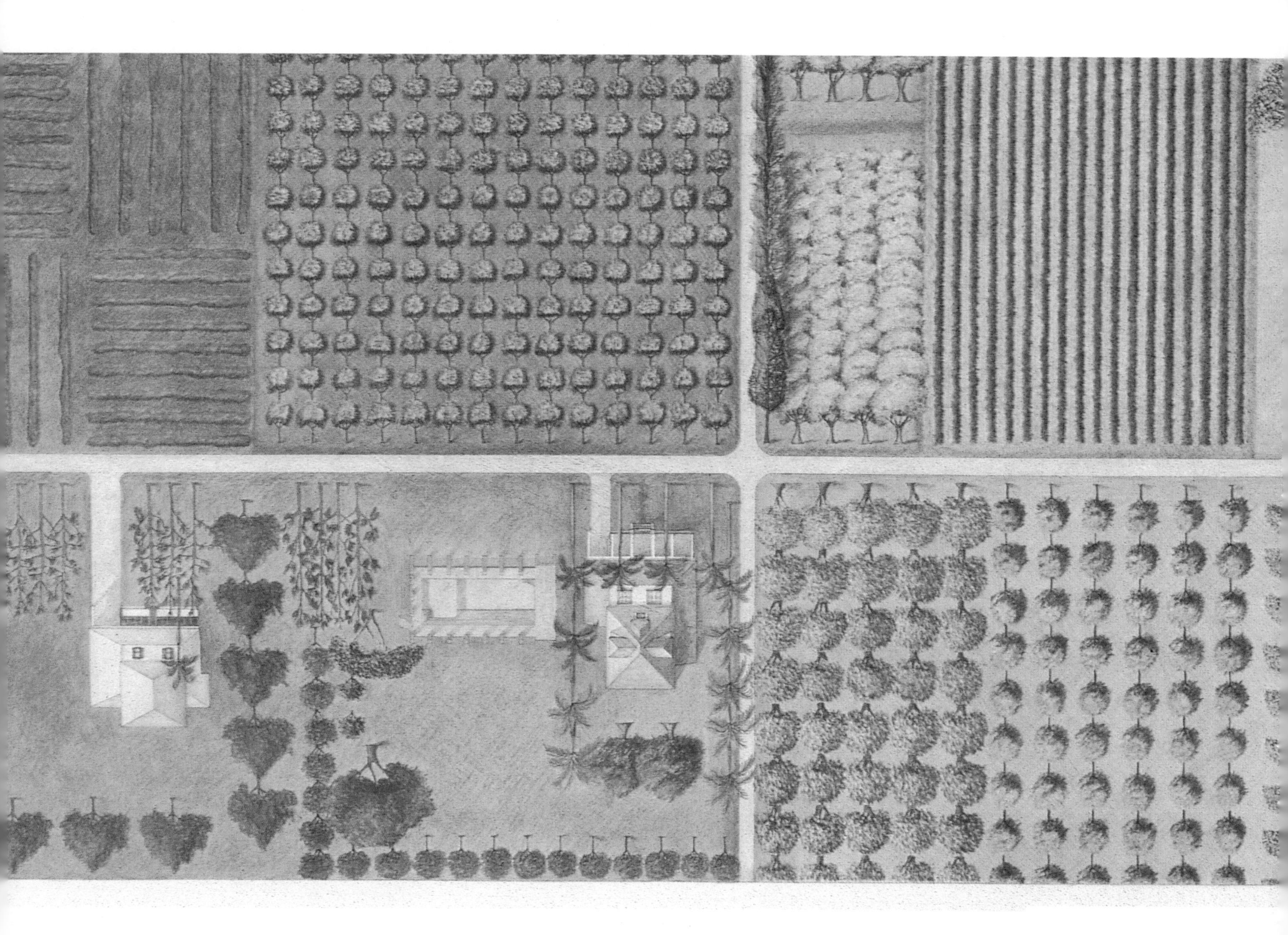

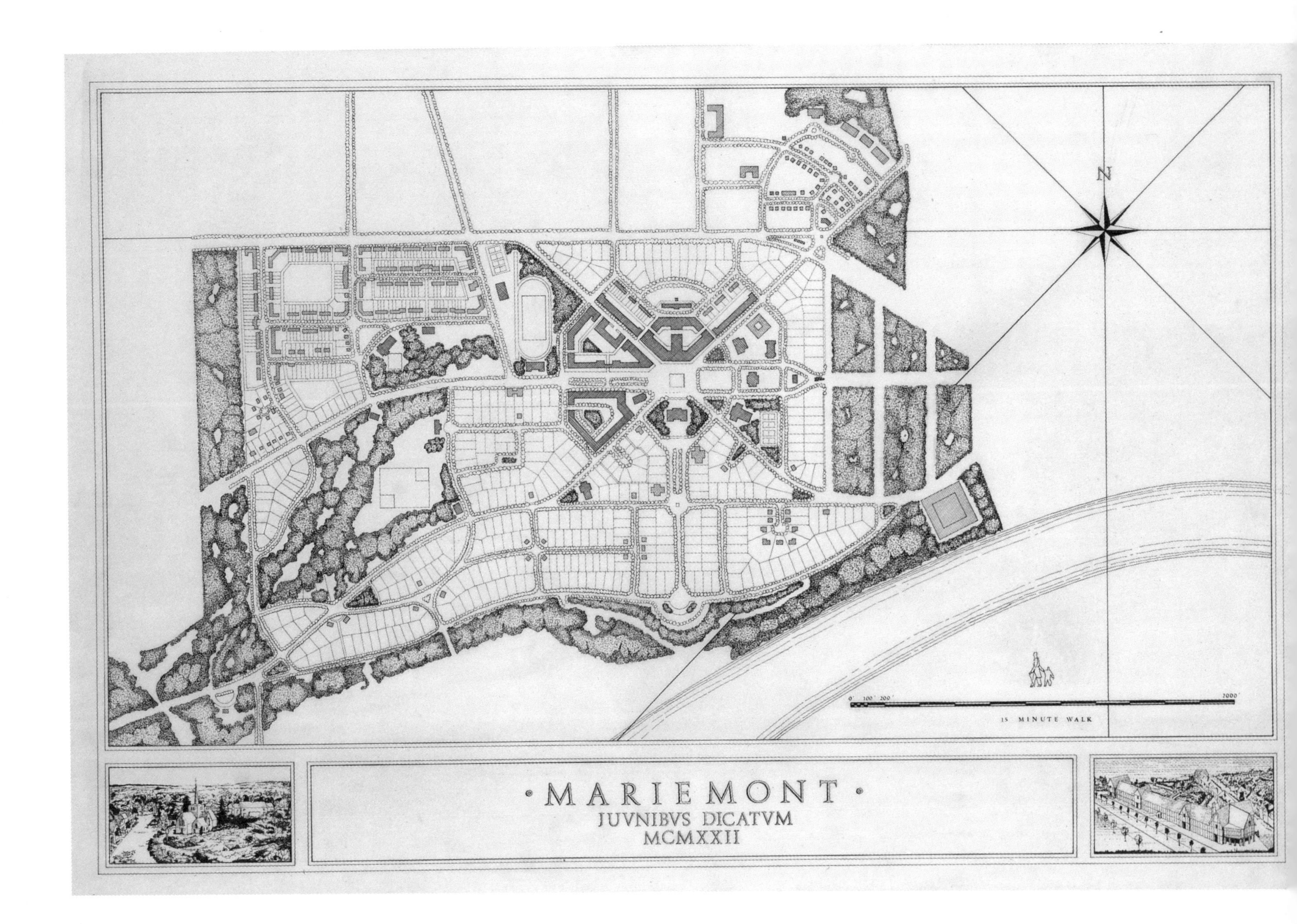

135. Felix Pereira. **John Nolen's plan for Mariemont, 1922,** 1988. Ink on mylar, 34 x 22"

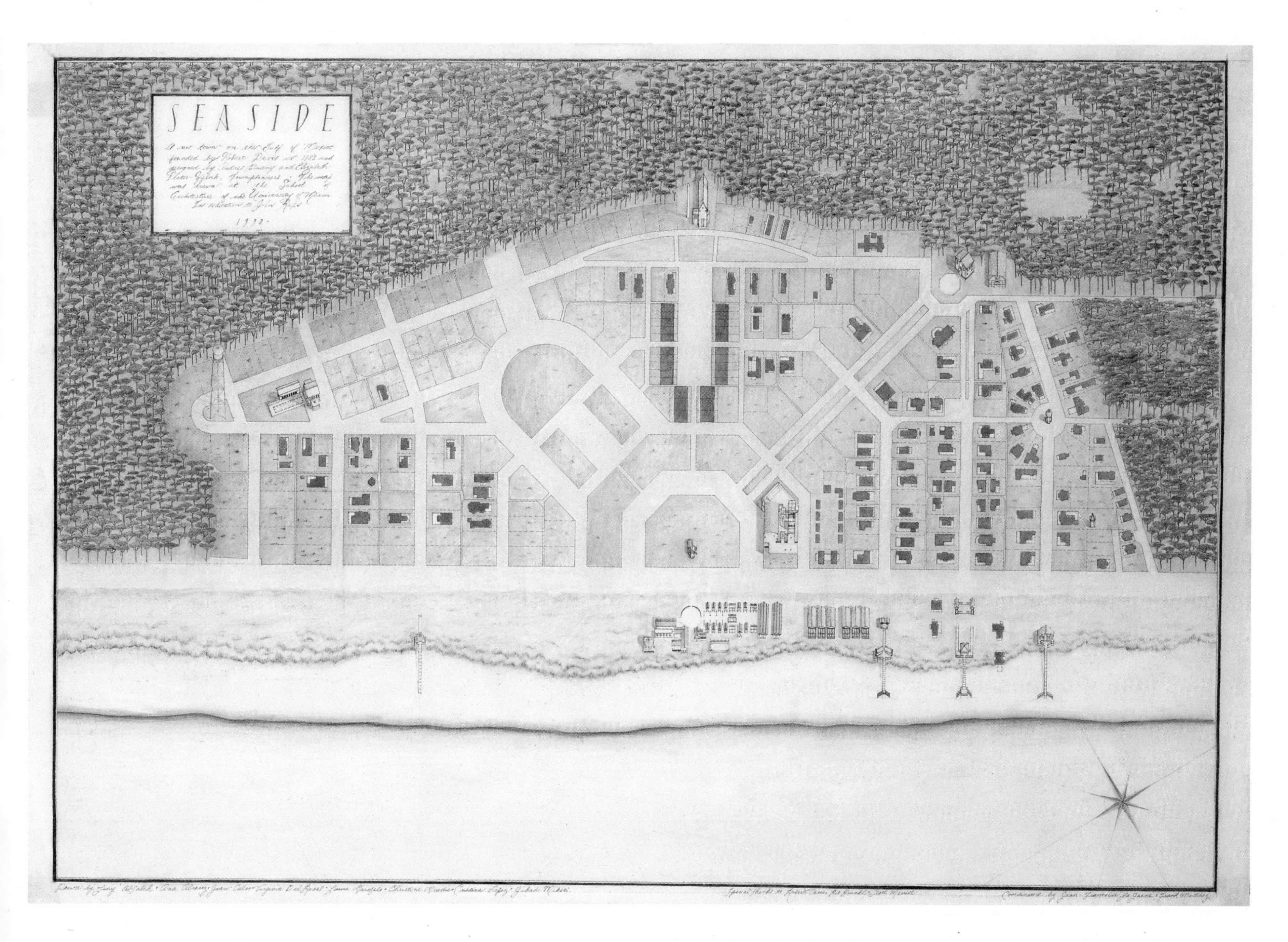

137. Jean-François Lejeune, Frank Martinez, Luay Al-Saleh, Ana Alvarez, Juan Calvo, Virginia del Rosal, Laura Garofalo, Christine Gradie, Christine Lopez, Jihad Mikati. **Seaside (Duany Plater-Zyberk, architect), plan,** 1990. Colored pencil, 41 x 29"

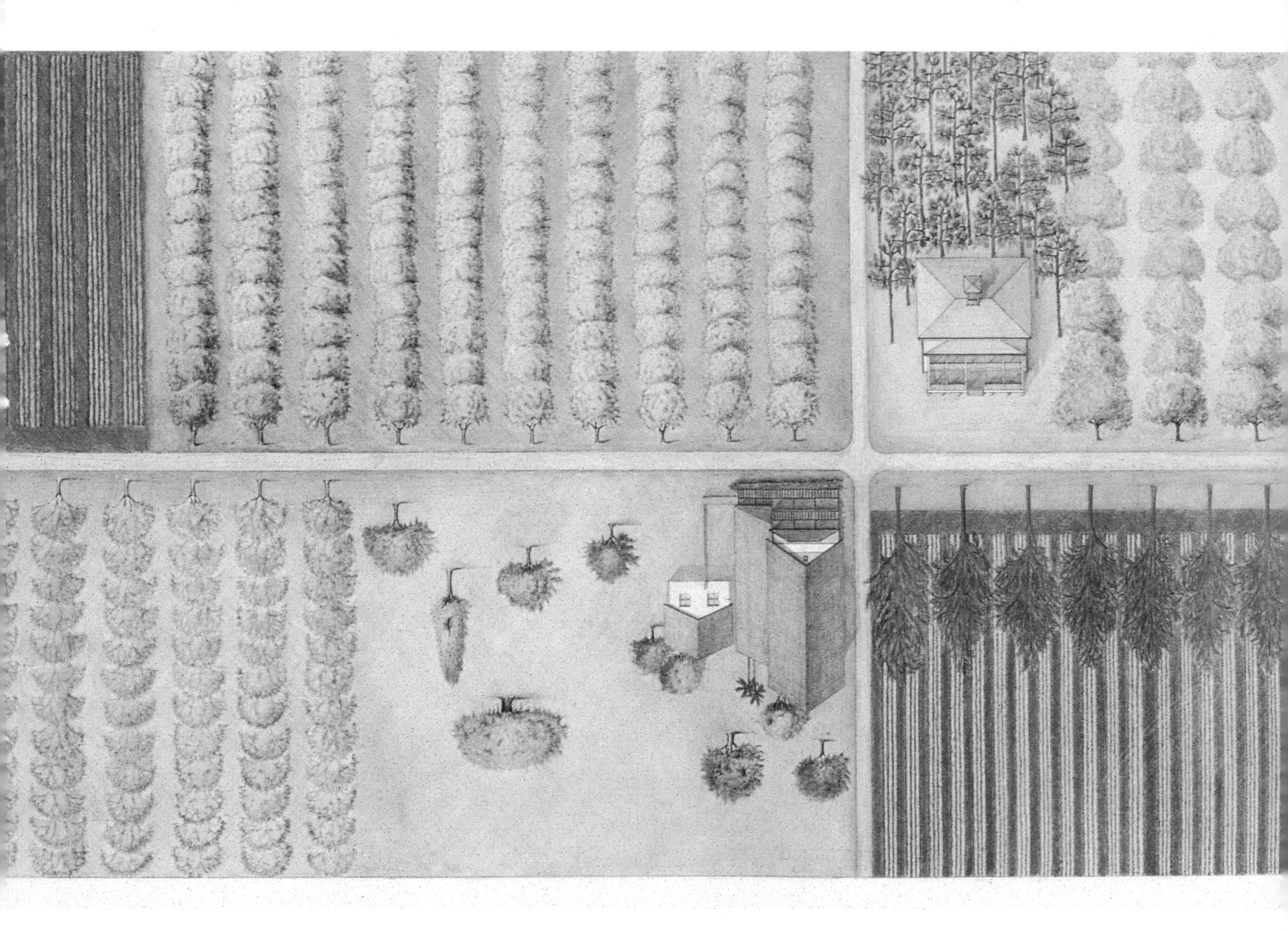

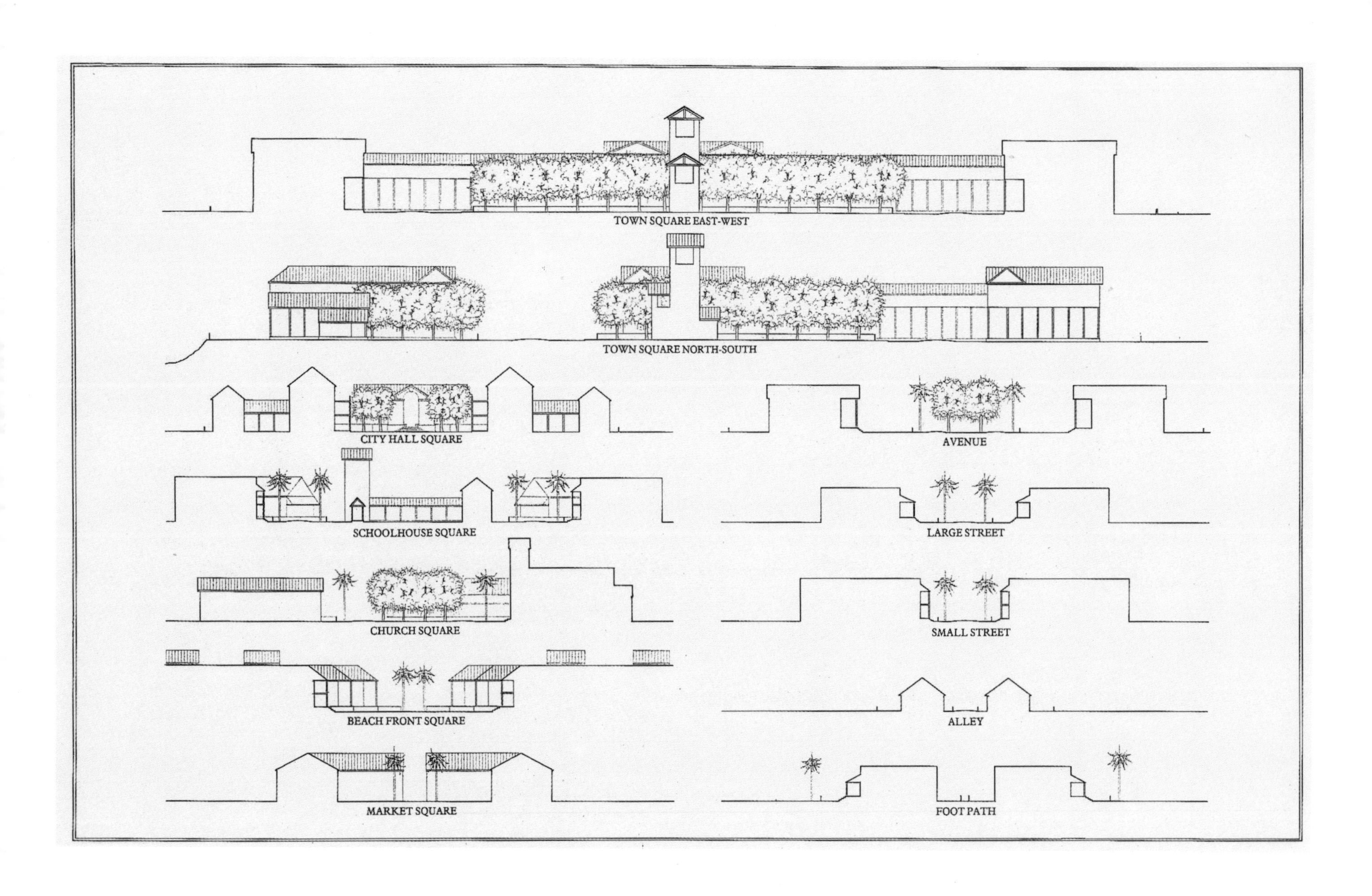

138. Duany Plater-Zyberk. **Seaside street sections, public spaces,** 1982. Ink on mylar, 36 x 24"

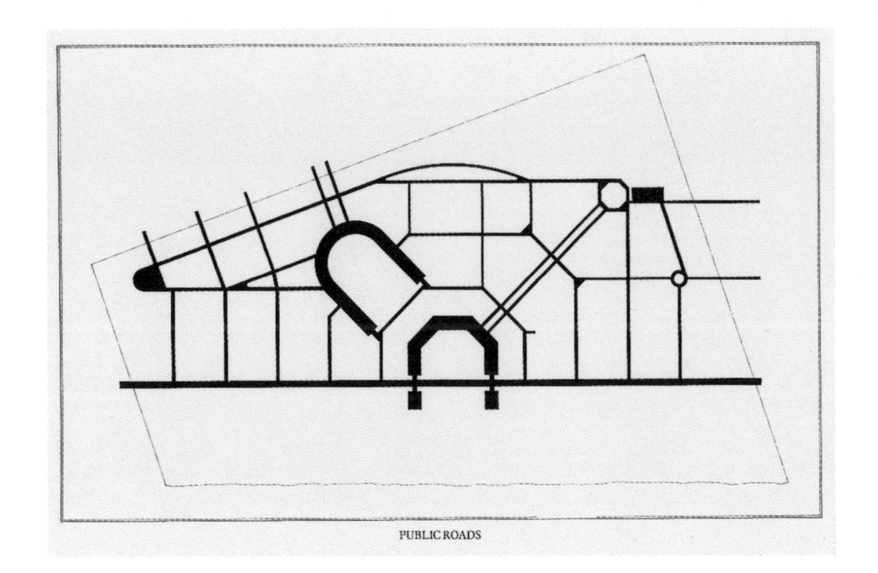

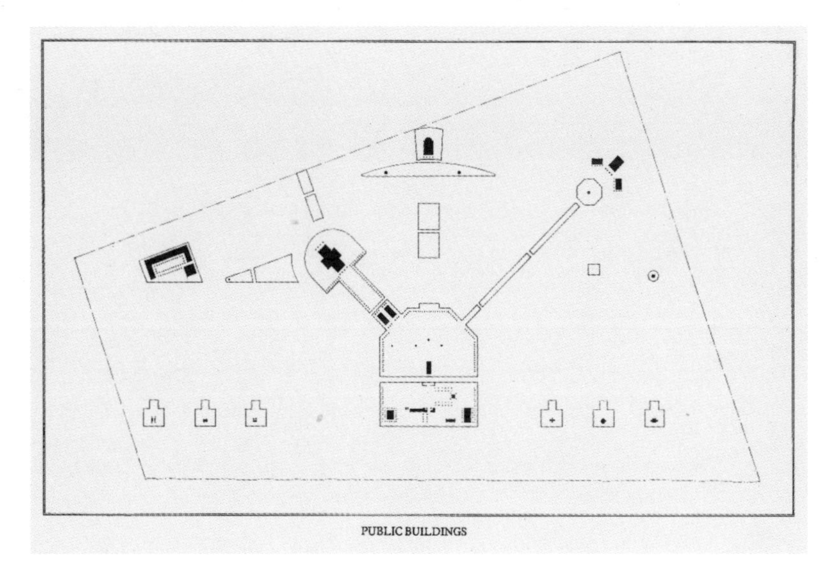

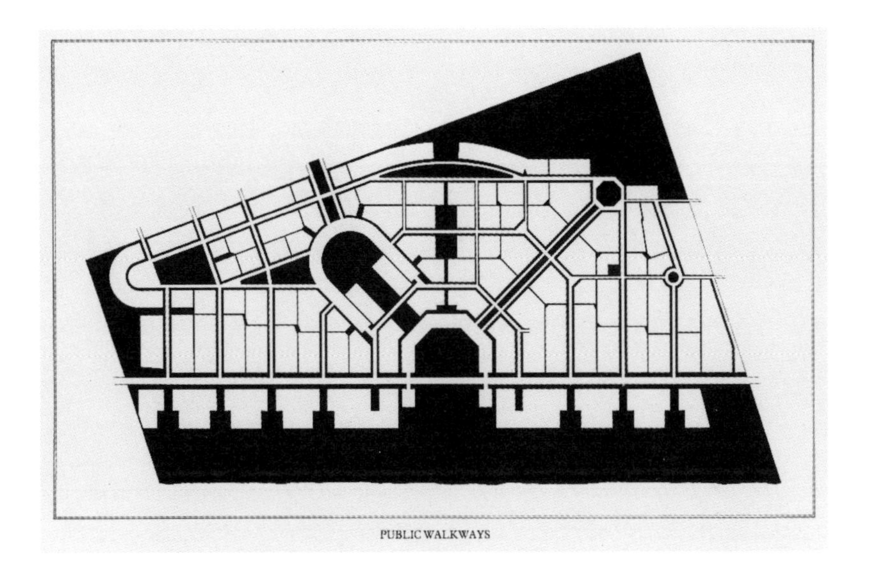

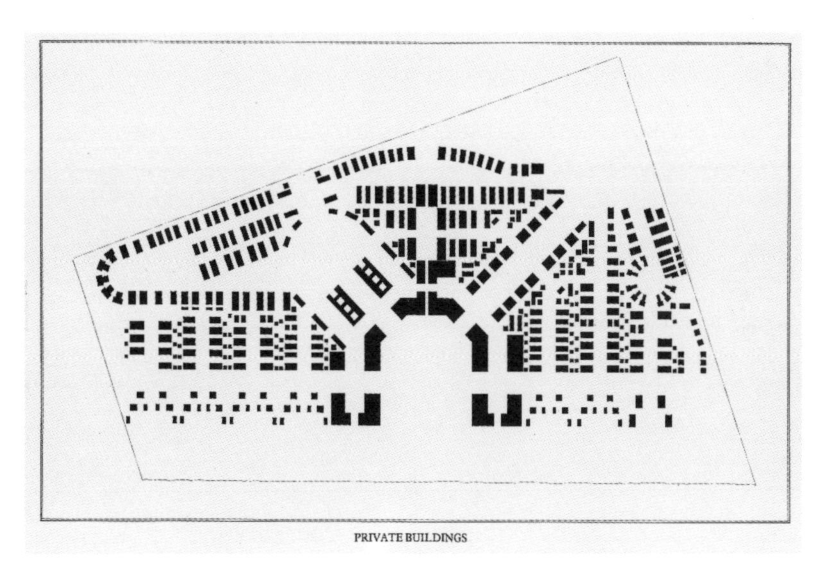

139 (upper left). Duany Plater-Zyberk. **Seaside code diagram, public roads,** 1982. Ink on mylar, 14 x 8 1/2"

140 (lower left). Duany Plater-Zyberk. **Seaside code diagram, public walkways,** 1982. Ink on mylar, 14 x 8 1/2"

141 (upper right). Duany Plater-Zyberk. **Seaside code diagram, public buildings,** 1982. Ink on mylar, 14 x 8 1/2"

142 (lower right). Duany Plater-Zyberk. **Seaside code diagram, private buildings,** 1982. Ink on mylar, 14 x 8 1/2"

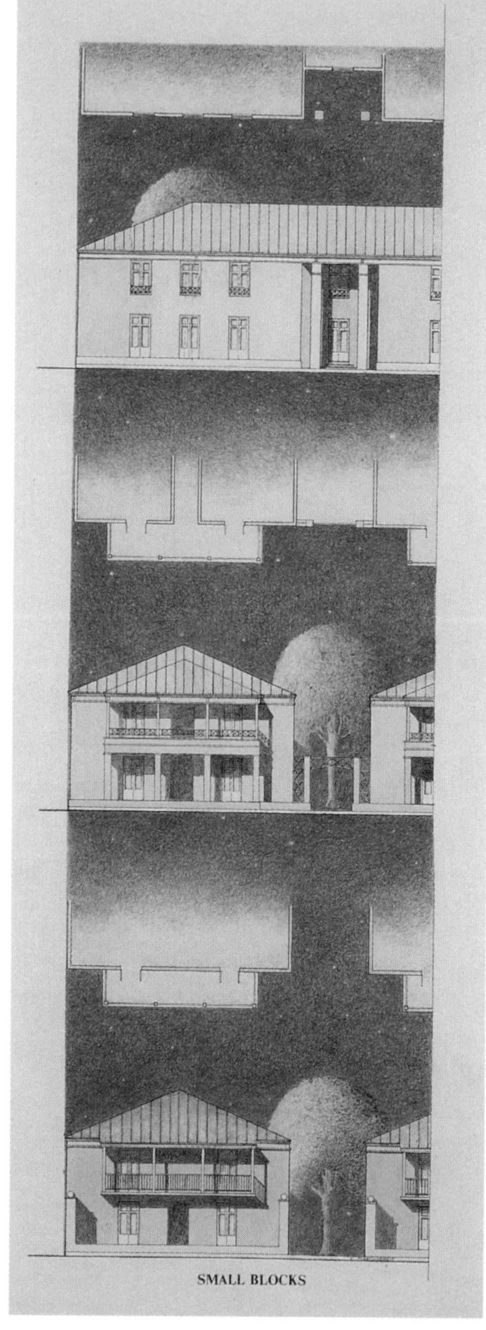

143 (left). Rosario Marquardt. **Lakes of Orlando (Duany Plater-Zyberk, architect), large blocks,** 1985. Colored pencil, 16 x 33″

144 (right). Rosario Marquardt. **Lakes of Orlando (Duany Plater-Zyberk, architect), small blocks,** 1985. Colored pencil, 10 x 31″

145. Rosario Marquardt. **Lakes of Orlando (Duany Plater-Zyberk, architect), civic building,** 1985. Colored pencil, 23 x 31"

146. Rosario Marquardt. **Andres Duany (diptych after Lorenzo Costa)**, 1985. Colored pencil, 14 x 21"

147. Rosario Marquardt. **Elizabeth Plater-Zyberk (diptych after Lorenzo Costa)**, 1985. Colored pencil, 14 x 21"

THE REGULATING PLAN OF

THE TOWN OF WELLINGTON, FLORIDA

SEPTEMBER 14TH 1989

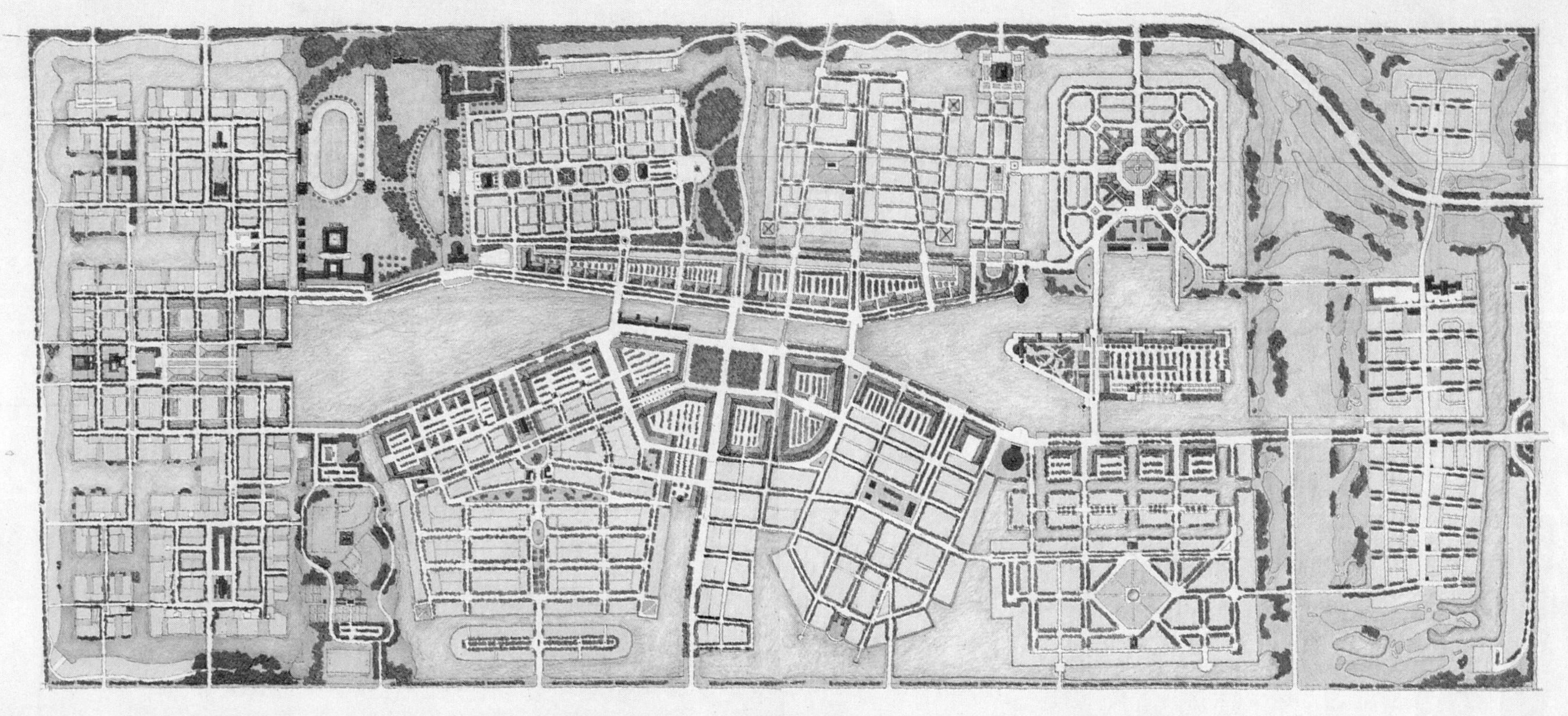

Corepoint Corporation, Owner

Andres Duany & Elizabeth Plater-Zyberk, Town Planners

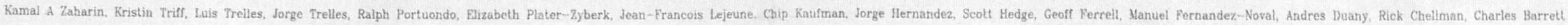

148. Charles Barrett, Rick Chellman, Manuel Fernandez-Noval, Geoff Ferrell, Scott Hedge, Jorge Hernandez, Chip Kaufman, Jean-François Lejeune, Raphael Portuondo, Jorge Trelles, Luis Trelles, Kristin Triff, Kamal A. Zaharin. **Wellington (Duany Plater-Zyberk, architect), plan,** 1989. Colored pencil, 61 x 33″

149. Charles Barrett. **Wellington neighborhood (Duany Plater-Zyberk with Jorge Hernandez and Jean-François Lejeune, architect),** 1989. Colored pencil, 17 x 12″

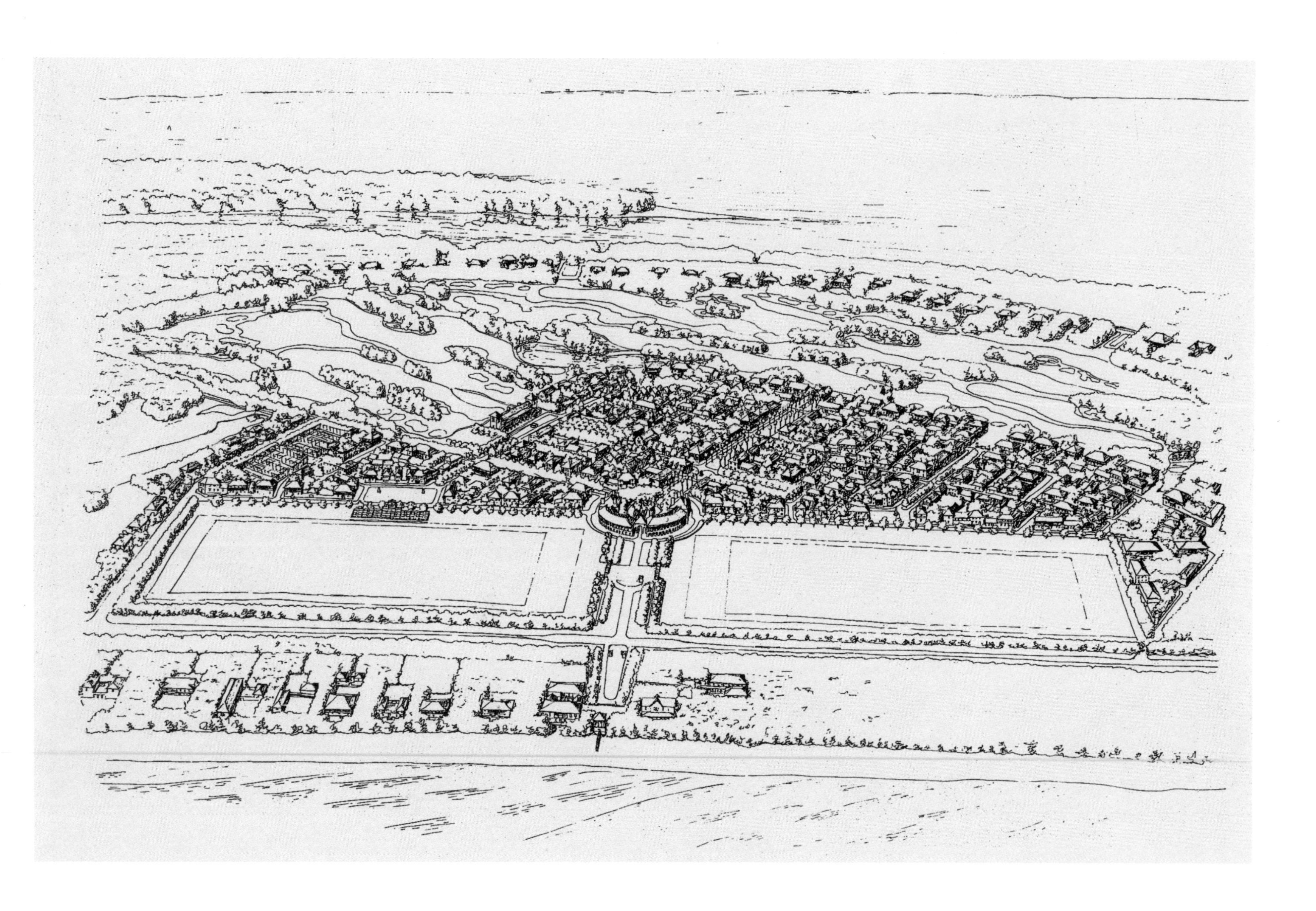

150. Charles Barrett. **Windsor (Duany Plater-Zyberk, architect),** 1990. Ink on paper, 23 x 15″

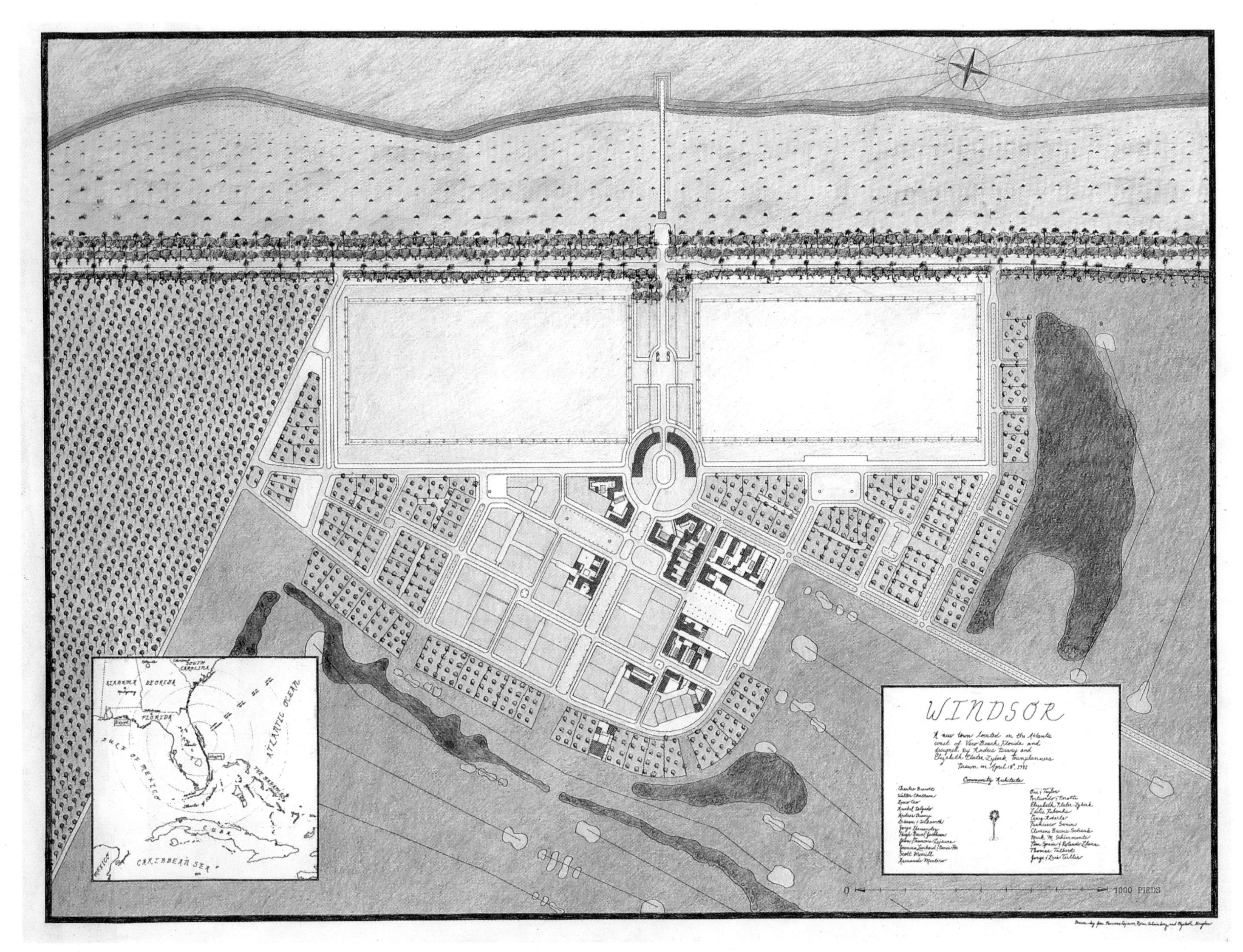

151. Jean-François Lejeune, Elizabeth Guyton, Victor Morales, Karen Scheinberg. **Windsor (Duany Plater-Zyberk, architect)**, plan, 1990. Colored pencil, 24 x 18″

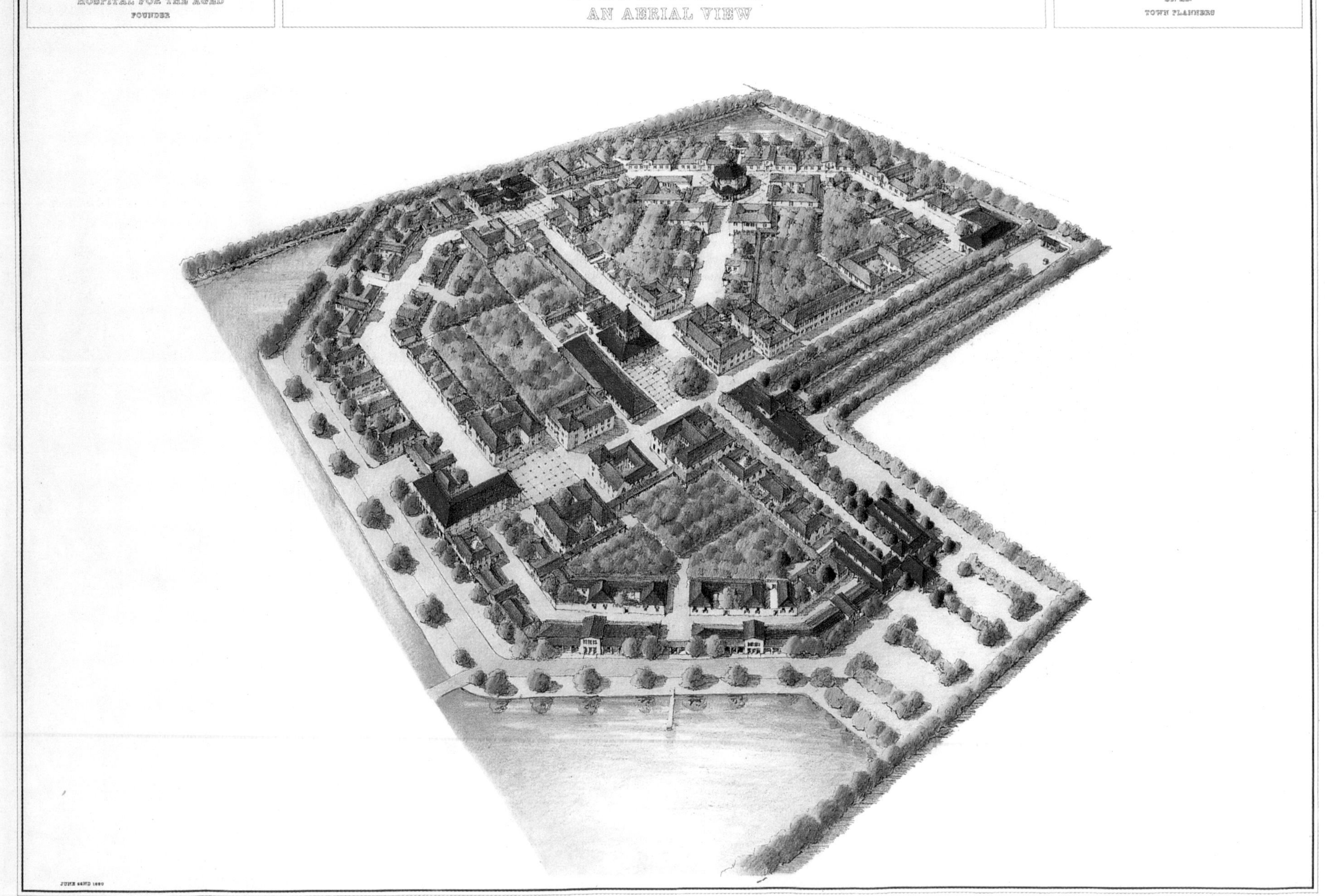

152. Charles Barrett. **Pathways (Duany Plater-Zyberk, architect)**, 1990. Colored pencil, 36 x 27″

153. Duany Plater-Zyberk. **Kemer, Turkey,** 1991. Colored pencil, 36 x 24″

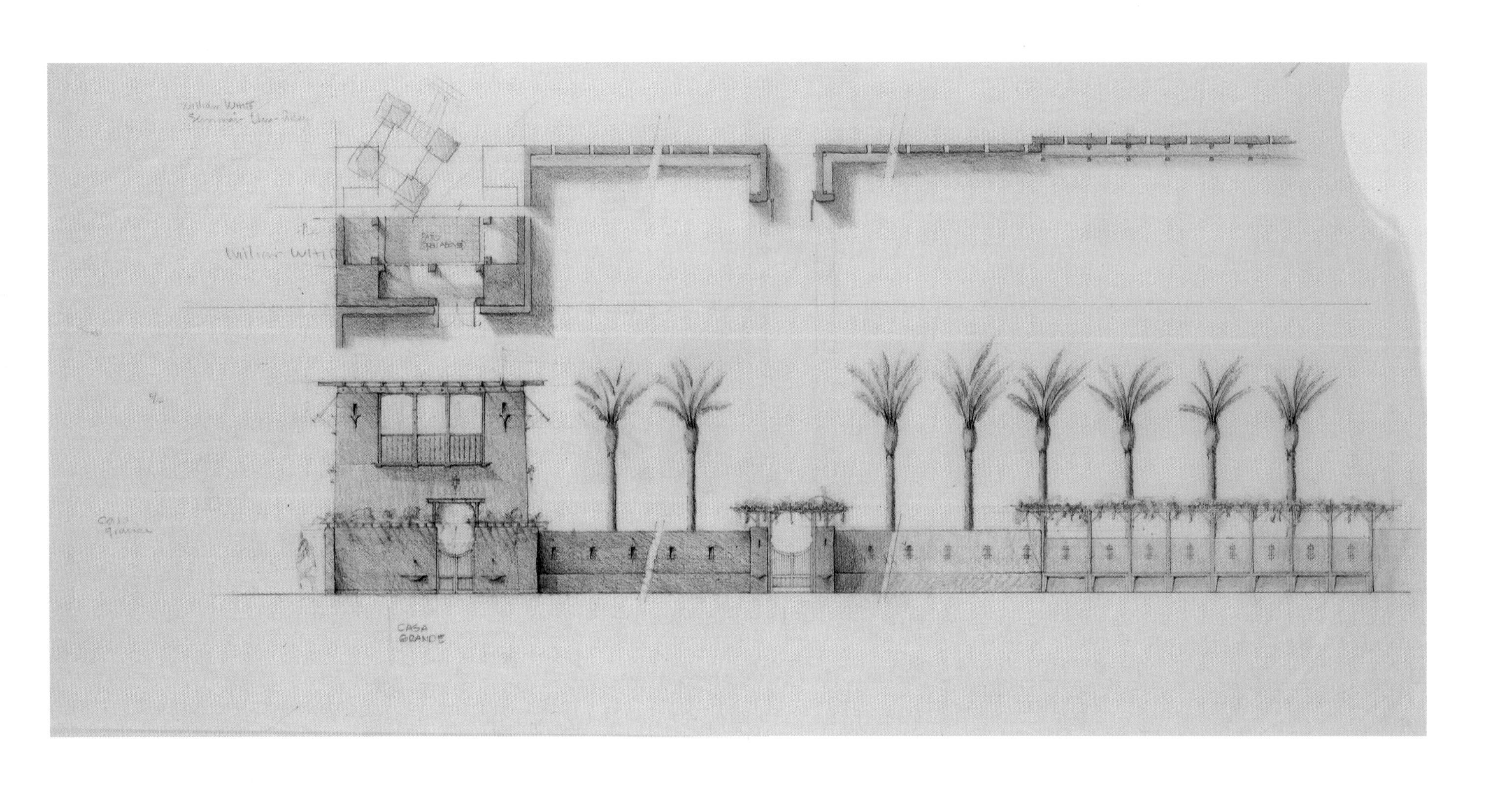

154. Juan Carruncho. **Rosa Vista (Duany Plater-Zyberk, architect), Casa Grande,** 1993. Colored pencil on trace, 28 x 12"

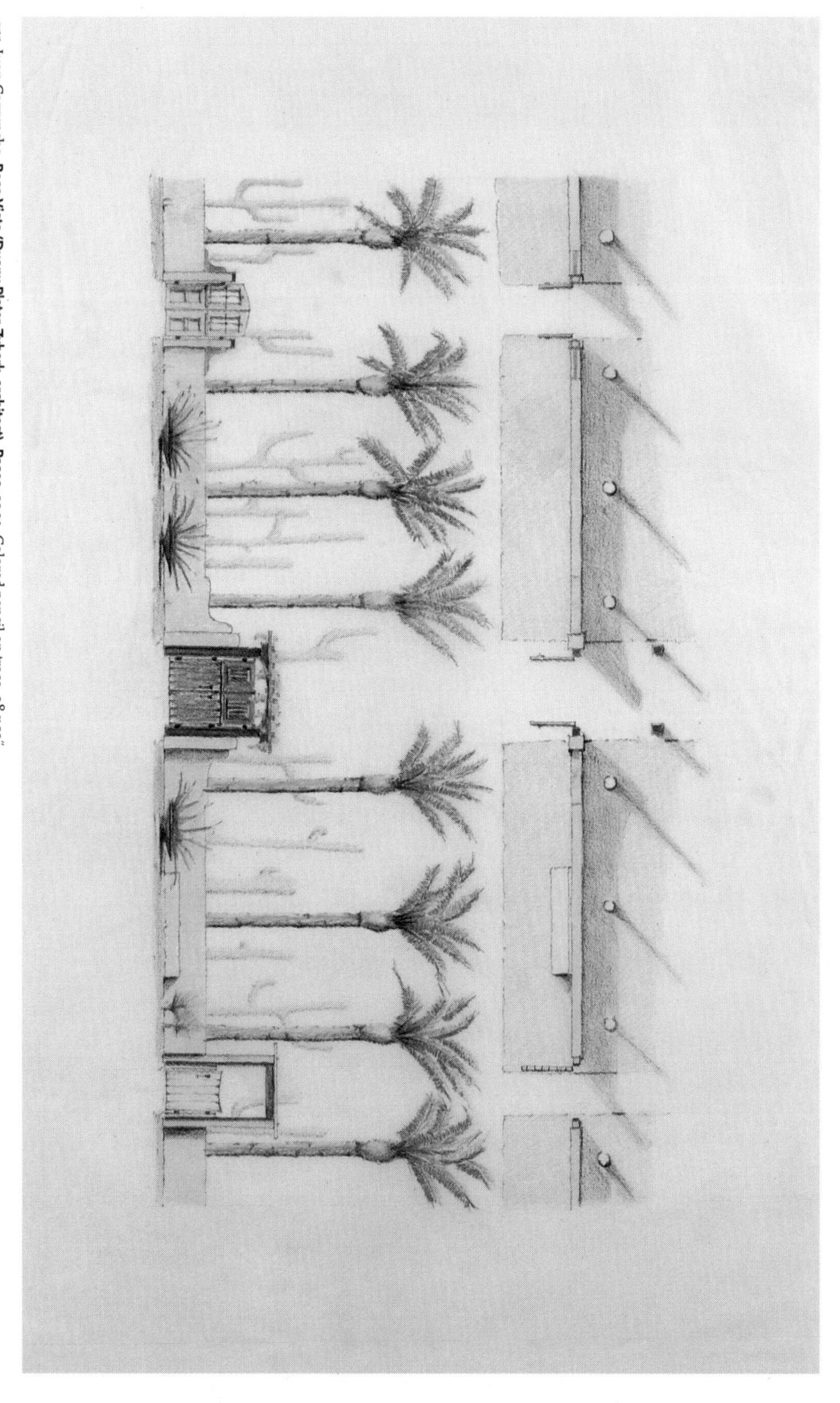

155. Juan Carruncho. **Rosa Vista (Duany Plater-Zyberk, architect), Paseo,** 1993. Colored pencil on trace, 28 x 12"

156. Juan Carruncho. **Rosa Vista (Duany Plater-Zyberk, architect), intersection,** 1993. Colored pencil on trace, 20 x 18"

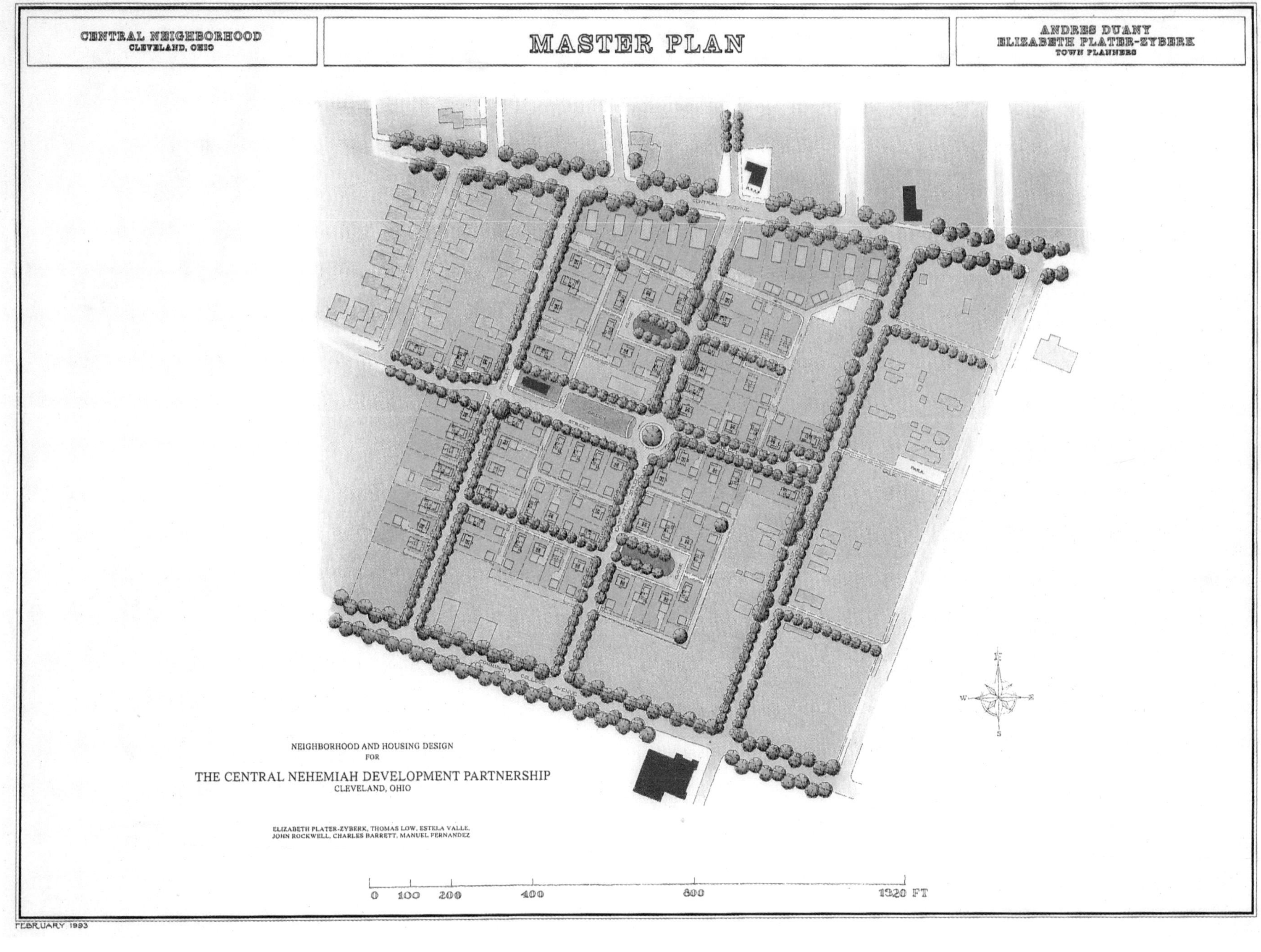

CENTRAL NEIGHBORHOOD
CLEVELAND, OHIO

MASTER PLAN

ANDRES DUANY
ELIZABETH PLATER-ZYBERK
TOWN PLANNERS

NEIGHBORHOOD AND HOUSING DESIGN
FOR
THE CENTRAL NEHEMIAH DEVELOPMENT PARTNERSHIP
CLEVELAND, OHIO

ELIZABETH PLATER-ZYBERK, THOMAS LOW, ESTELA VALLE,
JOHN ROCKWELL, CHARLES BARRETT, MANUEL FERNANDEZ

0 100 200 400 800 1320 FT

FEBRUARY 1993

157. Duany Plater-Zyberk. **Nehemiah central neighborhood, Cleveland, master plan,** 1993. Colored pencil, 24 x 20″

CENTRAL NEIGHBORHOOD
CLEVELAND, OHIO

A NEIGHBORHOOD STREET

ANDRES DUANY
ELIZABETH PLATER-ZYBERK
TOWN PLANNERS

AUGUST 1992

158. Charles Barrett. **Nehemiah central neighborhood street (Duany Plater-Zyberk, architect), Cleveland,** 1992. Colored pencil, 18 x 12″

ANDRES DUANY & ELISABETH PLATER-ZYBERK
ARCHITECTS & TOWN PLANNERS
ARMANDO MONTERO
ASSOCIATED ARCHITECT
OSCAR MACHADO
PROJECT MANAGER
ISKANDAR SHAFIE ESTELA VALLE
KAMAL SAMARIN

FARM WORKERS HOUSING
SOUTH DADE

EUGENIO SANTIAGO
STRUCTURAL ENGINEER
VICTOR REEVE
ELECTRICAL & MECHANICAL ENGINEER
RANDALL ATLAS
SECURITY CONSULTANT
HARRISON RUE
DEVELOPMENT CONSULTANT

DECEMBER 28, 1992

159. Duany Plater-Zyberk. **Farm Workers' Housing, South Dade,** 1992. Colored pencil, 36 x 24″

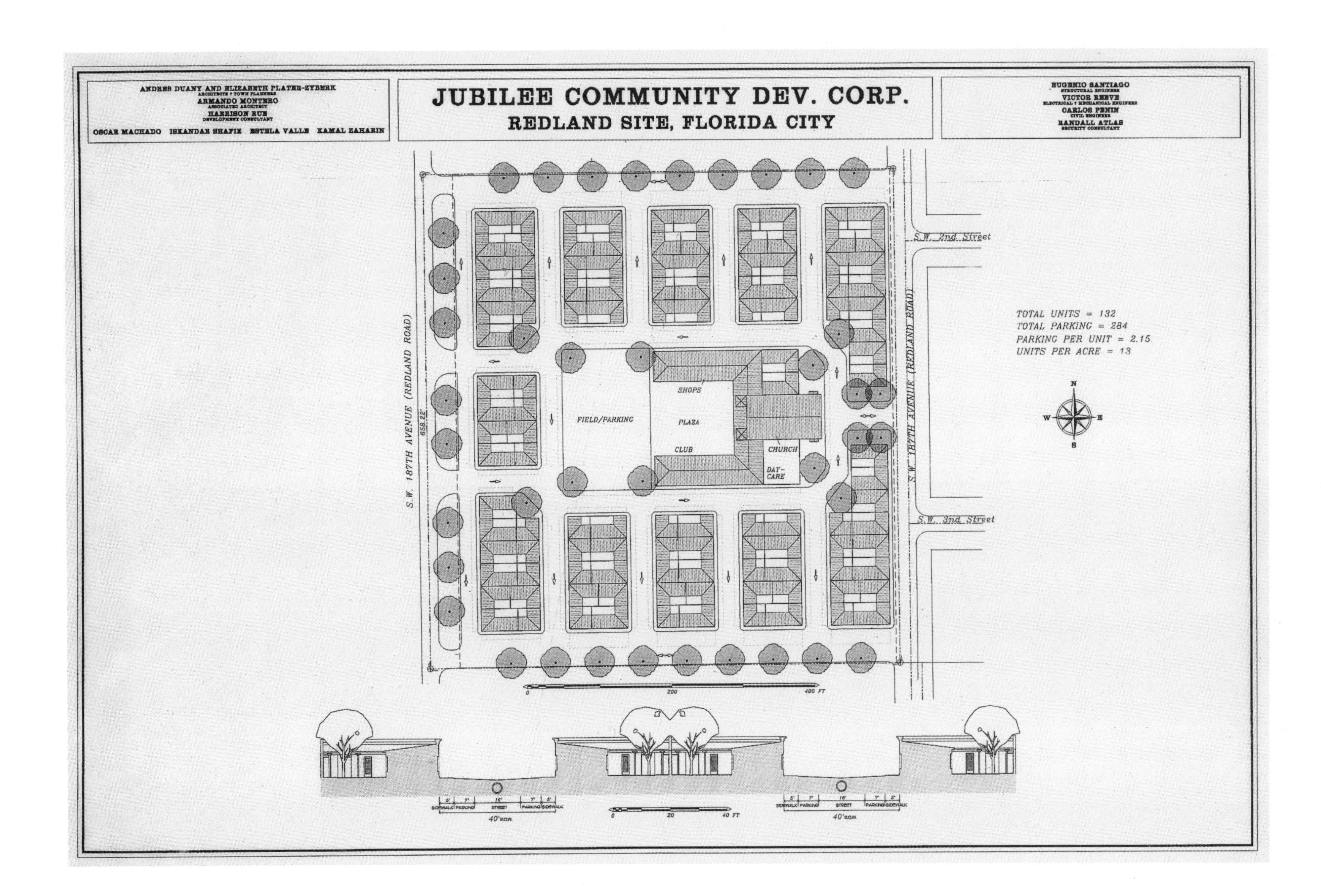

160. Armando Montero, Oscar Machado, Iskandar Shafie, Harrison Rue, Estella Valle, Kamal A. Zaharin. **Jubilee Community (Duany Plater-Zyberk, architect), Redland,** 1992. Ink on mylar, 36 x 24"

161. Jason Dunham, Chris Ritter, and David Williams. **Everglades pines,** 1993. Colored pencil, 10 x 8″

162. Jason Dunham, Chris Ritter, and David Williams. **Everglades planes,** 1993. Colored pencil, 10 x 8″

163. Jason Dunham, Chris Ritter, and David Williams. **Everglades Hammock,** 1993. Colored pencil, 10 x 8″

Catherine Lynn

Stone by Stone: John Ruskin's Path

> There is the strong instinct in me which I cannot analyse to draw and describe the things I love . . . a sort of instinct like that for eating or drinking. I should like to draw all St. Mark's and all this Verona stone by stone, to eat it all up into my mind, touch by touch.
>
> John Ruskin to his father, from Verona, June 2, 1852[1]

John Ruskin drew to see, drew to understand. Drawing was the tool upon which he was most dependent as he tried to make sense of the largely unresearched history of the Byzantine, Medieval, and Renaissance buildings of Venice, drawing, redrawing, comparing their every detail, studying each to learn anew to build for nineteenth-century England. "He is drawing perpetually . . . fragments of everything from a Cupola to a Cart-wheel," his father wrote from Venice in May of 1846.[2] Ruskin drew to think, drew to teach himself to derive from visual experience meaning that he could translate into the words that were to fill his many volumes on architecture.[3] Within them, long passages read like sketches for paintings: he describes, for instance, what he sees as he approaches Torcello in the opening pages of the second volume of *The Stones of Venice* as if he is telling the reader how to draw it, or making notes to himself for finishing at leisure sketches begun in the field.[4] Growing as much of it did from drawing, his critical writing was the first about architecture ever to attract a sizeable readership among a lay public. His words let them see it. During his own day, his influence in America was perhaps even broader than it was in England. Soon it extended to German architects who revolutionized their profession.

Something very like Ruskin's fever of drawing animates the school of architecture at Miami. From the moment undergraduates arrive, they are pushed to draw freehand. Close by, they draw the works of architects – the local products of their profession – and the works of nature – the palms, ficus, and live oak trees that press right up to studio windows, the leaves, blossoms, and fruits that instantly appear on drafting tables. Promptly students find themselves in the Everglades, in the citrus groves, in the agricultural Redland of South Florida, drawing, drawing, as are the young instructors at their sides. And they continue to do so for their full five years, dodging the traffic of downtown Miami, the skateboarders on South Beach, the tourists in Key West. A great many travel with their ever-drawing mentors to the ancient Spanish towns of the Caribbean and Central and South America. And some go to Rome. They can amaze even themselves with the pictures they bring back.

They are practicing as all student architects must. Architects must practice drawing as musicians must practice scales. It teaches them to think visually, something earlier education rarely will have done. They must produce technical drawings. They must learn to show clients buildings that do not yet exist. But there is greater emphasis at Miami than elsewhere on drawing what *does* exist as a way of understanding it themselves, and of letting others know *how* they see it, what they perceive to be important about it, what it means to them. Drawings can do this as no words – or photographs – can.

Very close looking and highly detailed drawing are encouraged at Miami. John Ruskin drew with a precision that sometimes seems fanatic. In an appendix to *The Stones of Venice,* he wrote of the plates he had prepared: ". . . their truth . . . is carried to an extent never before attempted in architectural drawing." They represented "the architecture itself with its actual shadows at the time of day at which it was drawn, and with every fissure and line of it as they now exist."[5] Writing to a friend in 1849 he defended this attention to detail:

> Such a degree of accuracy as this may perhaps at first appear ludicrous – but I have always held it for a great principle that there are no *degrees of truth;* and from habit I have made it just as easy to myself to draw a thing truly as falsely.[6]

In Italy, he drew at first for himself, nurturing his skill to teach himself about the place he loved. Then an urgency to use drawings to communicate what he'd learned took over. Daily, he hastened to transfer sketches onto etched and engraved plates, "biting them [bathing them in acid] in the wash-hand basins of hotel bedrooms."[7] In 1851 he wrote to his father:

> Until now I have drawn everything with the sole view of learning what things were; the moment I had got all the information I wanted, the sketch was thrown aside and only preserved as a memorial of certain facts. I have now arrived at a time of

1 *Editors' introduction to Ruskin,* The Stones of Venice, *vol. 2 (1853), as published in* The Works of John Ruskin, *Library Edition, ed. E. T. Cook and Alexander Wedderburn (London: George Allen; New York: Longmans, Green, 1903–12; hereafter* Works*), vol. 10, xxvi. The context for this excerpt from a letter to his father is:* I don't think myself a great genius, but I believe I have genius; something different from mere cleverness, for I am *not* clever in the sense that millions of people are – lawyers, physicians, and others. But there is the strong instinct in me which I cannot analyse to draw and describe the things I love – not for reputation, nor for the good of others, nor for my own advantage, but a sort of instinct like that for eating or drinking . . .

2 *J. J. Ruskin, Venice, May 25, 1846, as quoted in editors' introduction to Ruskin,* The Seven Lamps of Architecture *(1849), in* Works, *vol. 8, xxiii. The context for this excerpt:* He is cultivating art at present, . . . searching for real knowledge, but to you and me this is at present a sealed book. It will neither take the shape of picture nor poetry. It is gathered in scraps hardly wrought, for he is drawing perpetually, but no drawing such as in former days you or I might compliment in the usual way by saying it deserved a frame; but fragments of everything from a Cupola to a Cart-wheel, but in such bits that it is to the common eye a mass of Hieroglyphics – all true – truth itself, but Truth in mosaic.

3 *The derivation of meaning from visual experience is a central task of the art historian as Vincent Scully has characterized his discipline, and I have used his terms to characterize Ruskin's method.*

> life when I feel that my knowledge must – if it is ever to be so – be expressed in an intelligible form, legible by others as well as by myself.[8]

Ruskin described how this new concern inspired a new care in finishing and presenting the drawings. He sent hundreds of drawings and prints home and used them to illustrate his books.

The most influential drawing in Miami has also progressed from private to public, from study to communication. Andres Duany and Elizabeth Plater-Zyberk looked very closely at familiar American places – not just at buildings – and drew them, especially the ones that grew out of the great American planning tradition of the early twentieth century. Their initial measurement and detailed recording of the widths of streets and sidewalks, the spacing of trees and buildings, the arrangements for parking, hardly count as drawings, and probably would not have made very pretty published pages. But the close observation and notation of carefully quantified details were as crucial to their learning process as were to his John Ruskin's obsessive recording and comparison of every bit of carving on every stone in Venice. Then they were quick to grasp the importance of expressing what they had found so that it would be intelligible not just to other architects, but also to a much broader public.

Their drawings, and those of the talented colleagues whose skills they tapped, brought fresh visions of the familiar places to eyes long dulled to their virtues. Using drawings that were readily accessible to people uninitiated in the conventions of architectural and engineering offices, they empowered developers, citizen groups, and finally government officials to understand that there were still viable alternatives to strip and desolate suburb. They tell their students to value the skill, unique to architects, of enabling others through their drawings to see, *as* they have seen, places of the past as well as of the future. And, clearly, they have seen these places with love.

In the competitive, rather cynical, self-protective climate of the architectural profession of the 1970s, Duany and Plater-Zyberk's initial revelation of this love was in itself an act of courage. Some of their colleagues cultivated cool aloofness to architecture as a social art, an objective distance from it, and most of all, a smug superiority to pre-Modern buildings and to all urban situations – and almost inevitably to the people who were fated to live in their experiments. The world in which they trained and worked had little time for Ruskinian advice like this:

> You must love the creation you work in the midst of. For, wholly in proportion to the intensity of feeling which you bring to the subject you have chosen, will be the depth and justice of your perception of its character.[9]

This was Ruskin's exhortation to London's Architectural

4 *Ruskin,* Stones of Venice, *vol. 2, in* Works, *vol. 10, 17–18.*

5 *Ruskin, appendix to* Seven Lamps, *as quoted in editors' introduction to* Seven Lamps, *in* Works, *vol. 8, xlv.*

6 *Ruskin to George Murray Smith, Geneva, June 5, 1849, in "Letters on* The Seven Lamps of Architecture," *in* Works, *vol. 8, 277.*

7 *Editors' introduction to* Seven Lamps, *in* Works, *vol. 8, xlv.*

8 *Ruskin to his father, October 19, 1851, as quoted in editors' introduction to* Stones of Venice, *vol. 2, in* Works, *vol. 10, lxii–lxiii. Following the extract in this text, the letter continues:* The drawings which I now am making here will be brought home, not only finished, but framed, ready to be sent to the engraver the moment they are unpacked. They will also be much more popular in form and manner – many of them like the little vignettes to Roger.

9 *Ruskin, "Influence of Imagination in Architecture," address delivered to the Architectural Association, January 23, 1857, lecture 4,* The Two Paths *(1859), in* Works, *vol. 16, 370.*

10 *Ruskin, "Modern Manufacture and Design," lecture delivered at Bradford, March 1, 1859, lecture 3,* Two Paths, *in* Works, *vol. 16, 342–43.*

11 *Ruskin,* Seven Lamps, *in* Works, *vol. 8, 104.*

Association in a talk of 1857. Although they may not be so rhetorical, many who teach at Miami seem by their example and their enthusiasm to guide their pupils to love what they've seen and what they envision.

The modesty of the buildings the Miami faculty have admired is once again evocative of Ruskin's enthusiasms. He looked forward from 1859 to a period

> . . . in which domestic life, aided by the arts of peace, will slowly, but at last entirely, supersede public life and the arts of war. For our own England, she will not, I believe, be blasted throughout with furnaces; nor will she be encumbered with palaces. I trust she will keep her green fields, her cottages, and her homes of middle life.[10]

Florida's "homes of middle life" – the Cracker houses – and town planning of the early twentieth century were well outside the norms of the era's architectural taste when Duany and Plater-Zyberk began to study them. Today, with their colleagues, they continue to lead students to the gems, natural and manmade, that they recognize in the jarring landscape of a South Florida more intrinsically threatened by buildings than by hurricanes. And again, Ruskin's words of the 1840s echo in the school's concerns today, even though they describe a very different landscape:

> . . . how much oftener man destroys natural sublimity, than nature crushes human power. It does not need much to humiliate a mountain. A hut will sometimes do it . . . A single villa will often mar a whole landscape, and dethrone a dynasty of hills.[11]

Sensitivity to landscape, enthusiasm for the modest and vernacular, emotional commitment to beloved buildings may bring Ruskin to mind at Miami. But in this contemporary school of architecture they are complemented by cooler and more clinical concerns for proficiency in the mechanics and technologies of the profession as well as at the drafting table and the computer. While these last have their inevitable places, it is the school's purposeful nurturing of the investigative, interpretive, expressive, and emotional powers of drawing that is more distinctive. This nurtures in turn an appreciation of the expressive power of architecture itself, as creative art – not merely functioning technology, not theoretical act of criticism – that again distinguishes the school and suggests identification with John Ruskin. But above all, it seems Ruskinian in its focus on drawing from nature.

Certainly there is no avowal of allegiance by faculty members past or present to a gospel according to Ruskin. Historicizing here tends toward the Classical rather than toward Ruskin's beloved Gothic. But pivotal members of the faculty do seem to share Ruskin's central belief in the primacy of art in architecture and of drawing in the education of architects. It seems only coincidental that they have put in practice his teaching methods. By chance they might endorse, though few will have read, his assertion of 1858:

> A student who can fix with precision the cardinal points of a bird's wing, extended in any fixed position, and can then draw the curves of its individual plumes without measurable error, has advanced further towards a power of understanding the design of the great masters than he could by reading many volumes of criticism, or passing many months in the undisciplined examination of works of art.[12]

Ruskin's writings do not enjoy at Miami anything other than the general neglect they are accorded in every other school of architecture. Students perhaps read about Ruskin, about the influence of his dictum ". . . all beautiful works of art must either intentionally imitate or accidentally resemble natural forms"[13] on Frank Lloyd Wright's "Organic Architecture." Studying the Bauhaus, they may find Ruskin's name first on Walter Gropius' list of those who "sought, and in the end discovered, the basis of a reunion between creative artists and the industrial world"[14] – an honor that must surely disturb the shade of a man whose antagonism toward the machine and modern industry was unswerving.

But they rarely read the prose that taught architects and amateurs to judge buildings in moral terms. Accustomed by sermons to make moral judgments, Ruskin's generation was easily persuaded by his example to evaluate architecture the same way, to call a wall "honest," materials "true."[15] He was borrowing heavily from a critical vocabulary introduced to English architectural discussion by A. W. N. Pugin in the 1830s. But Ruskin must be given the credit for fixing in architects' minds the moralistic habit of thought that found expression in the vernacular of the drafting room and permeates Modernist criticism to this day. Only when John Ruskin began to speak this way about architecture did a great many people pay attention and imitate him. He made his mark by 1850 with rhetoric like this:

> . . . a direct falsity of assertion respecting the nature of material, or the quantity of labor . . . is, in the full sense of the word, wrong; it is as truly deserving of reprobation as any other moral delinquency; it is unworthy alike of architects and of nations.[16]

Today, architecture students may come across this gleam from "The Lamp of Truth" in an anthologized snatch of *The Seven Lamps of Architecture* (1849), or they may read the famous chapter on "The Nature of Gothic" from the second volume of *The Stones of Venice* (1853), an essay to which William Morris credited much of the inspiration for his brilliant career, but they hardly ever encounter *The Two Paths* (1859).[17] This is not surprising since only one of the five lectures that comprise *The Two Paths* was delivered specifically to architects, and that lecture focused on a subject of little interest to their profession in the present day: the sculptural

12 *Ruskin, "Education in Art," lecture, 1858, in* Works, *vol. 16, 149.*

13 *Ruskin,* Stones of Venice, *vol. 2, in* Works, *vol. 10, 156.*

14 *Walter Gropius, "The Theory and Organization of the* Bauhaus*" (translation of "Idee und Aufbau des Staatlichen Bauhauses Weimar" (1923), in* Bauhaus 1919–1928, *ed. Herbert Bayer, Walter Gropius, Ise Gropius (New York: Museum of Modern Art, 1938), 21. Reviewing the prehistory of the Bauhaus, Gropius writes:* The second half of the 19th century saw the beginning of a protest against the devitalising influence of the academies. Ruskin and Morris in England, van de Velde in Belgium, Olbrich, Behrens and others in Germany, and, finally, the Deutsche Werkbund, all sought, and in the end discovered, the basis of a reunion between creative artists and the industrial world.

15 *Roger B. Stein,* John Ruskin and Aesthetic Thought in America 1840–1900 *(Cambridge, Mass.: Harvard University Press, 1967), 73, 46. Stein writes:* By appealing to the ideals of men, Ruskin subordinated architectural questions to moral ones and thus broadened the basis of interest in art. Ruskin helped convince the majority of Americans . . . that architectural questions had an important bearing on their moral life.

16 *Ruskin, "The Lamp of Truth,"* Seven Lamps, *in* Works, *vol. 8, 59.*

17 *Ruskin,* The Two Paths, Being Lectures on Art and its application to Decoration and Manufacture, Delivered in 1858–9, *in* Works, *vol. 16.*

decoration of buildings. But for Ruskin, this was what distinguished true architecture from mere building.

Indeed, this now-neglected book is primarily concerned with the character of decoration, not only in architectural contexts but also in industrial ones, and the other four lectures apparently take the reader far afield from architecture. But it was the English debate about decoration and how students should be taught to design it that provided the platform upon which rested a good part of Modernist theory about architecture, and from which it borrowed vocabulary and patterns of thought for formulating that theory. *The Two Paths* was a key document giving voice to a minority opinion in the preliminary debate.

The intellectual heirs of Ruskin's opposition – the majority that carried the day as Modernists – borrowed heavily from Ruskin by making moral judgments about architectural questions. They listed him among their heroes, they caught his enthusiasm for the forthright, expressive qualities of Gothic architecture, and they quoted selectively from him.

But Modernists who claimed to have been greatly influenced by Ruskin precisely contradicted basic conclusions to which he had come in his earlier, better known works and upon which he dwelled with greatest emphasis in *The Two Paths*. The Modernists rejected his insistence on the centrality of ornament as the defining feature of true architecture, the feature that separated it from "mere engineering." In the mid-nineteenth century, proto-Modernists still concerned with the "problem" of ornament rejected in all contexts the identification Ruskin made in many contexts of truth with faithful representation of nature and of the human form. For ornament, they recognized truth and honesty only in the geometric or in "conventionalization." This was the nineteenth-century term for generalized, idealized, flattened representations somewhat abstracted from nature. They asserted that, in decoration, realistic depictions of natural objects lied to the eye: a painterly portrait of a leaf on a plate might, after all, fool a user who, thinking it real, might try to brush it aside. They used terms that sounded rather like Ruskin's own when they praised two-dimensional patterns for their forthright expression of flatness, for avoiding visual compromise of the solid surface. Later, the quest for architectural ornament "honestly" expressive of the age associated truth with more extreme abstraction from nature. And early-twentieth-century Modernists rejected all of what Ruskin's generation had called "surface ornament" as deceptive covering of material truth. Few, however, were so extreme as Adolf Loos, who equated ornament with crime in an essay of 1908, which Le Corbusier reprinted in the first issue of *L'Esprit Nouveau* in 1920.[18]

Reversing Ruskin, architects who read him most ardently and borrowed from him most freely in defining Modernism

18 *Adolf Loos, "Ornament and Crime" (1908), translated from* Trotzdem 1900–1930 *(Innsbruck: Brenner Verlag, 1931), quoted from Loos,* Samtliche Schriften, *ed. Franz Gluck (Vienna and Munich: Verlag Herold, 1962), vol. 1, 276ff, in Ulrich Conrads, ed.,* Programmes and Manifestoes on 20th Century Architecture *(London: Lund Humphries, 1970), 19–24.*

assigned to science – not to art – their primary allegiance. In *The Two Paths*, Ruskin's antipathy for the scientific model surfaces again and again, as here, from his lecture of 1857 to the Architectural Association:

> Man of science wrestles with man of science for priority of discovery, and pursues in pangs of jealous haste his solitary inquiry. You alone are called by kindness, – by necessity, – by equity, to fraternity of toil.[19]

But the scientific model emerged as the seductive one in schools of architecture. The equation of science with truth – truthful objectivity – conversely cast doubt on the value of subjective thinking, on knowledge that cannot be quantified or easily tested within a classroom. The old identification of Art with Truth and Beauty was called into question and finally rejected in Modern thinking where art itself found new definitions.

Modernist theories about painting and sculpture owe an important debt to the same nineteenth-century discussion of ornament that shaped Modernist architectural theory. As Linda Nochlin has written:

> It is in the unlikely soil of the decorative arts – furniture, carving, crafts, pottery, book illustration, textiles, weaving and wallpaper – that the seeds of the avant-garde mystique were sown in the second half of the nineteenth century. It is here that . . . the anti-narrative, anti-anecdotal, anti-naturalist, anti-illusionistic, anti-historical bases of Modernist High Art are first and most clearly articulated, and first accepted; and it is in this area that the Realist virtues of probity, honesty, sincerity, straightforwardness and directness are "trans-valuated" so that they now have their present "avant-garde" meanings.[20]

It was also the unlikely soil for the first clear articulations of essential elements of Modernist architectural theory, especially its preference for abstraction. This preference emerged from a great national debate in England that spurred the nation to practical action during the second quarter of the nineteenth century. Discussion of what character was proper to ornament and how students should be taught to design was carried far beyond artistic circles to the very halls of Parliament. England's industrial lobby convinced the government that the fortunes of much of the nation rested upon the quality of surface ornament on textiles, wallpapers, carpets, and china. In the trade wars, England was under heavy assault from the Continent, especially from France. The French, like other European powers, had established schools that educated artists for industry. French products dazzled the buying public with the verisimilitude of their depictions of flora, fauna, and the human form. To compete with these accomplishments, the English parliament was persuaded to fund an elaborate system of government schools of design to train specialists for industry. And it also supported a program to train teachers to instruct ordinary students to draw and to distin-

19 *Ruskin, "Influence of Imagination in Architecture," in* Two Paths, *in* Works, *vol. 16, 374.*

20 *Linda Nochlin* Realism *(Middlesex, England, and New York: Penguin Books, 1971), 224–25.*

guish good design from bad – which was, in practice, to appreciate and buy the kind of design being taught in the government schools. It is not coincidental that they recognized a superiority of abstraction over realism: simple, abstract decorations were relatively easy to churn out on the machines that were the pride of the technologically advanced English factories. Machines had trouble copying the intricate mimetic decorations of French manufactories where the human hand still played a more prominent part in finishing goods.

A great many practical people sought economy of motion and expenditure to make English goods look better to consumers. They spoke, debated, and published long and earnestly about whether and how the nation could train a corps of designers for industry, and they came up with the notion that it was necessary to identify and segregate rules for teaching "Design" (where abstraction was the desideratum) from those for teaching "Art" (where realism still seemed best). Their thoughts were widely reported in the popular press and a rough consensus on the basic ideas that should be taught to future employees who were so key to the national economy did emerge among participants in the design training movement, and they put it to the test in the state-sponsored schools.

Perhaps the most useful and long-lived document that brings together the fundamental precepts the design school masters generally were teaching during the 1850s is *The Grammar of Ornament* by Owen Jones, first published in 1856 and seldom out of print since.[21] In the original oversized edition, one of the early masterpieces of chromolithography, 150 plates were arrayed with nearly 2,400 samples of ornament. On many pages, specimens of brightly colored patterns in rows of neat little rectangles are just about the size of glass plates for microscopes. They were collected from every accessible corner of the world, drawn from the depths of time and the breadths of place that the preceding four centuries of exploration had revealed to Europeans. For working designers it remains a guide to styles, a compact source of images to be imitated or adapted.

In organizing this book, Jones took as his model the scientist. He collected data from which to deduce general, universal principles – which he denied were laws. But the way he wrote about them surely brings natural law to mind. In the preface, Jones called it a collection in which he had ventured "to select a few of the most prominent types in certain styles ... in which certain general laws appeared to reign independently of the individual peculiarities of each." He headed a short list of the "main facts" he had "endeavored to establish" with these two:

> That whenever any style of ornament commands universal admiration, it will always be found to be in accordance with the laws which regulate the distribution of form in nature.

21 *Owen Jones,* The Grammar of Ornament *(London, 1856). I have used the third edition (London: Bernard Quaritch, 1868) for all references in quotations from this work, hereafter* Grammar.

> That however varied the manifestations in accordance with these laws, the leading ideas on which they are based are very few.[22]

So few indeed were those ideas that Jones could proceed to list them as thirty-seven "General Principles in the Arrangement of Form and Colour, in Architecture and the Decorative Arts, Which are Advocated Throughout this Work."[23] In fact, he crammed into the first thirteen of these his bases for formal design, since propositions fourteen through thirty-seven give his ideas on color, which were closely adapted from the optical theories of Michel-Eugene Chevreul (1786–1889) and George Field (1777?–1854).[24] Reducing to thirteen the big ideas that students of ornament needed to know simplified things rather comfortably. Two of Jones' propositions proved especially potent in the guidance of nineteenth-century taste and in the subsequent formulation of Modernist preferences for abstraction: Proposition Eight, "All ornament should be based upon a geometrical construction," and Proposition Thirteen, "Flowers or other natural objects should not be used as ornaments, but conventional representations founded upon them sufficiently suggestive to convey the intended image to the mind, without destroying the unity of the object they are employed to decorate." This was easily translated by the shopping housewife: forego the lovely French cabbage roses for the parlor curtains; buy the ones with unidentifiable flora that look pressed flat, rearranged perfectly, and boldly outlined; or better still, go for the purely geometric pattern – a diamond diaper perhaps. The system instilled aesthetic confidence in an emerging consumer class and furnished manufacturers with home-grown design-school graduates, so that they no longer had to import more expensive designers from the Continent. Limiting the body of expertise made it easy to recognize professional competence. It was a great comfort to the entire nation.

But not to John Ruskin. The whole elaborate process of setting up a system for training designers separately from artists and identifying them as a lesser class than artists – practicing a lesser art – dismayed him. He took exception to the notion that Design was something different from and not as good as Art. That notion rested squarely on the assumption that Architecture should be separated out from Art, from which followed Owen Jones' Proposition One: "The Decorative Arts arise from, and should properly be attendant upon Architecture." Architecture, not Art, note. Training for designers, education for artists. Ruskin was alarmed by such distinctions and distancings within the design schools.

The Two Paths is in large part his criticism of the fundamental assumptions and the very foundation of the government design school system, of the process of regimenting and oversimplifying a very complex subject. The book is, in a way, Ruskin's attempt to complicate the system. He argues that

22 *Jones,* Grammar, *2.*

23 *Jones,* Grammar, *5–8.*

24 *Catherine Hoover Voorsanger, "Dictionary of Architects, Artisans, Artists, and Manufacturers," in* In Pursuit of Beauty: Americans and the Aesthetic Movement *(New York: Metropolitan Museum of Art/Rizzoli, 1986), 444–46.*

architecture and the decorative arts are part of a great wholeness of art and that the education of designers must be reintegrated with the education given to painters and sculptors.

But the reductive simplifications of design education in England in the nineteenth-century carried the day for a while. Although the design education system was ultimately abandoned by the nation, its image of businesslike professionalism, of a no-nonsense group that could invoke science in justifying its methods and show a government committee on a few pages just what it was going to teach, lingered as a seductive model for later architectural educators.

Ruskin delivered key lectures that went to the heart of his criticism of the government's design education establishment within its own halls. He was invited to speak at its schools and museums on august occasions, for he was extravagantly admired and widely read within them. He shared their interest in ornament, and within the pages of treatises on design published by the government's school masters, indeed upon the pages of Owen Jones, appear sentences that seem interchangeable with statements published by Ruskin himself. Avowals of allegiance to the study of nature resonate through all the era's manuals of design, though for nearly all their writers, except Ruskin, study of nature inevitably moves straight to some degree of abstraction. While Ruskin and the spokespeople for the schools of design agreed on some of the details, they were far apart in their fundamental assumptions. The assumption that design is a separate and lesser thing than "real" art is evident in the very establishment of separate schools of design. In *The Two Paths*, Ruskin attacked the fundamental error of that assumption from many angles.

He proposed that students who wished later to specialize in a particular branch of design be educated with painters and sculptors and exactly as they were. They must all learn first to paint and carve directly from nature before any of them turned to the more specific problems of design. Then to the truly educated artist, not to an automaton trained to obey a narrow set of rules derived from historical precedent, would be left the complex decisions about whether to ornament with naturalistic, conventional, or geometric forms, or whether to ornament at all. And those decisions would depend upon the subjective judgments of the artist with a finely tuned eye open to myriad and rich possibilities. The character of the material at hand, the distance from the human eye of a surface for which ornament was contemplated, and the use to which the building or object was to be put would factor into the choices. The decisions were not to be made before the fact, not to be constricted by narrow formula, because

> . . . the principles on which you must work are likely to be false, in proportion as they are narrow; true, only as they are founded on a perception of the connection of all branches of art with each other.[25]

25 *Ruskin, "Modern Manufacture and Design," in* Two Paths, *in* Works, *vol. 16, 319.*

So Ruskin said in "Modern Manufacture and Design," the third lecture in *The Two Paths.* In complicating what seemed to have been so conveniently simplified by authorities, he reintroduced the possibilities for blunders that come with unlimited choice. He denied the prerogative of the experts to dictate, and to limit, a definition of good design. He gave the authority back to the artist.

While *The Two Paths* was one of Ruskin's most popular works during the nineteenth century, especially in America where it had gone through nineteen editions by 1891 and inspired a journal called *The New Path,* it has aged badly. It bristles with the racial prejudices of Imperial Britain, shaken during 1857 by the mutiny of its Indian troops, the Sepoys, against their English commanders. Dispatches from the subcontinent shocked London. They detailed the slaughter of whole families of British in Delhi during the spring, the starvation of English women and children besieged through summer's heat in Cawnpore and through the autumn in Lucknow. In the words of James Morris: ". . . the vision of European women and their children violated or murdered by mutinous ruffians touched atavistic chords of fury."[26] When Ruskin rose before the opening meeting of the Architectural Museum in London's South Kensington the following January, he was in the throes of that fury, and spoke to an audience that shared it. He railed against Indian "treachery, cruelty, cowardice, idolatry, bestiality, – whatever else is fruitful in the work of Hell."[27]

The words come from the opening lecture of *The Two Paths,* "The Deteriorative Power of Conventional Art Over Nations." Here Ruskin associated "sin" with "geometry," "formula," and "legalism" in ornamental design. He illustrated his notion that these qualities had a morally deteriorative effect on those who produced and used them by depicting as corrupt and evil the "Hindoos," whose sophisticated designs were based on geometry, historical precedent, and law. He judged their products devoid of natural feeling. He depicted them as a criminal race, then contrasted the Indian producers of geometric design to the Scots, whom he held up as models of Christian virtue, and whose crude arts he judged to be in direct harmony with nature. Nor did Ruskin fail to cite the bravery of Scottish troops in putting down the Indian mutinies. In juxtaposing the ways of the Scots and the "Hindoos," Ruskin insisted that their manners of designing not only reflected, but also formed, their characters. One race had taken the wrong path.

The "two paths" Ruskin offered aspiring students of design presented a ". . . choice, decisive and conclusive, between two modes of study, which involve ultimately the development, or deadening, of every power he possesses . . . the way divides itself, one way [that of studying, celebrating, and following

26 *James Morris,* Heaven's Command: An Imperial Progress *(New York and London: Harcourt Brace Jovanovich, 1973; Harvest HBJ edition, 1980), 232.*

27 *Ruskin, "The Deteriorative Power of Conventional Art Over Nations," inaugural lecture at the opening meeting of the Architectural Museum, South Kensington Museum, January 13, 1858, lecture 1,* Two Paths, *in* Works, *vol. 16, 263.*

nature as a true artist] leading to the Olive mountains, one [the adherence to arbitrary rules of geometry and imitation of past models of design] to the vale of the Salt Sea."[28] Ruskin recognized "the dependence of all noble design, in any kind, on the sculpture or painting of Organic Form."[29]

> If the designer . . . exercises himself continually in the imitation of natural form in some leading division of his work; then, holding by this stem of life, he may pass down into all kinds of merely geometrical or formal design with perfect safety, and with noble results.[30]

While tying his argument to racial character might have helped at the moment to drive home his point, it subsequently undercut the power of *The Two Paths* to convince readers of the rightness of its basic theses. By linking to this lesser theme his greater vision of design as part of the unity of art, Ruskin rendered this published collection of his speeches virtually unreadable for many who have come to it latterly. Marginalia scrawled across photocopies of this text when it was assigned to recent students – "Ruskin is an imperialist, racist pig" – at least attest to his continuing power to provoke reaction at a gut level. Time-with-its-prejudices-bound as he clearly was in so many instances, he makes it difficult to argue, as I do, for the prescience of his larger theses, and for the revaluation of art within architectural thinking and of drawing from nature within the architectural curriculum.

Ruskin's insistence on the primacy of art within the design process proved to be something of a thumb in the dam holding back the flood of reaction against art and beauty – or at least Art and Beauty in the terms of the pre-Modern world – that swept through Modernist architectural thinking. In the 1890s, the Belgian architect Henry van de Velde proclaimed that the engineer was the true architect of our times.[31] Adolf Loos, searching the past for germs of incipient Modernism, declared that it had been "the great achievement of the nineteenth century to have brought about the clear separation between art and design."[32]

Yet Ruskin's old insistence that art retain primacy in design had a direct effect on the organization of the Bauhaus in 1919: in the early curriculum, Walter Gropius required all aspiring architectural designers to take courses in painting and sculpture. Gropius, however, in his attempt to integrate art and design, was dealing with an art that was newly perceived in Modern terms as giving priority to abstraction. During the intervening sixty years, abstraction had come to dominate the Modernist understanding of "Art" through an intellectual process that, as we have already been reminded, also owed its origins to the nineteenth-century English theories of Decorative Art. Ruskin's German readers may have invoked him as a mentor when they identified architecture with art, architectural education with that of the artist, but

28 *Ruskin, preface to* Two Paths, *in* Works, *vol. 16, 253–54. After the sentence quoted, he concludes the preface:* There are few cross-roads, that I know of, from one to the other. Let him pause at the parting of The Two Paths.

29 *Ruskin, preface to* Two Paths, *in* Works, *vol. 16, 251.*

30 *Ruskin, "The Deteriorative Power of Conventional Art Over Nations,"* Two Paths, *in* Works, *vol. 16, 288.*

31 *Alexander Dorner cites van de Velde's proclamation in "The Background of the* Bauhaus,*" in* Bauhaus 1919–1928, *12.*

32 *Adolf Loos,* Trotzdem 1900–1930, *72, as paraphrased/translated by Herwin Schaefer in* Nineteenth Century Modern *(New York: Praeger, 1970), 186.*

they forgot him completely when they limited Bauhaus design to abstraction.

Despite the Bauhaus proclamation that the reintegration of all the arts was high on its list of goals for the education of its students, participants in the Bauhaus proved themselves to be adamant campaigners against "Art." Among them Herbert Bayer is conspicuous. *The Way Beyond Art*, a book of 1947 about his work and writing, documents his vehement renunciation of the value of art in shaping buildings and "designs."[33] And where Modernists continued to work consciously to maintain a close association between art and architecture, narrowness of vision of the kind Ruskin deplored nevertheless ran apace. So the authoritarian handbooks on how to do – or to recognize – "good design" that were once produced so profusely by the Museum of Modern Art now invite parody. How glibly they canonize abstraction, how ridiculously blind to all the richness of life they now seem to be.

That abhorrence for Art and for ornament, the latter too often misunderstood as art applied, and alien, to architecture, characterized the Modernist architectural profession and the curriculum of its students. Indeed, Modernism's preference for the methods of science over those of art insinuated itself into all aspects of American architectural education during the Second World War, so that every student, now Ruskin's "man of science," was determined to outdo all the others by discovering an original, personal style all his own. With it came a radical renunciation of the rich precedents of the past and of its cumulative wisdom. Most of all, students and teachers alike left behind the "fraternity of toil" that Ruskin had admired among architects and became truly solitary – disastrously for architecture, which by its very nature is a community's art. So, in their planning charrettes, all working together, where sorority has joined (as Ruskin could never have foreseen) the fraternity of toil, and in their studios that produce beautiful pictures of living things, the architects of Miami have happened, it would seem, upon the path not taken, and have abandoned at last the other, which Ruskin said led to death.

33 *Alexander Dorner,* The Way Beyond Art: The Work of Herbert Bayer *(New York: Wittenborn, Schultz, 1947).*

Bibliography

Chris Abel. "Work of El Wakil." *Architectural Review,* November 1986, 52–60.

Mohammad Al-Asad. "The Mosques of Abdel Wahed El Wakil." *Mimar* 42 (March 1992): 34–39.

Rex Beach. *The Miracle of Coral Gables.* New York: Currier and Harford, 1926.

Roberto Behar and Maurice Culot, eds. *Merrick and Coral Gables.* Forthcoming.

Frank E. Brown. *Roman Architecture.* New York: Braziller, 1961.

Michael Crosbie. "School Reflects a Local Culture." *Architecture,* August 1987.

Marjory Stoneman Douglas. *The Everglades: River of Grass.* New York: Rinehart, 1947.

Andres Duany. *An Architecture for Key West: A Proposal for the Return to Civilian Use of the Former Submarine Base.* Miami: University of Miami, 1976.

Abdel Wahed El Wakil. Introduction to *Hassan Fathy.* London: Academy Edition/St.Martin's Press, 1988.

Robert P. Emlin. *Shaker Village Views: Illustrated Maps and Landscape Drawings by Shaker Artists of the 19th Century.* Hanover and London: University Press of New England, 1987.

Stephen Falatko. "Classical Education." *Architecture,* November 1994.

David Gebhard and Deborah Nevins. *200 Years of American Architectural Drawing.* New York: Whitney Library of Design for the Architectural League of New York/American Federation of Arts, 1977.

Werner Hegemann and Elbert Peets. *The American Vitruvius: An Architects' Handbook of Civic Art.* 1922. Reprint, New York: Princeton Architectural Press, 1988.

Jan Hochstim. *The Paintings and Sketches of Louis I. Kahn.* New York: Rizzoli, 1991.

Steven W. Hurtt and Dhiru A. Thadani, eds. *Making Towns: Principles and Techniques.* College Park, Maryland: School of Architecture, The University of Maryland, 1994.

John Brinckerhoff Jackson. *Landscapes: Selected Writings of J. B. Jackson.* Edited by Ervin H. Zube. Amherst: University of Massachusetts Press, 1970.

Owen Jones. *The Grammar of Ornament.* London, 1856. 3rd ed., London: Bernard Quaritch, 1868.

Peter Katz. *The New Urbanism.* New York: McGraw Hill, 1993.

Spiro Kostof. *The City Shaped.* Boston: Little, Brown, 1991.

———. *The City Assembled: The Elements of Urban Form Through History.* Boston: Little, Brown, 1992.

Alex Krieger with William Lennertz, eds. *Andres Duany and Elizabeth Plater-Zyberk: Towns and Town Making Principles.* Cambridge, Mass.: Harvard University Graduate School of Design; New York: Rizzoli, 1991.

Leon Krier. *Houses, Palaces, and Cities.* New York: St. Martin's Press, 1984.

———. "The Reconstruction of Vernacular Building and Classical Architecture." *Architects' Journal,* September 1984, 66–70.

Susan Lambert. *Reading Drawings: An Introduction to Looking at Drawing.* New York: Pantheon Books, 1984.

Phillip Langdon. *A Better Place to Live.* Amherst: University of Massachusetts Press, 1994.

Jean-François Lejeune, ed. *The New City 1: Foundations.* Miami: University of Miami, 1991.

———. *The New City 2: The American City.* Miami: University of Miami, 1994.

Jean-François Lejeune and Maurice Culot, eds. *Miami: Architecture of the Tropics.* Brussels: Archives d'Architecture Moderne/Miami Center of the Fine Arts, 1992.

Rosario Marquardt. "Rosario Marquardt." *Arquitectonica: Art and Architecture* 4 (October 1989): 5–24.

David Mohney and Keller Easterling. *Seaside: Making a Town in America.* New York: Princeton Architectural Press, 1991.

Deborah Nevins and Robert A. M. Stern. *The Architect's Eye: American Architectural Drawings from 1799 to 1978.* New York: Pantheon, 1979.

John Nolen. *New Towns for Old: Achievement in Civic Improvement in Some American Small Towns and Neighborhoods.* Boston: Marshall Jones, 1927.

Arva Parks. *Miami the Magic City.* Miami: Centennial Press, 1991.

John W. Reps. *The Making of Urban America: A History of City. Planning in the United States.* Princeton, N.J.: Princeton University Press, 1965.

———. *Views and Viewmakers of Urban America: Lithographs of Towns and Cities in the United States and Canada, Notes on the Artists and Publishers, and a Union Catalog of Their Work, 1825–1925.* University of Missouri Press, 1984.

Aldo Rossi: Buildings and Projects. Edited by Peter Arnell and Ted Bickford. New York: Rizzoli, 1985.

Aldo Rossi. *The Architecture of the City.* Translated by Diane Ghirardo and Joan Ockman, revised by Aldo Rossi and Peter Eisenman. Cambridge, Mass.: MIT Press, 1982.

———. "New School of Architecture at the University of Miami." *Arquitectonica: Art and Architecture* 5 (February 1990): 25–34.

John Ruskin. *The Works of John Ruskin.* Library ed. Edited by E. T. Cook and Alexander Wedderburn. London: George Allen; New York: Longmans, Green, 1903–12.

Vincent Scully. *The Shingle Style: Architectural Theory and Design From Richardson to the Origins of Wright.* New Haven: Yale University Press, 1955; new ed., with *The Stick Style,* New Haven: Yale University Press, 1971.

———. *American Architecture and Urbanism*. New York: Praeger, 1969; new ed., New York: Holt, 1988.

———. *The Shingle Style Today*. New York: Braziller, 1975.

———. Introduction to *The Travel Sketches of Louis I. Kahn*. By William G. Holman. Philadelphia: Pennsylvania Academy of the Fine Arts, 1978.

———. "Something New Under the Sun: Ca' Ziff." *Metropolitan Home,* June 1991, 49–57.

———. "Urban Architecture Awakens from a Bad Dream." *City Journal* 4, no. 4 (Autumn 1994): 75–80.

Gavin Stamp. *The Great Perspectivists.* New York: Rizzoli, 1982.

Robert A. M. Stern and John M. Massengale. *The Anglo-American Suburb.* New York: St. Martin's Press, 1981.

Charlton W. Tebeau. *The University of Miami: A Golden Anniversary History 1926–1976.* Coral Gables: University of Miami Press, 1976.

Raymond Unwin. *Town Planning in Practice.* London, 1909. Reprint, New York: Princeton Architectural Press, 1994.

Robert Venturi. *Complexity and Contradiction in Architecture.* New York: Museum of Modern Art, 1966.

William Whyte. *City: Rediscovering the Center.* New York: Doubleday, 1988.

Bertram Zuckerman. *The Dream Lives On: A History of Fairchild Tropical Garden 1938–1988.* Miami: Fairchild Tropical Garden, 1988.

A Note on the Type

This body text of this catalog is set in the typefaces **Scala** and **Scala Sans**, designed in 1991 and 1993 by **Martin Majoor** of Arnhem, The Netherlands. The sans serif font, used for titles, is **Bell Gothic**, designed in 1938 by Chauncey H. Griffith for the Bell Telephone Company.